# MISALLIANCE

# MISALLIANCE

*A STUDY*

*OF FRENCH POLICY IN RUSSIA*

*DURING THE SEVEN YEARS' WAR*

*L. Jay Oliva*

NEW YORK UNIVERSITY PRESS  1964

To *Warren B. Walsh*

# PREFACE

THE RELATIONSHIP between France and Russia during the Seven Years' War has been ignored since the turn of the twentieth century. At that time several French historians, writing to justify the wisdom and necessity of another Franco-Russian alliance in their own day, shaped the concept of the Franco-Russian *rapprochement* of the Seven Years' War. Albert Vandal and Alfred Rambaud, writing in the shadow of France's humiliation by the newborn German Empire, found the secret of France's weakness in its stubborn refusal to throw over old policies and to unite boldly and wholly with the rising power of the Russian Empire in 1756. The chief target of their wrath was the secret organization and diplomacy of Louis XV. History has left substantially unjudged the insistence of these great historians, both writing after the consummation of the Franco-Russian alliance of 1890–1894, that France could have saved the peace of Europe and its own fortunes had she long ago allied herself directly with Russia to preserve the peace.

Any claim that the Franco-Russian ties of the Seven Years' War could have been ultimately more beneficial to France than its traditional system of alliances should be based on more than wishful thinking or hindsight. It is the purpose of this study to analyze the origins, content, character, and results of French policy in Russia from 1755 to 1762, in order to discover whether there ever existed in the Franco-Russian relationship any elements of mutuality, desirability, or durability.

The Russian calendar in this period of the eighteenth century was eleven days behind its Western counterpart, and dates in this study have been transferred to the latter style wherever possible.

In the preparation of this work I am indebted above all to Warren B. Walsh of Syracuse University for his continuing guidance and friendship, and to those who read the manuscript in whole or in part: Leo Gershoy of New York University, Kenneth I. Dailey of the University of Oklahoma, Nelson M. Blake and A. Robert Schoyen of Syracuse University, and Samuel B. Hand of the University of Vermont. Special thanks are due Vincent P. Carosso and Bayrd Still of New York University for their advice and encouragement. The excellent staffs of the *Archives du Ministère des Affaires Etrangères,* the *Archives Nationales,* and the *Bibliothèque Nationale,* as well as those of other French libraries, have worked diligently in my behalf.

I gratefully acknowledge the financial help of Syracuse University, the Syracuse University Research Institute under the direction of Warren B. Walsh, and the Alliance Française de New York which provided a Fribourg Fellowship for research in France. I wish to thank the *Catholic Historical Review* and the *Polish Review* for permission to use materials that have appeared in their pages in different form.

Finally, I would like to recognize the financial sacrifices and enduring patience of my parents over many years, and the graciousness of my wife in welcoming and softening the disciplines of academic life. I am also indebted to my wife for the preparation of the index.

*L. Jay Oliva*

*Wappingers Falls, N.Y.*
*February 14, 1964*

# CONTENTS

# ABBREVIATIONS

The names of the several archives and archival divisions upon whose materials this study is heavily based have been abbreviated in footnotes as follows:

| | |
|---|---|
| *AMAE CP D* | Archives du Ministère des Affaires Etrangères, Correspondance Politique, Danemark |
| *AMAE CP Po* | Archives du Ministère des Affaires Etrangères, Correspondance Politique, Pologne |
| *AMAE CP Pr* | Archives du Ministère des Affaires Etrangères, Correspondance Politique, Prusse |
| *AMAE CP R* | Archives du Ministère des Affaires Etrangères, Correspondance Politique, Russie |
| *AMAE CP S* | Archives du Ministère des Affaires Etrangères, Correspondance Politique, Suede |
| *AMAE MD F* | Archives du Ministère des Affaires Etrangères, Mémoires et Documents, France |
| *AMAE MD R* | Archives du Ministère des Affaires Etrangères, Mémoires et Documents, Russie |
| *AMAE Pers* | Archives du Ministère des Affaires Etrangères, Dossiers Personnels |
| *AN AE* | Archives Nationales, Affaires Etrangères |
| *AN CC* | Archives Nationales, Correspondance Consulaire |
| *AN MM* | Archives Nationales, Ministère de la Marine |
| *BN SM MF* | Bibliothèque Nationale, Salle des Manuscrits, Manuscrits Françaises |
| *BN SM NAF* | Bibliothèque Nationale, Salle des Manuscrits, Nouvelle Acquisitions Françaises |

# MISALLIANCE

CHAPTER 1

# A Secret Mission

THE YEAR 1748, as every other year, was one of conclusions
and of beginnings in European affairs. While the dust was
settling on the conference tables beneath the spire and dome
of the Aix-la-Chapelle cathedral, Europe was, all unknowing,
in the throes of great changes.

The thirty years that preceded the settlement of 1748
began in diplomatic confusion and ended prosaically with the
European powers returned to their long-accustomed places.
The settlement of Utrecht in 1713 and the death of the Sun
King produced at first a volatile state in European relations.
The end of Louis XV's minority, however, was the signal for
the return to the old systems of alliances. After 1725 Europe
gradually assumed its ancient shape and disposition. France
grew strong again under the able leadership of Cardinal
Fleury, recovering colonies and commerce after the ravages of
the grand siècle. This restoration of French power under a
young and promising king was viewed with some alarm in
London and Vienna. French recovery caused a reversion by
Great Britain to her Austrian alliance. The sea power of Britain
and the land power of Austria could once more surround
France and protect the Low Countries. Prussia, Austria's natu-

ral rival for the control of Central Europe, was thus driven for protection and for hope into the arms of France. On the periphery of Europe, renewed French support of Sweden, Poland, and the Ottoman Empire against Austria and Russia rounded out the revitalized system of alliances.

These alliances seemed natural and satisfactory. They remained so as long as the real intent of the participants was to keep the peace. By 1741, however, this intent to keep the peace had disappeared in most European capitals. Under pretext of a contested succession in Austria, the right of Maria Theresa to inherit from her father, all Europe fell to war.

The conference that met at Aix-la-Chapelle in 1748 to end this world war actually produced only an armed truce. France lost territory in North America but secured the return of much of the French Empire from the British because of the successful war waged by Marshal de Saxe in the Low Countries. The war, in effect, had proved nothing. As to Austria, Maria Theresa kept her throne but lost Silesia. This lush province was ceded to Frederick of Prussia. Russia, which had sold its troops to the British for the defense of Hanover, received nothing but its subsidies.

After 1748, when the rancors of war could give way to more sober counsels, certain realities became evident. Austria had been convinced by French military successes of the futility of defending the Low Countries. The substance of Austrian opposition to France was fading. Further, Austria knew that its continued existence as a Great Power would be determined by its attitude toward Silesia. Austria could not and would not accept its permanent loss. Prussia, of late the upsetter of thrones, was now the most ardent defender of the *status quo*. Any alterations in the present arrangement of Europe would raise the question of Prussia's tenuous legal hold on Silesia. Britain had attempted to find its rewards for aiding the Empress-Queen in raiding French properties around the world, but had been balked by its vulnerability on the Continent. If Hanover could be guaranteed against the French, Britain might begin to pick more successfully at French dominions.

France had as its self-assigned task after 1748 the maintenance of its system: influence in Turkey, Sweden, and Poland and alliance with Prussia. Through this system the delicate balance of 1748 could be assured. France could relax and enjoy the fruits of its growing commerce and delightful civilization. The war had been a warning to France. Only tardily and by chance did France avoid worldwide disaster. Peace was France's need, and peace was its aspiration.

As to France and Eastern Europe, the French client states of Poland, Sweden, and Turkey had, since the successes of Peter the Great, been subjected to increasingly heavy Russian pressures. France was committed to the protection of these states on the expanding Russian frontier. The year 1748 had ended a long-wavering relationship between France and Russia. The approach of Russian troops hired by the British and sent toward the Rhine even as peace was being signed had awakened France to the new menace and hardened France against this intruder.

The threat of Russian troops to France had been doubly galling to Louis XV. It had been his gold upon which, in large measure, the present Empress Elizabeth had mounted to the throne in 1741, and his minister who had helped her determine to seize the crown from the German party. Elizabeth Petrovna, daughter of Peter the Great by his second wife, Catherine I, had been excluded from the throne after the death of her mother by a reversion to the heirs of Peter's first wife and then to the heirs of Peter's stepbrother. Elizabeth was inspired to overthrow the infant Ivan VI and his mother, Anne of Brunswick, by means of a midnight *coup d'état.* France had supported Elizabeth as the best guarantee of a Russian policy acceptable to French interests in Eastern Europe. Louis XV's sense of insult at the Tsarina's ingratitude was coupled with his contempt for Russia as a seller of mercenaries.[1]

The person responsible for the ingratitude of the Empress was the Grand Chancellor of Russia, Aleksei Petrovich Bestu-

---

1. The latest account of French policy in Russia from 1740 to 1746 is Sidney Horowitz, *Franco-Russian Relations 1740–1746* (Unpublished Ph.D. dissertation, New York University, 1954).

zhev-Riumin. At the age of twenty-one Bestuzhev had been
a member of the Russian observation corps at Utrecht, and
after the settlement had been in the service of George, Elector of Hanover and later King of Great Britain. Bestuzhev had
returned to service in the Duchy of Courland in 1718, and
was made a cabinet minister by Ernst Johann Biron during the
reign of the Empress Anne. He fell from power with Biron in
1740, but was rehabilitated by Elizabeth in 1741 and appointed
Grand Chancellor in 1744. He set the course of Russian policy
and cajoled the Empress, often against her inclination, to follow his desires. For fifteen years she left the foreign affairs of
Russia completely in his hands. Bestuzhev's phobias were
France and Prussia, and the Chancellor's cherished dream was
to unite Russia to Austria and Britain to destroy the power
of the Prussian king and remove French influence from the
states on the Russian border. The march of Russian troops in
return for British gold in 1748 was not simply a mercenary
adventure, despite the insistance of Western powers on view-
ing it as such. Regardless of his reputation for venality, Bestuzhev was never bought except when the proposals were of real
interest to him. The sale of troops was a commitment of Russia to Britain and a telling blow to Bestuzhev's internal enemies, who still clustered about the so-called French party in
Russia. The Grand Chancellor's aims were the severance of
diplomatic relations between Russia and France and the resulting isolation of his enemies. In these aims Bestuzhev succeeded admirably.

The French seized the opportunity afforded by the meet-
ings at Aix-la-Chapelle to have their revenge on the Russians.
The French well knew that Bestuzhev and his Empress were
intent on a place at the congress. Russia had never yet sat as
a full participating member of general European congress,
and pride vied with interest in motivating its desire to attend.
The French had plumbed this Russian sensitivity in the instructions to the French representative at the conference:

It is clear that Russia passionately desires to have her ministers
admitted to the conference at Aix-la-Chapelle. . . . They have
assured us that they will be occupied henceforth in seeking means

to make His Majesty forget what has passed. We have replied politely but very coldly that the King is persuaded by facts and not by words, and that the conduct of Russia in regard to France was so singular that it would require the strongest representations to efface all that they have done against us without the slightest provocation on our part. The King of Prussia, informed of Russian desires and fearing our agreement, has done . . . all that he can to incite us against this power.[2]

Frederick's incitements were hardly necessary. The French representative at the conference was insultingly terse when the matter of Russian participation was discussed. "If the mercenary powers are admitted to this peace, France will not conclude it."[3] Russia was not admitted. This repulse was followed rapidly by a mutual withdrawal of representatives from St. Petersburg and Versailles.

After 1748 the reactions from both French and Russians were severe. France proceeded officially to ignore the existence of the Russian state, and even the peculiar eighteenth-century civilities between sovereigns were abandoned. Russia became the refuge of French outlaws and French ne'er-do-wells, who passed off their smattering of learning as the deepest culture and made their livings as teachers and governors to the Russian aristocracy. Few decent gentlemen thought of visiting the barbarous court of St. Petersburg. Bestuzhev happily replied in kind. Heavy restrictions were placed on Russian visitors to France, and the very few noted French tourists who approached the Russian Empire were repulsed at the frontiers. The seizure of the Russian merchantman *Narva*, bound from Archangel to Lisbon, by the French man-of-war *La Victoire* was magnified by St. Petersburg into a general disregard for Russian commercial rights that would demand reprisals.

The passing years confirmed the reality of the rupture. On the official level, mutual antagonisms gradually melted into mutual indifference. There was, however, a trickle of un-

2. Memoir to M. Thiel, Aug. 30, 1748: *AMAE CP R,* Suppl. 7, 106–107.
3. Gaëtan de Raxis de Flassan, *Histoire générale et raisonnée de la di-* *plomatie française, depuis la fondation de la monarchie jusqu'à la fin du règne de Louis XVI* (Paris: Treuttel et Würtz, 1811), V, 404–405, note.

dercover activity during the years after 1748, of which only a few eruptions are observable. The cluster of persons who opposed the programs, ambitions, successes, or personality of Grand Chancellor Bestuzhev in Russia was by preference and by necessity the pro-French party. Attachment to French culture and French subsidies seemed naturally to accompany personal rivalries with the Grand Chancellor and the desire to destroy him. Bestuzhev's archrival, and thus the leader of the pro-French party in the Russian capital, was the Vice-Chancellor, Mikhail Illarionovich Vorontsov. This aristocrat had been instrumental in raising the Empress Elizabeth to the throne and, despite his general lack of capability, had been rewarded in 1744 with the post of Vice-Chancellor. From that post Vorontsov waged a steady if quiet campaign against his chief. It was characteristic of the Empress that she allowed this rivalry in the highest state offices to go unresolved. The victory that Bestuzhev effected by ending French ties in 1748 did not, as the Grand Chancellor hoped, destroy the Vice-Chancellor and his clique. It served merely to drive their opposition underground and to increase their fear and jealousy. There was a continuing rumor, assiduously propagated by Vorontsov but quite untrue, that France deplored the rupture between the two states and would be happy to repair it. Simply put, the anti-Bestuzhev, pro-French party in Russia maintained an undercover but continuing activity. They could wait and hope.[4]

Given the continuing aspirations of this pro-French group in St. Petersburg, it was not surprising that French knowledge of Russia during these years of separation was not solely reliant upon the formal reports of friendly foreign representatives at St. Petersburg. The visit to Versailles in 1754 of a renegade Frenchman serving in the Russian army was certainly an overture from the French party. The French were delighted to receive information on the condition of the Russian army and court, but the overtures were not reciprocated.[5]

France's sole concern with Russia during these interwar

4. P. J. Bartenev, ed., *Arkhiv Kniazia Vorontsova* (Moscow: Imperial Academy of Sciences, 1870–95), III, 640–670.

5. There are several versions of this visit. See *AMAE CP Pr* 10, 246 and 459–463; and Bartenev, *op. cit.*, IV, 46.

years revolved about the possibility of a Russian attack upon Sweden. Diverse methods were used to collect rudimentary military intelligence. Information elicited by the generous application of gold coin trickled through the Swedish, Polish, and Turkish embassies and into the French Foreign Ministry. Several Swiss merchants found it worthwhile to pinpoint Russian fortifications, troop concentrations, and fleet movements for the benefit of the French military.[6] The most satisfactory undercover source for the activities of the Russian court was a mysterious personality by the name of Michel de Rouen, who represented the French party in St. Petersburg. The French Ministry at Hamburg has left the best summary of the background of this shadowy character:

The person who has confided details on the court of Russia to me . . . is called Michel. He is the son of a Frenchman whom the Tsar Peter engaged for his service during his stay in France. . . . The father, living still, did not do well in Russia and set up his son as a merchant of notions at the court in Petersburg. Since he was raised in the palace he has been favored there and the nobles buy from him in preference to others. His successes have encouraged him and made him extremely energetic. He has already made seven or eight trips to France in great secrecy to buy merchandise and make purchases for members of the court. Thus, the nature of his commerce and the fashion in which he exercises it have spread and augmented the access which he has to the great houses of the court.[7]

That Michel was an agent of the French party in Russia, and particularly of Mikhail Vorontsov, was quite clear. Vorontsov, himself very active in commercial activities thanks to grants and monopolies from the Empress, used Michel as secretary and factotum for his public and private ventures. Michel's later activities demonstrated that his motive for these machinations was a commercial one. He hoped to draw from a renewal of friendly relations between the two powers a dominant role in their commercial affairs. His frequent visits to France were presumably commercial ventures which, in the face of Bestuzhev's harsh restrictions, were possible only un-

6. *AMAE MD R* 30, 211–213; and 9, 7–19. See also *AMAE CP R*, Suppl. 7, 180–189, 192–193, and 232–233.

7. Champeaux to the Ministry, Hamburg, Sept. 6, 1752: *AMAE CP R*, Suppl. 7, 234.

der the protection of his patron, the Vice-Chancellor. No journey to France passed without a visit to the French Ministry
of Foreign Affairs to deliver the opinion that Russia was ripe
for French friendship. Although the French court never acted
upon any of Michel's recommendations during this interwar
period, it found his information too interesting to discourage
completely. They had no intentions of reopening negotiations
with that ungrateful and barbarous court, but the French
found direct news of its activities somewhat comforting in the
existing vacuum.[8]

The man into whose hands these wispy threads of Russian
information fell ultimately by default between 1748 and 1755
was not even a member of the Ministry of Foreign Affairs.
This was Louis François de Bourbon, Prince de Conti. Conti,
the King's cousin, had earned a fine military reputation in the
War of the Austrian Succession, and was highly prized by
Louis as a private adviser on foreign affairs. The Prince maintained a large and lively court at the Maison Condé in Paris,
favorably rivaling the more formal life of Versailles. Conti's
interest in Russia at this time was peripheral to his interest in
Poland.

It was Conti's tragic flaw that he was unsatisfied with the
life of a military hero, a royal intimate, and a cultured gentleman. His ambition drove him toward a crown. He had offered
himself as a prospective bridegroom to the Tsarevna Elizabeth
of Russia during the reign of her predecessor, Anne of Courland, but had been refused. He had then determined, at least
since 1745, to be the next elected King of Poland. In that year
he had been approached by certain powerful elements of the
Polish aristocracy, who urged his candidacy to prevent the
crown of Poland from becoming hereditary in the Saxon house.
Conti had responded to the request with great enthusiasm.

The crown of Poland, however, was notoriously difficult

---

8. See Kasimir Waliszewski, *La Dernière des Romanov* (Paris: Plon,
1902), p. 395–96; Instructions to
L'Hôpital in Alfred Rambaud, *Recueil des instructions données aux*
ambassadeurs et ministres de France
(Paris: Felix Alcam, 1890) IX, 32–
34; *AMAE CP R*, Suppl. 7, 239–240;
and *BN SM NAF* 22009, 4.

to manage and required a good deal of preparation for its delivery. As the Count de Broglie, later an integral part of Conti's
plans, noted, "It was this which gave place to the formation of
a general political system of which the Prince de Conti was
the author." His plan was to bind Turkey, Sweden, and Poland
closely to France; to separate Austria from Russia, "pushing
the latter back into her vast deserts and relegating her to affairs outside the limits of Europe"; and to arrogate the Polish
crown to himself.[9] It was apparent from the beginning that
Russia was an obstacle to Conti's plans and would have to be
managed.

In pursuit of this will-o'-the-wisp crown Conti had the
sympathy of his royal cousin at Versailles. The King could not
officially sponsor Conti's candidacy for fear of offending the
Saxon king of Poland and driving him unequivocally into the
arms of Austria and Russia. Further, the King's son was married to a princess of the Saxon house. Secretly, however, under Louis's indulgent eye, Conti was allowed to play espionage
games in pursuit of a royal home in Eastern Europe. Soon the
Prince was the center of all that pertained to this area of
France's far-flung interests. Conti was allowed to influence and
guide the placing of official ministers and secretaries at the
embassies involved. With all the enthusiasm of a child with
secrets, he squandered the family fortune on an undercover
organization devoted to his interests. The Count de Broglie,
for example, son and brother of marshals of France and a career diplomat, was named Ambassador to Poland on March 14,
1752. Two days later he received a letter from Conti with a
note from the King enclosed. Louis asked him to conform in
the greatest secrecy to all that the Prince should order. Broglie
was incredulous, but a second note in the hand of the King put
the case more strenuously. As Broglie himself reported: "From
that moment the Count de Broglie obeyed and received from
the King through the Prince de Conti secret orders for projects

9. Memoir from the Count de Broglie   *secrète de Louis XV* (Paris: Henri
to Louis XVI, June 9, 1774: reprinted   Plon, 1866), II, 404–405.
in M. E. Boutaric, *Correspondance*

in Poland which he judged should be hidden from his ministers." Broglie was initiated into the so-called Kings's Secret.[10]

Conti's secret contacts expanded until they touched one
of the highest and most significant posts at the Ministry of
Foreign Affairs in the person of Jean Pierre Tercier, the *premier commis*. Tercier, a lawyer of Swiss parentage, had served
as secretary to the embassy at Warsaw during the War of the
Polish Succession. In 1749 he was awarded the post of *premier
commis*, which encompassed the functions of a permanent un-
dersecretary and was, according to Marion, "the fixed and
principal resource of all foreign policy." In 1754 Tercier received his secret orders: "Tercier will confer with the Prince
de Conti, place his trust in him, and conform to all that the
Prince advises on my behalf relative to the affairs of Poland.
He will keep all a profound secret toward everyone, without
exception." [11] The importance of Tercier to Conti's organization
could not be overestimated, for Tercier had immediate access
to all opinions and documents of the Ministry.

Those initiated into Conti's plans during these interwar
years soon included the ambassadors at Constantinople and at
Stockholm, the French Resident in Warsaw, several secretaries
at these embassies, and numerous officers and gentlemen of the
Polish nobility.[12] The whole structure of the Secret grew and
functioned unknown to the Secretary of State for Foreign
Affairs and the other ministers — and, indeed, unknown to all
those outside its carefully chosen ranks. The completeness of
this secrecy was astonishing.

As a result, by 1755 the agency in France with most concern in Eastern Europe and the only agency in France with
even a remote idea of affairs in Russia was that organization
under Conti and the King known as the Secret. Any alteration

10. Note from Count de Broglie to
Louis XVI, May 13, 1774: *ibid.*, II,
388. The organization has been called
the Secret Correspondence of Louis
XV, The King's Secret, or simply the
Secret.

11. Louis XV to Tercier, Fontain-
bleau, Oct. 31, 1754: *ibid.*, I, 197.
For a description of the post of *pre-*

*mier commis*, see M. Marion, *Dictionnaire des institutions de la France
aux XVIIe et XVIIIe siècles* (Paris:
Auguste Picard, 1923), p. 120.

12. List of the ambassadors, ministers, and residents admitted to the
Secret by order of Louis XV, February, 1775; reprinted in Boutaric, *op.
cit.*, II, 429–30.

in the relationship of Russia and Eastern Europe, and especially of Russia and Poland, was of immediate concern to this organization. Its ultimate aim seemed always to be the exclusion of Russian influence in Poland if any success was to be expected for a French candidate for the Polish throne. The fate of Stanislas Leszczyński was sufficient demonstration.

The deceptive reign of tranquillity that covered European affairs after 1748 was definitely shattered in 1755. Great Britain was plainly intent on reopening the colonial war. At the same time the Anglo-Austrian talks on the defense of the Low Countries had failed. Now the threat of Russian intervention in Poland and in the larger European picture as well suddenly loomed large; rumors of a British attempt to hire troops again for the defense of Hanover sped through Europe. In June of 1755 the British Ambassador, Sir Charles Hanbury-Williams, arrived in St. Petersburg with decisive instructions. Britain was willing to offer an immediate subsidy and annual payments to Russia to maintain troops on the Livonian frontier. Russia would be required to move against menaced points, and this meant Hanover, in event of an attack on the territories of the King of Great Britain or his allies. Russia naturally understood the enemy to be Prussia, although the negotiations never mentioned that kingdom by name.[13]

These negotiations obviously constituted a threat of Russian troop movements across Poland and to French ability to make successful war against Britain in Europe. In the existing delicate balance neither of these threats could be permitted. Thus, the British project was a blow at the *status quo* and the first and decisive act of the diplomatic revolution. Since the French were ignorant of the precise nature of Anglo-Russian commitments, they had of necessity to know more.

Lights burned late at Versailles in the early months of 1755. Discussions with the Austrians were being demanded by the growing Austrian party at the French court, which was

13. R. Waddington, *Louis XV et le renversement des alliances* (Paris: Firmen-Didot, 1896), p. 125; Constantin de Grunwald, *Trois siècles de diplomatie russe* (Paris: Calleman-Lévy, 1945), p. 82. For Williams, see D. B. Horn, *Sir Charles Hanbury-Williams and European Diplomacy: 1747–1758* (London: George G. Harrap, 1930).

fearful and suspicious of their Prussian ally. Kaunitz and the Austrians found hope in the fact of mounting crisis, feeling that a volatile state of affairs might lead France to consider more sympathetically Austrian requests for a *rapprochement*. To add to the crisis, the British naval war was raging. Now the Russians were once again prepared to stick their guns into European affairs.

Lights burned late also at the Maison Condé in the sleepy neighborhood of the Temple, but now not in customary revelry. The master of the household, the Prince de Conti, hitherto linked to his royal cousin in private and in secrecy, was suddenly projected into the center of the European situation. Conti and his group of crown seekers were the logical troupe to be consulted by the King on this dangerous Russian business. The King of France could never soil his honor by direct contact with the mercenary Muscovites. Investigation of the current status of Anglo-Russian agreement would have to be an undercover affair, and there was an undercover instrument at hand. The Prince de Conti and his Secret were entrusted with the task of discovering the extent of Anglo-Russian agreement.

Conti cast about for a suitable agent. A foreigner was needed, preferably an Englishman or someone close to it, since the British star was high over Russia. France was overrun with poor but noble sons of Scotland left over from many an ill-fated filibuster in favor of the banished Stuarts. Many of these were clustered in the entourage of the Prince de Conti, seeking some mission which would promise barrels of ducats, a reliable pension, and a substantial marriage at the end of the adventure. To the house of the Condé, therefore, in the last days of May, 1755, with empty wallet and high hopes, came a certain Chevalier Mackenzie Douglas. Alexander Peter Mackenzie Douglas of Kilden had been compromised in the Stuart uprising of 1745, escaped to France in 1747, and attached himself to the household of the Prince de Conti. Now, at age forty-two, Douglas was given his great opportunity. He evidently passed inspection, for Conti recommended him immediately through the King to the Secretary of State for Foreign Affairs, Antoine Louis Rouillé, as the man for the task.[14]

The role of Douglas was an anomalous one from the beginning. He was first a spy for the Secret, although not a full-fledged member, and second an undercover agent on official business operating with the knowledge and cooperation of the French Ministry. The Ministry accepted the secret mission of Douglas to uncover Anglo-Russian intentions without being aware of the real interests of his sponsor. Douglas was, therefore, as most agents of the Secret were wont to be, a dual agent. Even Douglas at this point was not aware of the purposes of Conti's organization, but was merely an instrument proposed by Conti for the accomplishment of some difficult business.

On June 1, Tercier, serving in his carefully concealed double role of foreign office executive and Secret secretary, sat down with Conti to draft instructions for the journey of a secret agent into the Russias. The appearances of negotiations between Britain and Russia, said the instructions, demanded French investigation. The absence of formal relations made normal methods impossible. Douglas would therefore travel as an ordinary English tourist visiting mines in Central Europe and Russia and buying furs. His investigations would begin in Courland, where he would determine the number of Russian troops and vessels stationed there. Douglas would then proceed to St. Petersburg, where he "will find out, as secretly as possible, about the success of negotiations for troops and the number of troops Russia actually has."

The agent was to risk nothing by ordinary mails, but was to "use a short and allegorical language which will be given to him." This code related to the fur trade. The British Ambassador, Hanbury-Williams, was the "black fox," and if British negotiations with the Russians were progressing well, then the "black fox would be expensive and they give the English the commission to buy them." If, on the other hand, no foreign

14. *AMAE Pers.* First Series 24, Douglas, 323–426.

power was dominant at the Russian court, then "ermine is in vogue." Bestuzhev was the "gray wolf." If the power of Bestuzhev was waning, Douglas would write that "the price of martens is going down," but if the Chancellor maintained himself, "the price of martens remains the same." Russian troops for hire were "little gray skins." The number of skins would be augmented by two-thirds and understood in terms of thousands to signify the number of troops sold to the British, "so that 10 skins signifies 30,000 men."

Letters sent by Douglas from St. Petersburg would be directed to a banking firm in Amsterdam, under sealed address to Avril de Charnacé, Rue Neuve des Petits Champs, in Paris. Two marks drawn thus, //, would signify letters to be forwarded to the Ministry of Foreign Affairs. Other letters would be sent to Tercier under the name of Mr. Hamilton. Finally, if nothing could be done in Russia, Douglas was to indicate that the climate in Russia was bad for his health. This code was printed in miniscule letters and hidden in a double–bottomed tobacco box.[15]

Douglas left Paris in the last days of June, 1755, traveling alone and under his own name.[16] By August 19 he was in Danzig, surveying the conditions and fortifications of the city as he had been requested and awaiting final orders.

If you and my other relatives and friends do not plan to interrupt my first project, I will undertake it. . . . The Russian resident here tells me that our Ambassador at Petersburg [Williams] is ill, which

15. This section is based on the instructions for the Chevalier Douglas going into Russia: *AMAE CP R*, Suppl. 7, 14–15 (reprinted also in Rambaud, *op. cit.*, IX, 10–14); and on "Manière allégorique d'écrire convenue avec M. °°° allant en Russie": *AMAE CP R*, Suppl. 8, 15–16.

16. The myth of the Chevalier d'Éon, who allegedly accompanied Douglas into Russia in 1755 in woman's guise and who was accepted into the chambers of the Russian Empress as a companion, is widespread but completely false. It has been given some credence because D'Éon did later serve in Rus-

sia and because on later duty in England during the 1760's he did assume female attire. He insisted until his death that he was a woman. The Russian myth stemmed from the fictionalized work by Frédéric Gaillairdet, *Mémoires du Chevalier d'Éon* (Paris: Bernard Grasset, 1866).

Waliszewski (*La Dernière des Romanovs* [Paris: Plon, 1902], p. 400) insisted that Douglas took the name Michel on the first journey. This confusion stems from the jumbling of the names Michel and Douglas in the Bibliothèque Nationale manuscript cataloguing.

gives me great discomfort. . . . The rumor is general here that he
has succeeded in consolidating the treaties between the two courts
and that Russian troops will be ready to march at the first need.
This success does not surprise me in view of his talents.[17]

In reply, Douglas received a sharp note from Tercier that
sent him on his way. Tercier implied that the whole plot had
probably leaked out because of a clearly momentary affair between Douglas and a young lady in Dresden. When Douglas
failed to meet her in Berlin as he promised, she became angry
and broadcast the nature of his mission, which he had fool-
ishly revealed to her. She had even written to the French Ministry to vent her spleen. Douglas, without reply, proceeded
quickly to Riga. Having crossed the frontier into the Russian
Empire on September 23, he went directly to work:

I have already informed myself on the matter of the furs, and in
view of my present financial situation it is useless for me to think of
succeeding. The black fox [Williams] is extremely expensive and
sought after here. . . . Martens are very much in vogue and gray
wolf [Bestuzhev] could not be at a better price. . . . My finances
do not permit me to send you any little gray skins: ten skins would
suffice if you were shorter, but as you are tall and heavy I would
need twenty or thirty skins.[18]

The information of Douglas was quite accurate. Bestuzhev
and Williams were in control in St. Petersburg. The prelimi-
nary agreement signed by these two on September 30 provided
for 30,000 troops to be garrisoned on Russian frontiers, with
a guarantee of 60,000 troops or more if English possessions in
Europe were attacked.

By October 4, Douglas had crossed northern Russia and
had entered St. Petersburg. This city of long, low palaces,
washed in pastel greens, yellows, and blues and placed carefully along the clean, reflecting canals, must indeed have impressed the urbane visitor. This bright city, youngest and best
planned in Europe, was under the eyes of the Chevalier Douglas in the moment of its creation. Brick, timbers, and excava-

17. Douglas to Hamilton, Danzig,
Aug. 23, 1755: AMAE CP R, Suppl.
8, 46–47.

18. Douglas to Hamilton, Riga, Sept.
23, 1755: ibid., Suppl. 8, 62.

tions spread out in profusion around the old center of Peter the Great. Rastrelli's striking Winter Palace was nearly completed on the mainland near the Admiralty, the green and white Stroganov dominated the Nevski Prospekt, the columns of the Bestuzhev and Vorontsov palaces were visible rising from the Kamenny Island, and the Razumovski Palace was already completed on the beautiful Fontanka Canal. Here, truly, was a city that a French noble of the century could appreciate, a city created for the court, a city devoted to splendor, pomp, enjoyment, and beauty. Even France could not boast such a city and had to flee the crowded lanes of Paris for the more courtly but bucolic Versailles.

Other eyes might have been less impressed here. Alexander Herzen a century later would describe the eighteenth–century society of this city as "a ship floating on the surface of an ocean; it has no real connection with the inhabitants of the deep beyond that of eating them." Herzen's famous judgment on the Russian court was also applicable to its capital. Those who sought the Russian people here as anything but crude intruders on a gigantic theater set would seek in vain. But, in the eighteenth century, few were seeking the people.

At the apex of the St. Petersburg pyramid was the Empress Elizabeth Petrovna, a beautiful but thickening figure plagued by advancing years, sporadic illness, and an inordinate attachment to the baser pleasures of this world. Dissipated by favorites and by power, her influence on affairs was irresolute and spasmodic. She was given to extremes in all things, but especially in pleasure and in religion. She was her father's daughter in few ways. She had no internal program for her empire and no foreign policy not made for her by subordinates. She grew old among her lovers, lamenting the passing of her beauty and fearing terribly the approach of death.

Beneath the scepter of the Empress was collected the court of St. Petersburg. Like its more glorious counterpart at Versailles, the court was the heart of the state. No self-respecting noble would be found living permanently outside St. Petersburg if he could afford the expenses of city life. The great mass of lands and peoples that was the Russian Empire lay in mystery and misery in the uncharted lands beyond the Neva. Only Moscow, the home of the conservative or recalcitrant aristocracy, stood forth to challenge the primacy of Peter's city, and even that challenge was primarily spiritual. The political condition of St. Petersburg at the time that Douglas first glimpsed its splendid expansion had been described by one of its more illustrious inhabitants, the Grand Duchess and later Empress Catherine:

> The Russian court was divided into two great factions or parties. At the head of the first . . . was the Chancellor Count Bestuzhev-Riumin; he was infinitely more feared than loved, excessively intriguing, suspicious but firm and intrepid, tyrannical in his principles, an implacable enemy and a devoted friend . . . always difficult to get along with and often taken up with trivial affairs. He was at the head of foreign affairs, having always to battle the entourage of the Empress. . . . He stood for the courts of Vienna, Saxony, and London. . . .
>
> The party opposed to Bestuzhev held for France, its protégé Sweden, and the King of Prussia. In the fore was Mikhail Vorontsov, who had taken part in the revolution and accompanied Elizabeth on the night she had seized the throne. . . .
>
> The rest of the court who followed the Empress consisted of the Shuvalov family . . . and the Razumovski. . . . All the others of the court ranged themselves on one side or the other, according to its interests or daily views.[19]

Catherine had described the rest of the court shrewdly. Most wavered from party to party, following the daily rise and fall of fortune of the greats. The Shuvalovs had come to their high place because Ivan Ivanovich had become the favorite of the Empress in her middle age. Such positions are always tenuous, based as they are on the whimsy and passing passion of the autocrat. Nevertheless, Ivan Shuvalov's cousins, Pëtr Ivanovich and Aleksandr Ivanovich, had not only used their personal avenue to rise high in the councils of the state, but had taken care to cement their positions. Pëtr was an army officer and artillery expert and came to play a dominant role in Russian foreign and domestic commerce. He had married a

19. A. N. Pipin (ed.), *Socheneniia Imperatritsy Ekateriny II* (St. Peters- burg: Imperial Academy of Sciences, 1907), XII, Memoirs IV (1), 201.

favorite companion of the Empress Elizabeth. Aleksandr was a Court Chamberlain and director of the Secret Chancery, the police. Ivan, the favorite since 1747, was a great patron of the arts, first director of the University of Moscow, and first president of the Academy of Art in St. Petersburg. The Shuvalovs were always in the position of maintaining their slippery status with the Empress while preparing for her perhaps abrupt departure. Such nervous lives are the fates of favorites.

The Razumovski were less fearful and consequently less active. Aleksei Grigor'evich Razumovskii, a handsome cossack of obscure origins, had been snatched from the imperial choir by Elizabeth as her first and favorite servant of the bedchamber in 1741. It is rumored that he secretly married the Empress in 1745, but he certainly never disturbed her in her other interests. As he grew older he was retired from his post as favorite and given the post of Court Hunter, living a graceful and noncommittal life, much loved and respected by the Empress. His brother Kirill Grigor'evich had shared in Aleksei's success: the Empress appointed him Hetman of Ukraine, a post he held for fourteen years. He, much more than his brother, watched the present and the future with a fearful eye.

Catherine neglected her husband and herself in her description. Beneath and in opposition to the Empress of Russia and her favorites was the Young Court, the imperial heirs. The Grand Duke Peter, born Karl Peter Ulrich of Holstein-Gottorp, was a peculiar figure, weak in mind and body. The reigning Duke of his beloved Holstein, he had also been the heir to the Swedish throne before being hauled off to Russia by his Empress-aunt. Elizabeth, searching for an heir, had been forced to adopt her sister's son. Peter was Prussian in politics and Lutheran in spirit, despite his forced conversion to Orthodoxy, and hated his Russian imprisonment and the barbarities of Orthodoxy with a passion. He had only two interests: his Duchy of Holstein and his hero, Frederick of Prussia. Peter's wife was the Grand Duchess Catherine, formerly Sophie of Anhalt-Zerbst, of minor Prussian nobility. She neither loved nor was loved by her husband, and her energies and ambitions were infinitely more active than his. Originally planted in Russia by the Prussian party, Catherine had grown more and more closely attached to Bestzuhev and the Englishman Williams, whom she thought could save her from the whims of her resentful husband and advance her cause in the future allocation of thrones. Husband and wife were united only in their desire to survive the intrigues of the court favorites.

It was this Young Court, the imperial heirs and their small following, that threw the Russian nobility in St. Petersburg into such paroxysms of indecision. The obvious and often manifested divergence of views between the Empress Elizabeth and her heirs posed terrible choices to the rest of the court, which had to balance present favors against future rewards. This struggle between holder and heirs, with its resulting fears and indecisions, was a major theme of Russian history during Elizabeth's reign.

Such was the political complexion of St. Petersburg when Douglas arrived in the capital. As the Scot correctly observed from Riga, Bestuzhev was in full control and at the height of his power. Austria was already well integrated into Russia's system by treaties concluded during the recent war. The Grand Chancellor had assiduously pursued the British alliance for over a decade, and now the subsidy treaty awaited only the ratification of the sovereigns. Bestuzhev's system, over the helpless Prussian sympathies of the Grand Duke Peter, was centered on opposition to Prussia and France. It seemed now that with the aid of Austrian armies and British gold Russia might pass to the offensive in Turkey, Poland, and Sweden. What neither France nor Russia knew was that the British were at that very moment negotiating with Bestuzhev's archenemy, Frederick of Prussia. If Bestuzhev had been a mind reader, he would have known that the British were already discussing the means to widen the understanding of the term "common enemy" in the Russian treaty, as the Russians clearly intended only Prussia. The British were well aware that the Anglo-Russian treaty could not really be considered binding if the Prussians should come to terms.[20]

20. Newcastle to Williams, Oct. 2, 1755, and Holderness to Williams, Dec. 26, 1755; both reprinted in Waddington, *op. cit.*, pp. 125, 224.

To all appearances, however, Bestuzhev's victory was untainted. Under these circumstances the stay of the French spy Douglas in the Russian capital lasted only sixteen days. Considering the short duration of this visit, a great deal was accomplished, even though Douglas was at the mercy of the British representatives in the Russian capital. It was the custom for visitors to come closely under the supervision of their nation's ambassador: Douglas, for example, received his mail in St. Petersburg through the British Resident. Since he posed as an Englishman, the Scot could be presented at court only by Hanbury-Williams.

Ambassador Williams knew of Douglas's arrival immediately, for the foreign population of St. Petersburg was too small to hide a newcomer. The ambassador was quite suspicious.[21] Douglas paid the customary call on "his" ambassador but found Williams "disdainful." The ambassador demanded letters from Britain that the visitor did not have and then accused Douglas of "being involved in the late unhappy Scottish affair." Williams refused Douglas an audience with the Empress and ordered him out of St. Petersburg and out of Russia within the week. Douglas drew the not unwarranted conclusion that Williams had an idea of his purposes. "I have a certain conviction that the Grand Chancellor and Williams have discovered a mystery in my travels in Russia, and think me representing the affairs of Prince Edward or of France."

But though the doors of the palace were officially closed to Douglas, the French party was delighted by his arrival. Through the instrumentality of Michel de Rouen, Douglas was introduced to the Vice-Chancellor Mikhail Vorontsov. The Vice-Chancellor and his household were incensed at the action of the British ambassador, and, as Douglas reported, "the beautiful ladies chided the Ambassador, asking him if he wished to reduce them to eating only English ragouts, or perhaps to enroll them all in the number of the Whigs." Vorontsov gave a large dinner party at which Douglas was the guest of honor

21. Williams to Holderness, St. Petersburg, Oct. 5, 1755: reprinted in A. I. Turgenev (ed.), *La cour de Russie il y a cent ans 1725–1783: Extraits des dépêches des ambassadeurs anglais* (Paris: E. Dentu, 1858), p. 143.

and at which many of the court appeared. The Empress herself learned of the visitor through Vorontsov and asked him to
appear at an Italian concert given under her patronage.

Beneath the surface formalities the French party was
vitally concerned with Douglas and his visit. Douglas found
the Shuvalovs, the Razumovskiis, the Narishkins, the Dolgoru-
kiis, and even the Grand Chancellor's brother Mikhail Petrovich desperately in search of support against Bestuzhev. The
Vice-Chancellor, reported Douglas, "was already carefully informed of my acquaintance with the Prince de Conti," no doubt
by Michel. Vorontsov was terribly concerned to discover "if I
had a letter from the Prince or some witness of his confidence
in me." The Russians were upset when no such letters could be
produced. Douglas was obliged to "give my word that . . . I
would return one more time, but recommended by my family
and friends."

Vorontsov continued to hint at his desire to be considered
with esteem by Conti and the French King. As the stay of
Douglas came to an end, Vorontsov finally found courage to
be explicit. He charged Douglas to tell the French ministry
that the "Empress of Russia had the most sincere will and
ardent desire to see a union established between the two
states." The Vice-Chancellor proposed that the French send
back a representative to Russia, once again in secret, who
would be authorized to treat for the reopening of relations.
The person so charged would write ahead to Vorontsov, identi-
fying himself as "he who was charged to procure a librarian
and send the Burgundy wines." Vorontsov would warn the
military governor at Riga to speed through anyone appearing
in that capacity.

Vorontsov was equally insistent that his chief, Grand
Chancellor Bestuzhev, be kept completely in the dark on these
matters. He was quite willing to acknowledge the power of
Bestuzhev to wreck his plans. "It is of the utmost consequence
that he never be informed of this coup until it is accomplished
and he learns of it from the lips of the Empress herself." When
asked by Douglas if he thought the British subsidy treaty
would impede these plans, Vorontsov said that it would be in

France's power to end that treaty and perhaps eliminate "that monster" Bestuzhev in the process.

The Chevalier Douglas, finally, was charged by Vorontsov with another mission of a less serious nature which the Vice-Chancellor felt would create good dispositions between the two courts. The Empress Elizabeth possessed an inordinate quantity of feminine vanity and had never, in her eyes, received proper treatment from a portrait painter. The Empress had been trying to secure the services of Louis Tocqué, the most famous portrait painter of his day, by unofficial contacts through the French financier Paris-de-Marmontel. Tocqué was uninterested in traveling to Russia. Now Vorontsov hoped that Douglas would bring weight to bear at Versailles to persuade the painter to please the Empress. Douglas promised to do his best to have a Frenchman on the scene before the appearance of a court painter from Vienna or London.

Thus, Douglas, come as a simple spy into Russia, found himself bound into events whose import surely overwhelmed him. The French party in Russia had seized upon this opportunity of his visit to press the reopening of relations with France and thus bolster their strength for an attack on Bestuzhev. Douglas had no orders and no advice for this development. He could only listen and promise to report to his employers. Douglas left St. Petersburg and, pursuant to the orders of his apparent ambassador, departed from Russia at Narva on October 22, 1755. A dashing trip brought him to Paris by December 29, where he reported fully and separately to both Conti and Rouillé within the week.[22]

While Douglas was making his speedy and successful scouting trip into Russia, a parallel mission began which throws much light on the status of the Secret with regard to Russia. The Prince de Conti, at the head of the Secret, seemed to have

22. This section is based upon undated notes by Douglas, 1755: *AMAE MD R* 5, 172; Douglas to Hamilton, Riga, Oct. 29, 1755: *AMAE CP R,* Suppl. 8, 89; Douglas to Hamilton, Narva, Oct. 22, 1755: *ibid.,* Suppl. 8, 86; and especially upon the memoirs of Douglas for his first visit, First Memoir, Paris, Jan. 6, 1755; and Second Memoir, Paris, Jan. 7, 1756; both *BN SM NAF* 22009, 9–35. For Tocqué, see Count Arnauld Doria, *Louis Tocqué* (Paris: Edition Beaux Arts, 1921), and Marc Furcy-Renaud, *L'engagement de Tocqué à la cour d'Elisabeth* (Paris: A. Colin, 1903).

decided to play a double game with his own agents. It was reasonably clear that Conti had not informed the Secret agents in Poland or at other courts, nor had permitted the Ministry to inform them, that the Douglas mission was taking place. This was first revealed when Louis de Cardevac, Marquis d'Havrincourt, French Ambassador to Sweden and an agent of the Secret since 1754, wrote to Tercier in November, 1755:

I heard the day before yesterday . . . that an Englishman named Douglas has shown up in St. Petersburg and has seen Williams, but that Williams refused to present him at court. . . . What I have concluded from all this is that this Englishman is nothing more than an adventurer, or worse, a liar planted to suggest that the King . . . is following some secret negotiation in Russia.[23]

Conti's reluctance to expose the Douglas mission to his own agents was also demonstrated in Poland. He did not notify Broglie, director of the Secret in the field. The Count de Broglie, having heard the rumors of Anglo-Russian talks and receiving no word from Conti or the ministry, was naturally fearful of Russian moves against Poland and inaugurated his own fact-finding mission. A certain Messonnier de Valcroissant entered Russia from Poland in December, 1755, after the departure of Douglas.[24] He was operating under orders given by Broglie under supervision of Durand de Distroff, French Resident in Warsaw and Broglie's chief agent of the Secret in Poland. Valcroissant's mission, already accomplished by Douglas unknown to the Polish agents, was to discover the state of Anglo-Russian negotiations and observe the size of Russian troop movements.[25]

Valcroissant pursued his mission inside Russian frontiers, collecting rumors, buying information, observing troop movements. While operating in Riga on December 30 he met a

23. Havrincourt to Tercier, Stockholm, Nov. 14, 1755: *AMAE CP R*, Suppl. 8, 100–101.
24. Albert Vandal (*Louis XV et Elisabeth de Russie* [Paris: Plon, 1911], p. 259) and Rambaud (*op. cit.*, IX, 5) placed Valcroissant's mission in 1754, before the visit of Douglas, making a sensible explanation of the journey impossible. For the date of the mission as December, 1755, see the letters of Valcroissant to Rouillé, beginning Mar. 10, 1756: *AMAE CP R*, Suppl. 8, 185–191.
25. Tercier to Douglas, Versailles, May 11, 1756: *BN SM NAF* 22009, 71.

certain Chevalier Luci of Metz. This meeting was unfortunate for Valcroissant. The Chevalier Luci operated under various pseudonyms, including the Chevalier de Leussy and the Baron de Leutreum. His real name was Claude de Tschoudi, and Luci the name he used in Russia. Characteristic of a large breed of Frenchmen of his day, Luci had enjoyed a wild career. Born in Metz in 1720, he had worked for a while in the Parlement of that city. A cousin of the librettist for Gluck's *Echo et Narcisse* and an amateur actor, he soon began to travel. While in Italy he got into serious trouble for authoring a work called *Le vatican vengée,* an apology for the Freemasons that the Pope condemned. He then fled into Russia where he joined a troupe of actors. Due to the patronage of Ivan Shuvalov, Luci soon became governor of pages at court and then secretary to Shuvalov for affairs of the University of Moscow.[26]

Luci, when Valcroissant encountered him in Riga, was on his way back for a short and secret visit with his family in France. The two men, fellow nationals, decided to share lodgings. The next day Valcroissant entrusted a letter to Luci, actually a coded message for Durand in Warsaw, asking his new friend to post it at Memel. This was a serious mistake. Luci, as Shuvalov later reported, "having remarked that the conduct of Valcroissant was observed at Riga and judging his mission to be a mischievous affair," sped his letter directly to his Russian patron.[27]

Valcroissant was quickly arrested in Riga. The Russians found, hidden in a jar of preserves, a letter from Durand containing instructions and some collected facts on Russian frontier forces. Valcroissant later reported, "I had a chance to burn my other papers and eat a coded letter." The spy was subjected to an examination by Ivan Shuvalov and Mikhail Vorontsov in a secret proceeding. The Russians had been watching this spy from Poland all along, but Vorontsov, out of consideration for

26. R. Aloys Mooser, *L'opéra comique française en Russie au XVIIIe siècle* (Geneva: René Kister, 1954), p. 20; Rouillé to D'Argenson, May 3, 1756: *BN SM NAF* 23975, 19; and Shuvalov to Rouillé, St. Petersburg, June 29, 1756: *BN SM NAF* 23976, 40.

27. Memoir for Rouillé, May 23, 1756: *BN SM NAF* 23975, 22–23; and Ivan Shuvalov to Rouillé, St. Petersburg, June 29, 1756: *BN SM NAF* 23975, 40.

a possible future friendship with France, had let him keep on. But in Revel and Riga, they charged, he had become too bold, bribing officers to deliver information and even attempting to buy defections from the Russian service. Valcroissant was also charged with sending military secrets out of Russia. The unfortunate agent was found guilty of spying and thrown into the Schlüsselburg fortress.[28]

Luci, the cause of Valcroissant's misfortune, proceeded boldly to France. Durand, always careful to protect the Secret, finally notified Rouillé at the ministry of the mission and its sad results. The officials at Versailles expected Luci at his home in Metz, "and the intention of His Majesty is that he be arrested on the spot and put away." Luci gave the French authorities no difficulties in finding him. Writing this time under the name of the Baron de Leutreum, he approached the Ministry of Foreign Affairs with an offer to report on the secrets of the Russian court, naturally for a reasonable fee. The ministry was only too happy to welcome this elusive fly into its web. On May 16 the Chevalier Luci was thrown into the Bastille.[29]

The problem of these two incarcerated agents would arise again. For the moment the Valcroissant mission, long shrouded in mystery and error, posed two problems. Why did the Russians choose to arrest Valcroissant in December, 1755, when Vorontsov had been able to protect and welcome Douglas in October? And, even more significant, why had Conti allowed the Secret in Poland to proceed with its own plans in Russia without informing them either that a mission was already underway or, once completed, that such a mission had been successfully concluded?

To the first question it may be answered that the Russians were at first wary of handling Valcroissant, thinking him perhaps a more official representative than he was. But he was French, as Douglas was not, which doubtless aroused suspicions in the anti-French camp which even Mikhail Vorontsov could not detour. Besides, Michel de Rouen had introduced

---

28. Valcroissant to Rouillé, St. Petersburg, Mar. 10, 1756: *AMAE CP R*, Suppl. 8, 191.

29. The documents on Luci in France are in *BN SM NAF* 23975, 10–29.

Douglas but had no knowledge whatever of Valcroissant. In addition, Valcroissant was operating from Warsaw, as the Russians well knew. The French agents in Poland were notoriously anti-Russian and had scored repeated blows against Russian interests since 1750. Lastly, Valcroissant was a blatant spy. Where Douglas had marched through the front door of the capital, Valcroissant had skulked about the frontiers. Once Ivan Shuvalov had been informed of Valcroissant's activities, it would have been difficult for anyone to divert attention from the case. As Shuvalov himself noted, the man's espionage activities passed the bounds of tolerance.

The second question demanded a more complex answer. The reasons for Conti's silence to the rest of the Secret in the field on the Douglas mission rested with the ambitions of the Prince. Conti's Secret in Poland, under the direction of Broglie, had been operating for years on certain basic propositions:

(1) That Conti should be elected to the Polish throne when next it fell vacant.

(2) That such an election was in the best interests of France because it would cement French alliances in Turkey and Sweden, would neutralize Austria, and would keep Russia out of Europe.

(3) That the most dangerous enemy of the stated propositions was the Russian Empire, whose agents and sympathizers in Poland had been operating with increased success against France since Peter the Great.

The Secret, therefore, operated in the firm belief that the dynastic ambitions of Conti in Poland and the national interest of France in general were united and mutually rewarding and would remain diametrically opposed to the ambitions of the Russian Empire.

However, unknown to the Secret agents in Warsaw, Constantinople, and Stockholm, Conti's dynastic ambitions were personal, flexible, and capable of being adapted to events. They were not created out of any great love for Poland or any profound awareness of France's best interest. The Count de Broglie in Poland had reason enough to suspect this, since all his diligent efforts to strengthen the Polish monarchy for effective resistance to the Russian party had been bitterly opposed by Conti for fear of strengthening thereby the Saxon house on the throne.[30] Subsequent developments left no doubt that Conti saw the possibilities after 1755 of another royal home in Eastern Europe or of a different and perhaps more realistic route to the Polish throne. It was within Russia's power to fill the vacant Duchy of Courland. It was even conceivable that it might soon again be within Russia's power to name the next King of Poland, and, of course, the Empress Elizabeth was to all appearances still unmarried. It was just possible that in the future state of affairs Conti might hope to be called to Courland, to the Polish throne, or even to the formerly attractive throne of Russia.

Future developments in the Secret indicate that Conti kept the Douglas mission a secret from his agents in the field precisely because he preferred two irons in the fire, the future of either being to his advantage. He did not want to frighten his agents in Poland by an abrupt change of face toward Russia, but neither did he want to close out the possibility of future Russian usefulness by subjecting Douglas to the violently anti-Russian Warsaw agents under Broglie. The Secret in Poland would find it difficult enough to handle a Franco-Russian rapprochement if such ever developed. There was no sense in arousing their fears or facing them with incongruities before such an event was even a prospect. The result was to prepare a split in the efforts of the Secret: French agents working for the dynastic ambitions of Conti to placate the Russians and French agents working in their national interest to resist them. These two threads could only be reconciled while Conti held the reins, since it was a personal bond only that united the efforts of the Secret.

It was in this indecisive state of affairs that the year 1755 drew to a close. New forces in Europe were preparing to intervene to determine the future of these small beginnings.

30. Albert, Duc de Broglie, *Le secret du roi: correspondance secrète de Louis XV avec ses agents diploma-* *tiques* (Paris: Calmann-Lévy, 1878), I, 101–3.

CHAPTER **2**

# A Return Visit

THE IMMEDIATE RESPONSE of the French authorities to the message carried by Douglas from the French party in Russia will never be known. Douglas made his reports in early January, 1756, but important events suddenly altered the situation into which they were received. The Austrian Ambassador, attempting to press France into a neutrality treaty so that Austria could proceed with the recovery of Silesia, revealed that the Prussians were secretly negotiating with the British. The second movement of the diplomatic revolution was under way.

France was loath to believe that its Prussian ally would deal so treacherously, but began to take precautions by turning a kindlier ear to Vienna. A minister was dispatched posthaste to renew the Franco-Prussian alliance at Berlin. It was too late. On January 27, 1756, Frederick of Prussia announced the signing of the Treaty of Westminster with Great Britain, mutually guaranteeing their German lands. Thus, Britain could protect Hanover and Prussia protect Silesia. The diplomatic revolution was in full swing.[1]

---

1. General coverage of the events of the diplomatic revolution will be found in Albert, Duc de Broglie, *L'alliance Autrichienne, 1756* (Paris: C. Lévy, 1895); R. Waddington, *op. cit.,* and Sergei M. Solov'ëv, *Istoriia Rossii s' drevneishikh vremën* (Moscow, 1871), Vol. XXIV, Chap. 1.

Even observers less politically aware saw that Britain had finessed Frederick into an alliance. Duclos noted in his memoirs that "the Russians, whom the English had invoked, frighten Frederick, and he reasonably fears to be crushed among so many powers." [2] Although Frederick evidently expected France to accept the new dispensation in good grace, since it was by no means intended as an offensive alliance against her, France was in no position to welcome diplomatic isolation. The commercial and colonial war which was raging with Britain was no less real for being unofficial. France now pursued its Austrian negotiations with much more interest and much less choice.

France could draw some minor consolation from these events. If Britain had pressed Prussia to a treaty, there was every possibility that Russia would take this betrayal of its troop commitment to the British very badly. There might be an excellent opportunity to convince Russia to throw over this commitment and retreat from involvement. It was in this light that the Chevalier Douglas received a short note from Secretary of State Rouillé notifying him that he would undertake a return visit to Russia immediately. His mission was simple. The Anglo-Russian subsidy treaty was to be jettisoned and the influence of Grand Chancellor Bestuzhev reduced. All the rest in Russia could await more opportune times. [3]

In late January, Tercier, in his double role as representative of the Ministry and of the Secret, and the Sieur Nicolas Monin, confidential secretary of the Prince de Conti, began preparing instructions for the second mission of Douglas into Russia. Douglas was again an agent of both the Ministry and the Secret, but this time he was informed of the long-range aims of the Secret on Conti's behalf. His primary mission from the Ministry of Foreign Affairs was to convince the Russians that their treaty with the British had been betrayed and that they should repudiate their troop commitments. At the same time he was given secret orders to take every opportunity to

2. C. P. Duclos, *Mémoires secrètes sur les regnes de Louis XIV et de Louis XV* (Lausanne: Mourer, 1791), II, 399.

3. Rouillé to Douglas, Feb. 9, 1756: *BN SM NAF* 22009, 37–39.

prepare for Conti the Russian army command, the Duchy of Courland, and ultimately the Polish throne. Once again the second set of orders was issued unknown to all in the French Ministry except Tercier.[4]

The official instructions from the Ministry made it quite clear that the breaking of the subsidy treaty, not the reopening of relations, was the purpose of this mission. Practically every secondary account has described the purpose as the restoration of official contact, but such was not the case. France wanted neutrality from Russia and expected and hoped for no more. Douglas was commissioned to offer secret subsidies to Russia to make up for the loss of British payments if the subsidy treaty was repudiated. Of course, he was not to offer these subsidies unless the Russians raised the issue. He was also instructed to use mild threats to Vorontsov about possible belligerent feeling in Poland and in Turkey if the British ties were not jettisoned. Discretion in all this was of the utmost importance to avoid frightening French allies in Sweden, Poland, and Turkey by the prospect of a Franco-Russian deal.

As to the possible reunion of the two courts, that was relegated to the distant future. If Vorontsov pressed the matter, Douglas was provided with a complicated plan for the exchange of consuls that was designed to prolong negotiations for an indefinite time. France was not interested at that time and under those conditions in parading any activities in Russia before the public view. This second journey of the Chevalier Douglas was generated by the Anglo-Prussian treaty, as his first journey had been generated by the Anglo-Russian treaty. Neither was undertaken from any inherent mutual interest nor from any hope for future "systems." Circumstances beyond France's control had caused her to send a French agent into Russia. External circumstances were to determine his fate.[5]

Secretary of State Rouillé notified Vorontsov that Douglas was on his way back into Russia with the agreed password:

4. Instructions, January, 1756: reprinted in Rambaud, *op. cit.*, IX, 18–27.
5. For testimony on the purpose of this mission, see Memoir in Foreign Affairs, Versailles, Feb. 9, 1756: *BN SM NAF* 23975, 2–4; and Rouillé to Douglas, Feb. 9, 1756: *ibid.* 22009, 39.

"The person whom Your Excellency commissioned to choose you a librarian and to send you some Burgundy wines is charged to witness my esteem to you." [6] The Scot left Paris for the second time on February 14, 1756.

While Douglas was making his way across a frightened Europe, the British were busy in St. Petersburg attempting the reconciliation of their two latest treaties. The Anglo-Russian treaty provided for action against the "common enemy," by which the Russians happily understood the King of Prussia. The Treaty of Westminster made this interpretation useless to the British, and they were pressing for a more general understanding of the treaty. [7] They were attempting to reconcile the irreconcilable. They had actually betrayed Grand Chancellor Bestuzhev by the Prussian move, and the Russians knew it. The French were still naïve enough to think that Russia recognized money but not its own interests and that it would require a secret mission to direct Russian attention to the proper course. Such was not the case. On February 19, long before the Chevalier Douglas reappeared in St. Petersburg, the good sense of the Russians had accomplished his mission for him.

The Empress of Russia, to leave no place for misunderstanding and to avoid all mistake, sends notification that in case of the diversion to which she is engaged by the convention just concluded, it can and must be applied only when the King of Prussia will attack the states of the King of England or of his allies. [8]

On March 25 the Empress Elizabeth held a full-scale Council meeting, at which the Grand Duke Peter, Grand Chancellor Bestuzhev and his brother Mikhail, Vice-Chancellor Vorontsov, Aleksandr and Pëtr Shuvalov, and Field Marshal Stepan Fëdorovich Apraksin were present. The results of this meeting clearly sealed the doom of the British alliance and signaled the beginning of disaster for the Grand Chancellor. The members of the Council, excluding always the Grand

6. Rouillé to Vorontsov, Feb. 9, 1756: *ibid.* 22009, 41.
7. Exchange of letters between Holderness and Williams from Oct. 2, 1755, to Dec. 26, 1755: Waddington, *op. cit.*, pp. 125 and 224.
8. Most secret declaration annexed to dispatch of Williams to Holderness, Feb. 19, 1756: *ibid.*, p. 350.

Duke, agreed to treat with Austria as soon as possible for an offensive alliance against Prussia, to which Russia would contribute as many as eighty thousand troops.

The Council further decided that France was not to be feared at present, since the British war occupied the French sufficiently. The members also recommended that their ministers at foreign courts be respectful and courteous with the French representatives to gain the neutrality of France in the Continental war which was inevitably coming. The arguments of some historians that France could have allied with Russia to force Austria and Prussia to keep the peace were demolished at this early date by the obvious intentions of the Russians to wage a war. It was interesting, too, that the Russians wanted no more from the French than the French wanted of them — neutrality. The Russian Council went on to agree that Poland was to be prepared for the passage of Russian troops and that Turkey and Sweden would have to be kept at peace. The aims of the war, according to the council, included the defeat and weakening of Frederick of Prussia, the restoration of Silesia to Austria, the cession of East Prussia to Russia (which would exchange it with Poland for Courland and a border "rectification" with Poland in the Ukraine).[9]

The decisions of the group were implemented immediately. Negotiations began among Bestuzhev, Vorontsov, and the Austrian Ambassador, Prince Nicholas Esterhazy, unknown to the British Ambassador, Williams. An offensive Austro-Russian treaty was discussed, based on a mutual contribution of eighty thousand men and a simultaneous attack on Prussia. Hostilities were to be continued until Silesia was secure and East Prussia was in Russian hands. These territorial compensations were not embodied in the final treaty, probably due to Austrian beliefs that they might be able to cede less and to Russian expectations that they might be able to extract more. In the middle of these discussions, Esterhazy received orders

9. Notes of the Russian Council of Mar. 25: reprinted in Solov'ëv, *op. cit.*, XXIV, 26–28.

from Kaunitz in Vienna to slow down the Russian talks until some definite arrangements with France could be made.[10]

Meanwhile, news of the British difficulties with the Russians came to the French Ministry of Foreign Affairs, probably from Michel de Rouen or perhaps from Vorontsov himself, and were rapidly transmitted to Douglas en route:

This letter will inform you of the state of that affair which you left when you returned from your first journey. Following the news that your family originally heard, we find that there is argument and division in a family that you knew there. You have already seen the beginnings of it. We are assured that it is growing.[11]

Bestuzhev was indeed disturbed. He had pressed the British alliance as the logical conclusion to the Austrian union of preceding years, only to find that the British had betrayed his devotion at the moment he was ready to unleash Russian power in Eastern Europe. Bestuzhev clung tenaciously to the possibility of salvaging some part of the British tie, but even the veteran diplomat Williams was shocked by the message he was required to deliver to his former collaborator:

His Britannic Majesty considers neither useful nor necessary any commentary on the treaty between His Majesty and the Empress of Russia recently concluded. He can see only that the Russian court revokes a formal engagement which cannot be modified, to come to the aid of England in case of an attack by any enemy whatever.[12]

At the same time the Chevalier Douglas notified Vorontsov of his imminent arrival by the appropriate passwords, and on April 21 he was in St. Petersburg. His purposes were now confused, since his primary mission had already been effected by the Russians. His first message to Vice-Chancellor Vorontsov treated of the disadvantages of the British alliance — which the

10. Letters of Esterhazy and Kaunitz, Apr. 1 to May 2, 1756: reprinted in Alfred von Arneth, *Geschichte Maria Theresia* (Vienna, 1863–1879), V, 46–48. For a discussion of Austrian policy in Russia during this period, see Yevgerii N. Shchepkin, *Russko-Avstriiskii soyuz vo vremia semiletnei voiny, 1746–1758 gg.* (St. Petersburg: V. S. Balashevi, 1902.)

11. Tercier to Douglas, Mar. 25, 1756: *BN SM NAF* 22009, 56.

12. Holderness to Williams, for delivery to the Grand Chancellor, Mar. 30, 1756: reprinted in Waddington, *op. cit.*, p. 352.

Russian government had already seen — and asked for the removal of Bestuzhev — which the Vice-Chancellor had been pursuing unsuccessfully these many years. There was little of startling content. Douglas wandered aimlessly while the Easter festivals kept official business at a standstill, and he delivered a few presents to the outstanding members of the French party.[13]

Fate and the unexpected once again intervened, and once again significant European events determined the course of the Scot. On May 1, in French Secretary of State Rouillé's residence at Jouy, the misnamed First Treaty of Versailles was signed between France and Austria. By Austrian shrewdness and by French design, the treaty was defensive. France was thoroughly uninterested in agreements to make war on the Continent, wishing merely to rectify the diplomatic imbalance that they felt had been created by the Anglo-Prussian treaty. Austria was to remain neutral in the present Anglo-French war, but was to join France against any new invader. France in turn promised to assist Austria in repulsing any aggressor. Twenty-four thousand troops were to be sent in aid, but by mutual agreement the troops might be replaced by a financial subsidy. France and Austria had come to some tentative agreements about French gains in the Netherlands and in Italy in case of a European war, but these were not embodied in the treaty.

The new Austro-French defensive treaty immediately threw the question of reopening relations between France and Russia into the foreground. Russia and Austria had long been bound by defensive treaties and shared a mutual hatred of Prussia. It behooved any healthily suspicious state to know what friends were doing, even if they qualified only as friends of friends. France needed to be aware of Austro-Russian plans and relationships, and this was nearly impossible without an official representative in St. Petersburg.

The Ministry and the Secret both immediately sent Douglas notice of the newly concluded treaty. The Secret, in the

13. Memoir for the Vice-Chancellor alone, St. Petersburg, Apr. 22, 1756: *AMAE CP R*, Suppl. 8, 207–208; and list of jewels bought by Douglas, Sept. 9, 1756: *BN SM NAF* 22010, 69.

person of Conti, went further and provided the Scot with the means to send rapid private couriers to Versailles. If France decided to accredit an official in Russia and quick communication became necessary, Conti wished to be ready. The Prince saw the Polish crown glittering more closely to his hand than ever before.[14]

Meanwhile, Douglas was passing through the court formalities in St. Petersburg. The British Ambassador, in his current confusion, did not impede his visit, and the Scot was received in audience by the Empress Elizabeth on May 6. "What a striking spectacle when the Empress deigns to honor the court with her presence. The majestic brilliance which radiates from her person announces the queen of all hearts." Vorontsov thought this reception to augur well for the reopening of relations with France. On the day after the audience, Douglas was again urged by the Vice-Chancellor to obtain accreditation as French chargé d'affaires in St. Petersburg. Vorontsov was already planning to send a member of his household, Fëdor Dmitrievich Bektiev, into France to be available for the same purpose.[15]

However, the French Ministry of Foreign Affairs was not so precipitate. "You should retain your incognito," they informed Douglas. "That way if these negotiations end badly you will not have compromised the King." [16] Douglas, not having received these orders, was begging the Ministry for permission to assume official status. The Vice-Chancellor, Vorontsov, needed this step, pleaded Douglas, because the British Ambassador and the Grand Chancellor were seemingly aware of the Scot's return and his motives and might expose the matter at court. If the French did not permit Douglas to reveal himself, the Chevalier argued, Vorontsov would lose face and Douglas might again be expelled from Russia. Vorontsov also desired more precise information about the new Franco-Austrian treaty. To carry these pleas and requests, Douglas sent Michel

14. Tercier to Douglas, May 3, 1756: BN SM NAF 22009, 65.

15. Douglas to Tercier, May 8, 1756, and Douglas to Rouillé, May 23, 1756: ibid. 22009, 95, 100.

16. Tercier to Douglas, May 11, 1756: ibid. 22009, 71.

on a rapid mission to Versailles. The merchant left Russia on May 24.[17]

Before the arguments propounded by Douglas could reach Versailles, the Ministry of Foreign Affairs had resolved upon its new course. Because of the requirements of the new Austrian attachments, the long, involved process for reopening relations with Russia that had been contained in the original instructions to Douglas were finally jettisoned. New instructions arrived in Russia empowering Douglas to treat for an exchange of chargés d'affaires. Douglas and Vorontsov quickly reached agreement on the exchange and even planned the joint naming of ambassadors for September 15, 1756, with the ambassadors to assume their posts by the following January.[18]

Letters of credence for Douglas as chargé d'affaires were sent by the French Ministry on June 16. Rouillé and others at Versailles were fearful that Bestuzhev would take the secrecy of these negotiations very badly. They ordered Douglas to deliver his letters to Bestuzhev if at all possible, in hopes of repairing some of the damage. However, the French Ministry still enclosed a second set of letters addressed to the Vice-Chancellor, in case Vorontsov continued to insist on operating the affair through himself. Meanwhile, Bektiev was leaving for France by way of Holland to obscure his mission. With the arrival of Michel in Paris on June 14, the Ministry sent copies of the First Treaty of Versailles, minus all secret articles, for Vorontsov's perusal.

Fëdor Bektiev, intimate friend and employee of Vorontsov and now chargé in France, arrived at his post on July 24. He presented his letters to Rouillé and delivered a blank check for the appointment of a French ambassador to Russia to be dated at his order. Bektiev's welcome was a mixed one, symbolic of the French distate and distrust of this hurriedly accomplished business. The first man to know of his arrival after the Minister was the Chief of Police. "You are informed that . . . a Russian gentleman named Bektiev has arrived in Paris, living at the

17. Douglas to Rouillé, St. Petersburg, May 23, 1756: *ibid.* 22009, 107–114.

18. Notes in the Ministry of Foreign Affairs, 1756: *AMAE CP R* Suppl. 9, 17.

Hotel Port Mahon, Rue Jacob. I feel it imperative to have his activities and connections observed, above all if he sees Kniphausen [the Prussian Ambassador] often." The necessary precautions were taken.[19]

At St. Petersburg the situation was much more explosive. The Empress Elizabeth was informed by Vorontsov of French dispositions and was delighted that her long sympathy for all things French could now be expressed. She ordered Vorontsov to inform Grand Chancellor Bestuzhev of the French negotiations so that he might receive the letters of credence from Douglas. When Douglas finally met Grand Chancellor Bestuzhev on July 24, after so much intrigue and deception, he found the redoubtable Russian minister annoyed but reasonable. He did not blame Douglas for the underhanded dealings, but said that "these were tokens of the scorn that the French court holds for him and his principles." While Douglas was happy to accept the reopening of Franco-Russian relations as the final nail in the coffin of the Grand Chancellor, Vorontsov, veteran of many an ill-fated intrigue against his colleague, was not so ready to dismiss Bestuzhev. Said he, mixing metaphors for emphasis, "It is necessary to walk with the Chancellor as on ice and moving sand."[20]

The month of June, while Douglas was sure of the satisfactory direction of negotiations but was awaiting official word of their consummation, was taken up with three problems: the first concerned Valcroissant, the French agent of the Secret in Poland, who had been imprisoned in Russia; the second concerned the French painter Tocqué; and the third concerned a secretary for the new French headquarters in St. Petersburg.

Valcroissant had been arrested in Riga on evidence provided by the Chevalier Luci, a French employee of Ivan Shuvalov. Luci was in turn arrested on his return to France. News of this arrest finally reached his patron, Ivan Shuvalov.

19. Rouillé to Berryer, Compiègne, August 11, 1756, and Berryer to Rouillé, Aug. 12, 1756: BN SM NAF 22009, 217–221. For the instructions of Bektiev, see Bartenev, op. cit., III, 422, and Solov'ëv, op. cit., XXIV,

68. The correspondence of Bektiev is reprinted in Bartenev, op. cit., III, 147–307, and VI, 208–320.
20. Douglas to Rouillé, St. Petersburg, July 31, 1756: BN SM NAF 22010, 25.

Immediately Shuvalov wrote to the French Foreign Minister, Rouillé, defending the actions of Luci in turning Valcroissant over to the Russians as a spy and recommending a mutual release now that relations between the states had so improved.[21]

Douglas advised Versailles that an exchange of prisoners might be the best solution. France should "cut off from her body a gangrened member and throw it away from her." The Ministry was of the same opinion and ordered the release of the Chevalier Luci on August 1, 1756. Tercier notified Bektiev that Luci had been released and shipped back to his Russian patrons and demanded the reciprocal release of Messonnier de Valcroissant. The spy Valcroissant was freed on September 10 and placed in the care of Douglas. Thus, the results of Douglas's first negotiation were successful. The new union of France and Russia had at least procured something as solid as the freedom of two unhappy spies.[22]

The second undertaking of Douglas in his new role was minor but similarly successful. He had been instructed on leaving for Russia the second time to explain to the Empress Elizabeth that distance and loss of clients impeded the painter Tocqué from going into Russia. "Petersburg must never think that in France we consider that they do not appreciate or reward talent in Russia. That is a particular truth which has no relation to the present conditions between the two states." [23] Vorontsov was unsatisfied with the explanation and told Douglas that the Russian court would provide as much cash as necessary to entice the artist. The shifting state of French official thinking on Russia after the Austrian treaty also changed their minds on this matter. Douglas and the French Ministry began to bring pressure to bear on Tocqué to visit Russia to keep the Empress happy. No doubt the promise of a substantial salary and a pension from the King of France helped. In any case, the

21. Ivan Shuvalov to Rouillé, St. Petersburg, June 29, 1756: *BN SM NAF* 23975, 39–40.
22. Rouillé to D'Argenson, July 28, 1756; D'Argenson to Bastille, Aug. 1, 1756; Tercier to Bektiev, Aug. 3,

1756; Valcroissant to Durand, Sept. 14, 1756: *BN SM NAF* 23975, 60–73. See also Douglas to Durand, Nov. 4, 1756: *BN SM MF* 10661, 85–86.
23. Instructions: reprinted in Rambaud, *op. cit.*, IX, 120.

Tocqués, man and wife, set out from Paris at the end of June and arrived in St. Petersburg on August 7.[24]

Tocqué was immediately presented to the Empress Elizabeth and placed near her for the day to view his subject. Tocqué, in his role at the court, played a minor but interesting part in the flow of reports to France. The artist seemed quite happy to have had his mind changed by the Ministry of Foreign Affairs. Douglas and the Ministry congratulated each other on the happy results of this cultural exchange.

Douglas had one last and most important affair to conclude before his official ratification as French representative in Russia. He had intended to bring with him as secretary on his second trip into Russia a young man whom he had met in the household of the Prince de Conti. The young man could not break away from family commitments at the time. This was the notorious Chevalier d'Éon de Beaumont. D'Éon was born in Tonnerre and practiced law in Lyons. His cousin was Tercier, the *premier commis,* who introduced him into Conti's service and ultimately into the work of the Secret. This was the same D'Éon whose mythical escapades in Russia disguised as a woman were so well circulated, and who actually did spend his last years in England in female disguise.[25]

Immediately after his arrival in St. Petersburg the Chevalier Douglas wrote to Tercier asking if D'Éon could possibly follow soon. D'Éon finally cleared up his affairs and left Paris on June 4, arriving in Russia on August 7.[26] The arrival of the Chevalier d'Éon in Russia signalled a new development in the Secret. This was not simply another secretary on his way to a new post; this was an agent of the Secret bearing new instructions to a key post. D'Éon had been ordered by the Prince de Conti to bring into Russia more strength and support for the particular program of the Secret there, unknown not only to

24. Vorontsov to Douglas, Mar. 6, 1756: *BN SM NAF* 22010, 36–39.
25. AMAE Pers 28, 109, 172, 181, 207.
26. Albert Vandal ( *op. cit.,* p. 266) noted that Douglas and D'Éon traveled into Russia together in April.

This was not the case. See D'Éon to Tercier, St. Petersburg, Aug. 8, 1756: *AMAE CP R,* Suppl. 8, 322; and Tercier to Hermann and Dietrich, June 4, 1756: *BN SM NAF* 22009, 126.

the Ministry but also to Broglie in Poland and the other members of the Secret in Stockholm and at the Porte. D'Éon and Douglas were urged to exercise all their ingenuity to acquire for the Prince de Conti the command of the Russian army and election to the Duchy of Courland. Thus, the "Prince planned to slide easily onto the throne of Poland, or even to marry the Empress Elizabeth." [27] The undercover projects which had been confided to Douglas by Conti's Secret on his departure for the second mission in Russia were now activated by the arrival of D'Éon.

The aims of the Secret diplomacy were now clearly split. The Secret now had two principal centers of operations, Warsaw and St. Petersburg. Each was charged with commissions that were not only different but also contradictory. The Count de Broglie in Poland, an outspoken critic of the Austrian alliance, was firm in the belief that the Austrian-French-Russian understandings were temporary and deceptive at best. Broglie was charged with the maintenance of the integrity of the Polish Republic, and recognized rightly that this charge, now as never before, meant dedicated opposition to Austrian and Russian meddling.[28] Russian troops were to be kept out of Poland and Russian pressures relieved against Sweden and Turkey. All this work would one day, Broglie was confident, erect Poland as a significant power in the French system and secure the Polish throne for a French candidate.

However, Conti had been considering the possibility of more immediate compensations and quicker routes to his goal. His failure to notify Broglie or his agents of the Douglas mission indicated that a plan was in his mind even then. When it became clear in May and June, 1756, that the Ministry intended to reopen relations with Russia through Douglas, already a Secret agent, Conti saw his opportunity. The Prince might well be able to approach Poland more realistically from the Russian side. Therefore, D'Éon and Douglas were instructed to press for Conti's appointment as Russian army commander, in the

27. Monin to Douglas, Paris, June 7, 1756: *AMAE CP R*, Suppl. 8, 273; see also D'Éon to Broglie, London, June 12, 1775: reprinted in Boutaric, *op. cit.*, I, 222, Note 2.
28. Broglie, *Le secret du roi*, I, 256–257.

hope that as payment the Prince would receive the Duchy of
Courland, Russian assistance in Poland, or, even more spec-
tacular, an imperial marriage.

What this meant in practice for the agents of the Secret
in Russia was an acceptance of the Russian alliance as solid
and promising, a willingness to see the power and authority of
the Russian Empire extended, and, naturally, a hope that her
armies would wage victorious war, across Poland or not. Thus,
Conti confirmed a new goal for the Russian branch of the
Secret that seriously clashed with the still active principles of
the Polish branch as embodied in the Count de Broglie. If
Conti's authority over these conflicting means to a single end,
his own aggrandizement, were ever to be removed, the two
branches of the Secret would erupt into open conflict.

During this period preceding official activity, the French
delegation in Russia was forced to face serious obstacles, on
both the official and Secret levels, to convincing the Russians
to fulfill the ambitions of the Prince de Conti in particular or
any French ambitions in general. Despite the progress of the
restoration of relations, there were outstanding areas of Russian
resistance that came to French attention:

(1) The traditional opposition of Conti's agents to Russian interests in Poland, which the Russians had long resented.

(2) The continuing opposition of the Grand Chancellor
Bestuzhev to France in general.

(3) The Young Court.

The Young Court — the Grand Duke Peter and the Grand
Duchess Catherine with their entourage — was the center of
most anti-French feeling at the Russian court. The Grand Duke
Peter was a Prussophile to the point of obsession; foreign
reports abounded with tales of his devotion to Frederick. The
Grand Duchess Catherine, clever, more subtle, and more effective, also feared the French. She was devoted to the British
Ambassador, Williams, and to the Grand Chancellor, and feared
that any renewed French influence would operate against her
future interests.

[Ivan Betskii] asked me what book I was reading and hearing that
it was a history of the secret intrigues of France, he said to me that
England's story did not fall far short of it and that he would send me
a copy. . . . He thought it desirable that harmony with France be
established, for, he said, the arts and sciences are more necessary to
us than anything else. But how, I asked, would a French ambassador
help towards this: would he give public lectures? He answered that
the French, if assured of protection, would establish themselves here
and would cultivate the arts and sciences. To introduce these people
the Ambassador is necessary. All this goes to prove what bad reasoning is employed apparently as better than nothing.[29]

Ambassador Williams used the opportunity and played
upon Catherine's fear of renewed French ties. "The arrival of
a French ambassador will not do me much harm, but I always
fear for you. His arrival is the one thing fatal to your interests.
Think this matter over and send me your reflections. I will send
you mine as to the best means of parrying this thrust."[30]
Catherine's attachment to the British and her desire to defeat
plans for permanent French influence in St. Petersburg were
compounded of equal parts friendship and self-interest. The
extravagant Grand Duchess, whose card games would later
embarrass even the opulent French Ambassador, was always
badly in debt. The inexhaustible source for her expenditures
was Lord Wolff, British Resident in St. Petersburg.[31] Williams
was also her bulwark against the eventualities of the death of
the Empress Elizabeth, so often seriously ill. Catherine was
already giving thought to limiting her infantile husband in the
event of a succession, since Peter might well be expected to
use his new power to revenge himself on his unloved wife.
Lastly, it was Williams who had brought the young and handsome Stanislas Poniatowsky to Russia as his secretary and
sponsored his love affair with Catherine.

What Ambassador Williams and Catherine feared in Aug-

29. Catherine to Williams, Aug. 14,
1756: reprinted in Earl of Ilchester,
*Correspondence of Catherine the
Great While Grand Duchess* (London: Butterworth, 1928), p. 30.
30. Williams to Catherine, Aug. 15,
1756: *ibid.*, p. 36.

31. Drafts of the Grand Duchess
Catherine on Wolff, July 21 to Nov.
11, 1756: reprinted in *Sbornik Imperatorskago Istoricheskago Obsch-
chestva* (St. Petersburg, 1867–1916),
VII, p. 73.

ust of 1756 was rapidly coming to pass: Bestuzhev was finding it impossible to save anything at all from the wreck of the Anglo-Russian subsidy treaty. Williams, always an enemy of the King of Prussia, went about his business with great distaste. His instructions obliged him to consider the treaty concluded by the deposit of the first subsidy payment with Lord Wolff. The Russians refused to take the money, and Bestuzhev told Williams coldly that he "thought it a little too late." The Vice-Chancellor, Vorontsov, was pressing his advantage, using the displeasure of the Empress and the disappointment of the Grand Chancellor to urge the recall of the British Ambassador. At this time the removal of Poniatowsky, whose influence with the Grand Duchess the Empress Elizabeth had always detested, was accomplished. He was sent back to Poland. Williams still held on and struggled to keep his place in the affections of Catherine and Bestuzhev, no doubt because the life of the Empress wavered precariously enough to give him hope of establishing Catherine in her place and reversing his defeats. Williams managed to maintain his bold front:

Is it possible to inform this court of anything without it becoming known to the Vice-Chancellor? Does he think that the confidante of Douglas will have my confidence? The two chancellors and I sometimes act as a triumvirate, and I raise no objections to the Grand Chancellor being Augustus. But I desire at least to be Antony, and during my stay here the Vice-Chancellor shall only be Lepidus.[32]

Meanwhile, the union of France and Russia continued to solidify. Douglas was notified by the Russian Vice-Chancellor that the proposed Ambassador to France was to be the Francophile brother of the Grand Chancellor and member of the French party, Mikhail Bestuzhev. Douglas replied with the information, still unknown to the Grand Chancellor, that the French Ambassador was to be the Marquis de l'Hôpital, then Ambassador of the King at Naples. The Grand Chancellor, stubborn to the last, posed an additional obstacle to the naming of ambassadors by making it necessary to have the signa-

32. Williams to Catherine, Aug. 15, 1756: reprinted in Ilchester, op. cit., p. 34.

ture of the Grand Duke Peter. Bestuzhev felt that the Grand Duke would never agree. The Empress Elizabeth finally forced the compliance of her recalcitrant nephew, but at the cost of further hard feelings between Empress and heir.

The Russian Imperial Council of August 23 resolved to tell the Austrian Ambassador, Esterhazy, that they would be pleased to entertain negotiations for the adherence of Russia to the First Treaty of Versailles, although they did not communicate with Douglas on this matter since he was not yet empowered to undertake such negotiations.[33]

In the midst of these activities in St. Petersburg, French and Austrian negotiators in Paris finally came to an agreement on the inclusion of Russia in their defensive alliance. The intent of Austria to bring France and Russia to its aid came closer to reality. Truly, France was being led down the garden path, because at the same moment the Austrians were discussing defensive commitments at Versailles, they were discussing offensive commitments at St. Petersburg. When Austria and Russia were prepared for their war on Prussia, they would be assured of French benevolent neutrality at the least, and, dependent on events, might even have active French aid in a "defensive" war. The French, on August 14, still intent on rebalancing Europe to preserve the peace, sent orders to Douglas to join the Austrian Ambassador, Esterhazy, in securing the adherence of Russia to the First Treaty of Versailles. Douglas, now in one of the most significant posts in Europe, was at the apex of his career.

At the same moment that instructions to Douglas for negotiating the Russian accession to the defensive treaty were on their way across Europe, Frederick of Prussia was taking steps which made them doubly important. Frederick was reasonably well informed of the Austro-Russian talks of an offensive alliance, even if France was not. On August 28 he demanded assurances from the Empress-Queen Maria Theresa that she was not plotting a war against him. No such assurances were forthcoming. Frederick demanded free passage for

33. For accounts of the Council, see "Tainaia Kantseleria," *Russkaia Sta-* *rina* (St. Petersburg, 1875), XII, 522–39.

his troops across Saxony in the first week of September and, not receiving it, invaded the Electorate of Saxony and put the Elector-King to flight. In the Saxon archives Frederick professed to discover proof of the Austro-Russian plot to partition his territories. The Saxon army was incorporated into his own, and Frederick proceeded immediately to the attack on Maria Theresa of Austria.

Frederick's fear of a very real Austro-Russian threat had led him to strike first. The Seven Years' War had begun, and under the most unfavorable circumstances possible from the French point of view. Frederick's invasion had, as the Austrians must have hoped only in their wildest flights of fancy, invoked the defensive commitments of France to Austria under the recent treaty. France was in the war. The inclusion of Russia in the defensive treaty between France and Austria now became for France no longer useful in keeping the peace, but absolutely imperative for the making of war.

The reopening of relations between France and Russia had happened almost accidentally, impelled in fits and starts by European affairs in which France had little part. The nature of its instrument, an unknown Scot spy suddenly turned diplomat, was a measure of its accidental nature. It was the fate of this union between France and Russia to be born in the threat of war and to be engulfed immediately by the confusions of that war. Alliances born under such threat almost always begin by submerging difficulties and differences in the first exuberance of war. Then the participants must proceed slowly and painfully to recognize and to cope with these differences emerging between them. The approach of victory or defeat or the prolongation of the war usually ends the deceptive unanimity of wartime enthusiasm and puts the true content of the alliance to the test. The story of French policy in Russia during the Seven Years' War was to be the story of the emergence and testing of such differences.

CHAPTER **3**

# The Diplomat

THE OUTBREAK of the Seven Years' War, planned by some, feared by others, discussed by all, nevertheless caught Europe unawares. Austria and Russia, which prepared it, did not begin it; Prussia, which did not want it, precipitated it; France and Great Britain, which had negotiated frantically to avoid it, were parties to it. Europe underwent a cumbersome shift from defensive to offensive alliances.

France was being dragged into a Continental war in which she had no interest. Her need for defensive allies in Europe had driven her into the arms of Austria, and Frederick's sudden attack on the Empress-Queen had invoked the defensive commitments of the Austrian treaty. To keep her newly acquired ally on the Continent, France would be obliged to make war on the King of Prussia. It was hard for French statesmen, even at the outbreak of the war, to see what practical good that could possibly do them.

In these fast-moving events the Chevalier Douglas had found himself precipitated from secret agent to diplomat of the King of France charged with a first-rate mission. Since Russia and France were both committed by treaty to aid Austria, it became expedient for France and Russia to mend their grievances and concert their efforts. A Russian attack on Prussia could mean a quick and successful war. Such Russian aid would entail the movement of an army, and the movement of an army would mean new pressures and old fears in Poland, Turkey, and Sweden. The diplomacy of France in these conditions would be sorely tested. Until an ambassador could be sent, that diplomacy was in the hands of the Chevalier Douglas.

The avalanching events of these months had thrown the French Ministry of Foreign Affairs into confusion and the King's Secret organization into a fright. The Ministry, having committed itself in the enthusiasm of the moment to a Russian alliance, had glimpses of fearsome shadows ahead. The Secret, from the exalted level of the King and Conti to the rough-and-tumble level of the field agents, knew that the future of Poland had to be handled very delicately. Douglas was instructed by the King to keep the Prince de Conti directly and promptly informed of all news from St. Petersburg.[1]

On September 11, when news of Frederick's attack on Austria arrived in St. Petersburg, orders were immediately prepared to set the Russian troops in Livonia, originally established there by the British subsidy treaty, in motion against Prussia. When the necessity and desirability of a Russian movement into Prussian lands became a fact, the French Ministry tried to impress upon Douglas the difficulties for Poland. It was illegal for any state, wrote Rouillé, to cross another without requesting and receiving permission. Douglas was to inform the Russians that such a request was required by the French. If such a request did not receive immediate approval in Warsaw, which it would not, Rouillé recommended that the Russians sail from Livonia to Danzig. Thus, all difficulty with the Poles and their watchdogs at the Sublime Porte could be avoided. "You must defend the King's credit in Poland at all costs."[2]

The Secret, represented in the field by the Count de

<hr>

1. Louis XV to Douglas, Sept. 23, 1756: *AMAE Pers.* 24, 396.

2. Rouillé to Douglas No. 3, Sept. 23, 1756: *BN SM NAF* 22010, 74.

Broglie, was equally insistent to Douglas on safeguards for Poland:

You cannot be too much concerned in making known to the Russian ministers how agreeable it would be to the King that of all the means they might choose to send troops against the King of Prussia, they choose those which will eliminate the march of Russian troops on Polish territory. . . . I have hurried to pass this advice to you so that you will know how important it is to the King that this new union with Russia never disturb in any way the good will he has always accorded Poland.[3]

With the official and the Secret diplomacy united at least momentarily in defense of Polish integrity, Douglas was faced with a troublesome task. He was charged with securing Russian adherence to the Versailles treaty of May 1, which seemed naturally to include French acceptance of the march of Russian troops. At the same time he was ordered to convince the Russians that they must sail or march around, not through, the Republic of Poland. Douglas begged for special funds for this work, maintaining that bribery was the keynote of the Russian court. "It cannot be presumed that I can surmount all the obstacles without making secret expenses . . . which I have done to the amount of 10,000 livres." Douglas further noted that the "secret subsidies which they [Austrians and British] dispense, above all among subalterns, leave them ignorant of nothing which occurs."[4]

As negotiations with France began, the Russians notified the French of their current status, assuring them that the British treaty was abandoned and that their army would move to avenge Saxony and defend Austria as soon as preparations were concluded and the season was congenial. Their statement on Poland, however, was not reassuring:

Although the idea of the Count de Broglie that our troops, in their march, touch Poland as little as possible, is agreed to in principle here and we would like to conform to it, it is nevertheless abso-

3. Broglie to Douglas, Dresden, Sept. 7, 1756: *AMAE CP R*, Suppl. 8, 385–386; this advice was repeated in another letter of Sept. 18, 1756: *ibid.*, Suppl. 8, 388.

4. Douglas to Rouillé, St. Petersburg, Sept. 25, 1756: *AMAE CP R* 51, 23–27.

lutely impossible in view of the country through which we must pass. You may give Broglie the strongest assurances that we will not abuse the necessity of our passage in any way. . . . Of course, we know that the most badly intentioned among the Poles . . . will take this march as a favorable occasion to sow complaints and discord between our two courts.[5]

When Douglas and Esterhazy met for the first time on October 1 to discuss the form of Russia's accession to their treaty, Douglas discovered an even more disturbing Russian approach to Poland. The Russian Ministry had written to Saxony and Austria to notify them of Russian intent to pass an army through Poland and that "notable prejudice would result for Poland if they impeded or opposed that operation." [6]

This Russian determination was received with varying degrees of hostility in France. The French Ministry now seemed prepared to back down before the Russian plans if a quick and harmless passage could be assured. Rouillé's aim was a speedy and successful war.[7] Within the Secret, however, no such concessions were considered. The Prince de Conti was busy with plans for the army, and the Secret was activated by the determined Broglie. The Count could not conceive of any Russian march through Poland being quick or harmless.

The Russians soon began to feel the results of the Secret's activity. Jan Klemens Branicki, Grand General of the Polish Crown, principal leader of the French party in Poland, and a member of the Secret, had already sent envoys to the Porte to alert the Turks on Russian intentions. Durand, French Resident in Warsaw and also a Secret agent, was busy urging the Primate of Poland to oppose the passage of troops with all his power. Durand had also contacted Charles de Vergennes, French Ambassador and Secret member at Constantinople, in the same cause. The Russians complained bitterly to the French Ministry about this pronounced opposition.[8]

5. Imperial rescript to Bektiev at Paris, St. Petersburg, Sept. 30, 1756: reprinted in Bartenev, *op. cit.*, III, 195.
6. Douglas to Tercier, Oct. 2, 1756: *AMAE CP R* 51, 40; see also notes in the King's Council, October, 1756: *BN SM NAF* 22011, 31.
7. Rouillé to Douglas No. 4, Oct. 11, 1756: *AMAE CP R*, Suppl. 8, 412.
8. Notes from the Russian Ministry, Oct. 9 and 18, 1756: *AMAE CP R*, Suppl. 8, 394–395 and 422–424.

Broglie, the leader of this resistance, made his reasons quite clear to Douglas. Russian answers to French questions about the troop passage did not satisfy him: "These are only words to which actions will never correspond." Broglie maintained that the problems of subsistence that the Russians posed for other routes did not exist. He was angry with Douglas, a member of the Secret, for neglecting what the Count considered to be his primary mission in that role:

It will be an unhappy state of affairs if our reconciliation with Russia, far from putting us in a position to ensure the tranquillity and happiness of Poland, serves only to impede us from working to preserve Poland from the yoke which the Muscovites have sought so long to impose upon her.

I suppose, Sir, that you are ordered to negotiate objects which seem to you more significant, and which, seemingly more relative to France, strike you as most essential. I suppose you expected to see these aims of lesser importance sacrificed to obtain ends you consider paramount. Let me remind you, Sir, that what is done in Poland, if you will take the trouble to examine the question, is of the final consequence.[9]

The Russians were greatly agitated by these signs of opposition to their plans. Chancellor Bestuzhev issued an open letter to the nobility of Poland announcing the impending visit of Russian troops and warning against any opposition.[10] The Russians continued to bring mounting grievances to Douglas, and he was at a loss as to how to answer them. His mission confused him, and properly so. The Prince de Conti, his guide thus far, was now silent and preparing to withdraw from affairs. Douglas did indeed, as Broglie accused him, think the Russian venture more important than any other, but primarily because he and D'Éon had been instructed by Conti to consider it so. His most important services for the Ministry only reinforced his belief that France was serious in her overtures

9. Broglie to Douglas, Dresden, Nov. 9, 1756: *AMAE CP R*, Suppl. 9, 6–7. Douglas was snubbed by Durand as well: "The last packet you sent me was on October 11, and was written in such a laconic style that it might well have come from Sparta." Douglas to Durand, Nov. 22, 1756: *BN SM MF* 10661, 87.

10. Circular to the Polish nobility, Nov. 14, 1756: *BN SM NAF* 22011, 82–86.

to Russia. Meanwhile, Broglie and his group, uninstructed and unsympathetic to Conti's new aims in Russia, held firmly to their old system in Poland. Conti's plantings were bearing their fruit of confusion: having split the efforts of the Secret, his approaching withdrawal was leaving the branches in certain contradiction. Thus, Douglas considered the new Russian ties important and useful to France and to Conti, while Broglie considered the old ties with Poland unchanged. The Russians, represented by the Russian Resident in Dresden, had at least a partial understanding of the problem:

I think that it is necessary to regard these schemes of Broglie and Durand as the consequences of their old system; after having worked for nearly five years to prevent any passage of Russian troops through Poland . . . they are now embarrassed by the difficulty of speaking one way and all of a sudden in another way to their partisans in Poland. They hate to destroy their own carefully laid work in Poland and Turkey, although the change of systems in Europe would be sufficient excuse.[11]

At this angry moment, with the disagreement between the two branches of the Secret emerging more clearly, events at Versailles were shaking the very foundations of the Secret. In November, 1756, three princes of the blood were energetically seeking the command of the French army that would march on Prussia in the spring. Prominent among the contestants was the Prince de Conti.[12] Louis XV, exercising one of the few untrammeled prerogatives which he still possessed, decided against the Prince de Conti. The Marquise de Pompadour, long jealous of Conti's close and puzzling influence with the King, had been influential in the refusal. Upon receiving the news, Conti angrily announced his retirement from all affairs and withdrew to the shaded splendors of L'Isle Adam. He forwarded all the documents and correspondence of the Secret to

11. Gross to Bestuzhev, Dresden, Oct. 22, 1756: *AMAE CP R* Suppl. 8, 429.
12. For an entertaining description of this contest, see the dispatch of Fontenoy, Saxon Minister in France, Dec. 1, 1756: reprinted in Jules Flammermont (ed.), *Les correspondances des agents diplomatiques etrangères en France avant la révolution* (Paris: Imprimerie Nationale, 1896), p. 171.

Tercier. Louis was equally annoyed with Conti over this dispute and made his feelings clear to Tercier:

I am sending you Conti's letter. Since I have not given him command of the Army of the Rhine . . . he says that he is dishonored. This is a word now in common use which never ceases to offend me. . . . One thing is certain, I will receive him if he calls, but I will never go out of my way for him, especially after his letters. . . . Our correspondence in Poland was on his behalf alone. Public affairs in Poland will go well enough without him, but I wish to change nothing; that is, I wish to sustain the Poles and ensure their free choice of a king.[13]

The Count de Broglie, in the midst of being expelled from Dresden by the Prussians and attempting to follow the fleeing Elector-King to Warsaw, was recalled to Versailles. Arriving on December 12 and receiving news of Conti's self-imposed retirement, the Count reported directly to the King. Complaining of the obvious contradictions between the new French system and his mission in Poland and pointing out Conti's removal, Broglie was already hinting at a transfer to the embassy at Vienna, a post he had long sought.[14] Actually, Pompadour had already acquired the Vienna embassy for her close friend the Count de Stainville, later Duke de Choiseul.

Louis insisted that Broglie remain in his post in Warsaw. As to Broglie's difficulties with the new alliances, the King assured the Count "that you are not alone, but such is my will and you must concur. As to Conti, it is he who has annoyed me. . . . I am master of my choice, so much the worse for him." Concerning a program for the Secret, Louis could only insist again that he wished to maintain both the Austrian alliance and the integrity of Poland. Methods for achieving these contradictory courses plainly eluded him. Said the King to Broglie: "Keep always at heart the union with Vienna; this is my work; I desire it and wish to sustain it. In these circum-

13. Louis to Tercier, Nov. 9, 1756: reprinted in Boutaric, op. cit., I, 212–213; see also subsequent letter of Nov. 13, ibid., p. 213.
14. Broglie to Louis XV, Versailles, Dec. 21, 1756: reprinted in Didier Ozanam and Michel Antoine, Correspondance secrète du Comte de Broglie avec Louis XV (1756–1774), (Paris: Societé de l'histoire de France, 1956), I, 1.

stances your presence at Warsaw is necessary; you are loved and esteemed by the Poles, and a new minister would be incapable of making them do well the things they must do without abandoning my party there, which I wish to sustain." [15]

If the King of France was less than lucid on his plans for Poland, surely Douglas in St. Petersburg could be excused his feelings of confusion. The inherent contradiction of attempting to placate both Russia and Poland was only aggravated by the removal of Conti. The King was an observer; in the end it was the active diplomats in the field, Broglie in Warsaw and Douglas in St. Petersburg, who would have to make practical decisions and stand responsible for their results. Theirs was not an enviable role.

On January 30, 1757, Louis XV directed Broglie to take command of the Secret with Tercier. Tercier would provide the necessary contacts with the Ministry while Broglie would command in the field. The Secret was now in the hands of an avowed enemy of the Austro-Russian alliance. The Count de Broglie was actually relieved that the personal requirements of Conti could finally be replaced by firm and fixed national purpose in defense of Polish liberties. Broglie had long been prone to substitute national purpose for flexible dynastic ambitions. Louis XV, himself confused by the requirements of the new system, could not or would not clarify his concept of the Secret beyond his desire to sustain the Poles' "free choice of a King." It was natural, therefore, that the Secret outside Russia henceforth bore the opinions, tone, and determination of the Count de Broglie.[16]

Although the unifying figure of the Prince de Conti had been removed, the Prince still retained contacts with the agents of the Secret in some quarters; most of them were graduates of the Maison Condé and personal friends of the Prince. This was especially true in Russia, where Douglas and D'Éon were actually clients of the Prince. Long after the direction of the Secret was handed over to the Polish branch, the agents in

15. Louis to Broglie, Dec. 24, 1756, and Jan. 22, 1757: reprinted in Boutaric, op. cit., I, 214 and 216.
16. Broglie to Louis, Jan. 30, 1757: reprinted in Ozanam and Antoine, op. cit., I, 12–13. See also Louis to Tercier, Dec. 26, 1756: reprinted in Boutaric, op. cit., I, 215.

Russia were awake to their old dynastic mission of finding Conti a congenial home in Russia, Courland, or Poland with Russian help.[17]

While the Secret labored through this crisis, Douglas was busy at St. Petersburg with the task of completing Russia's adherence to the alliance. This seemingly simple task was made complicated and dangerous by Russian plans. The Russians intended to show France that their adherence to the Franco-Austrian alliance would frighten the Ottoman Porte and perhaps force the Turks to war. Russia then hoped to receive a promise of aid from France against the Turks for such a possible war and thus rupture the ancient tie between France and Turkey that had bothered the Russians so much. Pressures to this end were generated rapidly by the Russian Ministry.

The Grand Chancellor began his campaign to raise the price of his alliance by seeming to attempt a salvage of some remnants of the British alliance. He proposed to Douglas that, out of consideration for the sacrifice of British subsidies which Russia had made, Hanover be excepted from their treaty and guaranteed from attack during the coming war. Bestuzhev clearly hoped to use this as a bargaining point to buy concessions against the Turks. Then, when Esterhazy brought his own charges of Turkish military preparations, Douglas had the distinct impression that Austria had joined Russia to force a break between France and Turkey. The campaign continued as Havrincourt reported from Sweden that the Russian party there under Nikita Ivanovich Panin had been spreading rumors everywhere that the Turks were massing on Russian frontiers.[18]

Foreign Minister Rouillé easily detected the aims of Russian pressures. He prepared orders for Douglas noting that it was "an indispensable necessity" that the Ottoman Porte be specifically excepted from the proposed treaty as it had been from the Anglo-Russian subsidy treaty, in order to give no offense to France's Turkish ally. Count Charles de Vergennes, French Ambassador to the Porte, had informed Rouillé that

17. Ozanam and Antoine, *op. cit.*, I, lvii, note 1.
18. Douglas to Rouillé No. 16, Oct. 9, 1756: *BN SM NAF* 22011, 4;

Havrincourt to Douglas, Stockholm, Oct. 29, 1756: *AMAE CP R* 51, 63. Both in code.

the Turks awaited this exception with some impatience. France would in no way commit itself against the Turks. As to Hanover, Rouillé insisted Russia had no right to be concerned. The Treaty of Versailles excused France's allies from participating in the British war. Therefore, Russia need not attack Hanover. No such guarantee of Hanover could be given by France, however, since any restriction on its ability to make war on Britain would be absurd. As a sop to Russian disapointment, Rouillé sent extracts of instructions being sent to French ambassadors on the passage of troops through Poland. Basically they reduced themselves to an acceptance of the march, though hedged about with solemn assurances to be given by the Russians. Rouillé hoped that this concession would be enough to divert the Russians from their Turkish plans.[19]

Rouillé also tried to explain to Douglas the absolute necessity for traveling in the wake of Austria in the Russian negotiations. The primary aim of French policy was to avoid the necessity, or even the possibility, of paying subsidies to the Russian army, "since it is not for France that their troops will march." Rouillé was enunciating an *ad hoc* policy which was to linger in France's attitudes well into 1759. "It is to this that you should ascribe the lack of instruction to which you have been subjected: the two Empresses being allied by treaty, it is between them that negotiations ought to be carried out."[20] This was the basis upon which France had decided to approach its relations with Russia: that since France and Russia were auxiliaries of Austria in the Continental war, Austria should bear the weight of negotiation. Rouillé was playing a tricky game to avoid supporting the ever greedy Russian Ministry; the less Douglas could say in negotiations, the better. This game was not nearly so clever as Rouillé thought; temporarily useful, it forecast disaster.

Unfortunately for the French, even the decisions and instructions which Rouillé had decided to outline for Douglas arrived in St. Petersburg too late to help the Scot. On Novem-

19. Rouillé to Douglas No. 24, Nov. 20, 1756: *BN SM NAF* 22010, 216; Rouillé to Douglas No. 7, Jan. 20, 1757: *AMAE CP R* 52, 63–66. Both in code.

20. Rouillé to Douglas, Nov. 27, 1756: *AMAE CP R* 51, 102.

ber 27, Douglas complained bitterly that, although he expected
the accession to be signed within the week, he had not had a
word of instruction from his Ministry concerning the exception
of the Turks or any other limitation which France desired. He
found himself completely at the mercy of the Austrian Ambassador, as Prince Esterhazy well knew. All this was the result
of Rouillé's calculated policy of keeping Douglas subordinate
to the Austrian diplomacy.

With the Russians and Austrians obviously aware of the
Scot's predicament, pressures on him continued to mount. He
heard rumors that Bestuzhev might foment an Ottoman invasion of Russia in order to destroy the Franco-Russian alliance.
Then the appearance of a Sieur Mazzini, suposedly a Prussian
agent ordered to impede the alliance, helped to stampede
Douglas into signing the accession. At this point Esterhazy,
Bestuzhev, and even Vorontsov sprang the trap that they had
been carefully preparing with their rumors and complaints of
Turkish unrest. Esterhazy advised Douglas that the only condition under which the Russians would ever sign the accession
to the Treaty of Versailles would be the inclusion of a secret
article providing for French aid to Russia in event of a Turkish
war. Douglas was thunderstruck. He had no orders on this
matter except to follow the lead of the Austrian Ambassador;
his instructions were still en route. Now that Ambassador
threatened to lead him over a precipice.[21]

Douglas resisted as best he could. He pleaded the absence
of instructions. He argued that the secret declaration belied
the public document and implied bad faith on the part of the
King of France. He even sought a statement in writing from
Esterhazy that France had transmitted instructions for such a
secret declaration through the Austrian court.[22] But the Russians had done their work well. Douglas, a diplomat of absolutely no experience, was panicked by fear that the alliance

21. Douglas to Durand, Dec. 27, 1756: *BN SM MF* 10661, 102–105; Notes at Versailles, Jan. 2, 1757: *AMAE CP R* 52, 11; Douglas to Havrincourt, Apr. 29, 1757: *ibid.* 51, 289–290.

22. Douglas to ministers of Austria and Russia concerning the signing of the secret act, Jan. 11, 1757: *AMAE CP R* 52, 31–34.

would fail on his account. In the end all that he could do was to reserve final ratification to the King. Fearing to take responsibility for so monumental a failure as the loss of Russia to the war, a loss never possible, Douglas signed the accession of Russia to the Treaty of Versailles and its secret clause on January 11, 1757:

Although it is stipulated in the act of accession that Her Imperial Majesty dispenses His Most Christian Majesty from defending and aiding . . . the states . . . of Her Imperial Majesty in case of attack by the Ottoman Porte or by Persia, His Most Christian Majesty promises and contracts himself, in case Her Majesty be menaced by an attack from the said Ottoman Porte, to employ all means to deter it; and if, on the contrary, the Porte . . . actually attacks the states of Her Majesty . . . His Most Christian Majesty engages to furnish to her, in place of 18,000 infantry and 6,000 cavalry, a monetary subsidy of 8,000 Imperial florins for each thousand infantry and 24,000 florins for each thousand cavalry, each month for as long as the war will last. In return Her Majesty engages . . . to aid His Most Christian Majesty with 24,000 infantry, or stipulated payments, if the states of France in Europe are attacked by England, excepting the present war and the war in America and other colonies.[23]

The last phrase had been inserted to salve the Scot's conscience; it meant nothing. Douglas knew that he had performed badly. The act he had signed could bring nothing but trouble. He had chosen to shift responsibility for the maintenance of the new alliances to shoulders more accustomed to bearing these diplomatic burdens. Russia and Austria were delighted with the opportunity of separating France from its historic alliance with their traditional enemy. They obviously hoped to pressure France into accepting the *fait accompli* or to win at least some concession in return for its removal.

Ironically, at the end of February some of Rouillé's instructions finally arrived in St. Petersburg, giving straightforward answers to the pleas of Douglas. Rouillé was shocked at Esterhazy's proposition of a secret declaration against the

23. Most secret declaration, St. Petersburg, Jan. 11, 1757: *AMAE CP R Suppl.* 9, 79–81.

Porte: "I am astonished that you even entertain such a proposition. The King absolutely forbids you to sign such an agreement." [24] How Douglas must have agonized over the decoding of that dispatch! Its contents terrified him; he generated numberless excuses; he clutched desperately at an alternative project proposed by Vorontsov that another act in the form of a letter from King to Empress be sent, in which the contents of the secret clause could be enclosed. All that he could really do was to await the arrival of Michel at Versailles and the recriminations that were sure to come.

Meanwhile, Austria and Russia had completed their negotiations for an offensive alliance against Prussia, and on January 22, 1757, the Treaty of St. Petersburg was signed. This treaty renewed the formal engagements of May 22, 1746, and then committed each state to provide eighty thousand regular troops. There was to be no separate peace. An invitation was extended to other powers, especially France and Sweden, to adhere to the treaty. Secret articles stipulated that Austria would pay Russia two million rubles when Silesia was returned and one million rubles a year while the war lasted. Austria also agreed to use her good offices to help Russia acquire Courland and a border rectification in the Ukraine. The means to that end were not detailed. [25]

Douglas sent as much information on these agreements as he could to his Ministry. He had only glanced at the documents over Esterhazy's shoulder. The Austrians and Russians followed the announcement of their treaty with a request that France assume some of the burden of Russian subsidies. However, Douglas had already been pushed far enough by these deceptive allies. "I continue to turn a deaf ear." In this, at least, he followed the wishes of his Ministry. Rouillé wanted nothing to do with Russian finances. "The affair of Austro-Russian subsidies is their problem. You do well to keep silent." [26]

24. Rouillé to Douglas, Jan. 22, 1757: *AMAE CP R* 52, 68.

25. Austro-Russian treaty of Jan. 22, 1757: reprinted in F. F. Martens, *Recueil des traités et conventions conclus par la Russie avec les puis-*sances étrangères (St. Petersburg, 1874–1909), IX, 352.

26. Douglas to Rouillé, Feb. 8, 1757, and reply of Feb. 16: *AMAE CP R* 52, 117 and 129.

On February 13, Michel arrived at Versailles with his packet containing the accession of Russia to the treaty and the attached secret clause against the Turks. Rouillé was the first to respond:

I cannot express our shock and pain at seeing this secret declaration. . . . We were sure all went well. All your agreements cannot justify a step which you must have known very well would be disagreeable to the King. I cannot hide from you that His Majesty is extremely upset at the ease with which you signed. . . . I send you, Sir, the ratification of the act of accession only. It is up to you to repair the fault. If you say Esterhazy got you in, then let Esterhazy get you out.[27]

The King was indeed upset. He knew, as Rouillé did not, that Douglas was a member of the Secret. It was astonishing that one of the King's inner circle, dedicated to the cementing of ancient ties, should have been guilty of such foolishness. "I . . . disapprove . . . strongly of this beautiful secret act which Douglas had the stupidity to sign," wrote the King in his role as Secret chief. "In the circumstances, what Rouillé proposes to write seems quite proper to me." [28] As the reproaches piled high around him, Douglas threw servility to the winds and said a few well-chosen words in his own behalf:

Had you given me some attention or the least hint of instruction . . . you would have spared yourselves the difficulty and embarrassment of repairing and disavowing my stupidities. . . . You are like the blind man's guide who leads him into the thickets, laughs in his face, and leaves him to get out as best he can.[29]

However, neither the Ministry of Foreign Affairs nor the King's Secret were really prepared to leave Douglas in the thicket. Rouillé's cavalier response was soon replaced by the realization that direct action was needed to kill the repulsive secret act. The first step, of course, was to inform Douglas officially that His Majesty could not accept the clause. The King desired to unite with the Empress, but the secret act could only impede that union. The second step was to make

27. Rouillé to Douglas, Feb. 16, 1757: *ibid.* 52, 134.
28. Louis to Tercier, Feb. 13, 1757: reprinted in Boutaric, *op. cit.*, I, 217.
29. Douglas to Tercier, Mar. 8, 1757: *AMAE CP R* 51, 253.

the refusal more palatable to the Russians. Ivan Shuvalov was selected for his influence with the Empress, and the King of France graciously bestowed upon him a collection of medals in token of his monumental contributions to the arts. Finally, the most intriguing step taken to destroy the secret act was the determination of Louis XV to write secretly and personally to the Empress Elizabeth. Louis, long convinced of his own genius for foreign affairs, decided to bring his prestige, reputedly high with the Empress, into the struggle. The thought so pleased him that if the first letter succeeded he had decided to continue the personal exchange between sovereigns.[30] Tercier wrote to Douglas:

> You will find here joined a letter in the hand of His Majesty the King for the Empress of Russia. His Majesty hopes thus to win the Empress to the accession. Since you have not been permitted to visit alone with the Empress, you cannot deliver it personally. As the King wishes this matter kept in the greatest secrecy . . . you will pass it through Vorontsov.[31]

The letter was a rousing success and accomplished its mission perfectly. Elizabeth melted under the glorious personal touch of His Majesty. Replying through the newly opened secret channel, Elizabeth wrote to Louis: "I have rati-

30. Louis to Tercier, Feb. 24, 1757: reprinted in Boutaric, *op. cit.*, I, 219.
31. Tercier to Douglas, Feb. 19, 1757: *AMAE CP R* 52, 145. This letter of the King is missing. Although the author has found many of these letters, others have disappeared. A clue is given in a note of the King to the Baron de Breteuil in Russia (Sept. 10, 1762, reprinted in Flassan, *op. cit.*, VI, 340): "I do not think the Chancellor Vorontsov is as afraid today as he was during the preceding reign to burn all my secret correspondence with the late Empress. Thus, you must insist in my name that he return to you all the pieces of it or that he burn them in your presence so that there remains no trace of them."
Some historians have confused the Secret organization with this undercover exchange of letters. They are unrelated except in the King's penchant for secret activities and in that some members of the Secret were useful in the exchange. The best survey of this question is M. Antoine and D. Ozanam, "Le secret du roi," *Annuaire-Bulletin de la Societé de l'Histoire de France*, 1954–1955. These gentlemen record the existence of a book called *Correspondance secrète de l'Imperatrice Elisabeth avec Louis XV, 1758* (Moscow, 1875), 688 pages. This book is also entered in E. Saulnier and A. Martin, *Bibliographie des travaux publiée de 1866 à 1897 sur l'histoire de France de 1500 à 1789*, I, No. 4053. (Paris, 1900). Unfortunately, no one has been able to unearth this volume.

fied without the least delay, conformable to your desires, the act of my adherence to the treaty. . . . For all the rest, that is compensated for by the wonderful fashion in which Your Majesty explains it to me." [32]

Final and formal ratification of Russia's accession to the Treaty of Versailles, with the secret act annulled, was signed on April 19, 1757. Douglas chose the Chevalier d'Éon to be the bearer of these documents and the letter of the Empress to Versailles. Russia naturally took the opportunity to ask again for French subsidies, feeling that their agreement to annul the secret act entitled them to compensations. They had in mind a loan of four to five million roubles to be repaid over a very long period after the war was concluded. They hoped "that the generosity of the King would match that of the Tsarina." [33] It did not.

D'Éon left Russia, carrying the altered Russian accession, on April 26. In his dispatch case he carried, in addition to the ratifications, the last hope of the Chevalier Douglas for a successful conclusion to his Russian mission. Testified D'Éon, "after a thousand intrigues Douglas and I had succeeded. . . . The secret object of my return to France in 1757 was to carry the assurance of the Empress to the Prince de Conti for the army command and for Courland." [34]

This seemingly astounding success came as unexpectedly as a thunderbolt. How the result was achieved remains a mystery, and whether the offer was seriously made by the Russians will probably never be known. Only a few threads of the negotiations remain. Douglas had been intent on placing money in unidentified hands "for our father" as early as December, 1756. [35] The suspicions of the ever watchful Count de Broglie had been aroused in April, 1757, when he came upon

32. Elizabeth to Louis XV, Mar. 14, 1757: *AMAE CP R* 52, 215; in the hand of the Empress. Nisbet Bain was under the impression that the secret agreement against the Turks remained in force. See R. N. Bain, "Russia Under Anne and Elisabeth," *Cambridge Modern History* (New York: Macmillan Co., 1909), VI, p. 321.

33. Douglas to Rouillé No. 23, Apr. 26, 1757: *AMAE CP R* 52, 357.

34. D'Eon to Broglie, London, June 12, 1775: reprinted in Boutaric, *op. cit.*, I, 222, Note 2.

35. Douglas to Tercier, Dec. 27, 1756: *AMAE CP R* 51, 142.

letters of Heinrich von Brühl, Prime Minister of Augustus III of Saxony and Poland. Broglie wrote to the King:

I saw in a letter from Poniatowsky to Brühl . . . several things which make me think that the Chevalier Douglas is occupying himself at Petersburg with the interests of Conti relative to Poland. The letter speaks clearly: "Douglas, having chatted a long time on these subjects and having treated me dearly, loaded me with compliments from Conti and told me that the Prince esteemed me greatly. . . ." It appears to me indispensable to order the Chevalier Douglas to cease occupying himself with ends not analogous to your will. . . . I fear strongly, Sire, that these indiscretions . . . of Douglas . . . might ruin Your Majesty's influence in Poland.[36]

By whatever means the task was accomplished, it is easy to imagine with what delight Douglas sent D'Éon on his way: the offer to Conti could recoup the losses inflicted on his future by the unfortunate affair of the secret act. If he had made a general shambles of his official mission, at least Douglas seemed to have succeeded gloriously in his secret mission. The Empress was indeed offering her army and the Duchy of Courland to the unemployed Prince. Unfortunately for Conti, the Empress and Vice-Chancellor Vorontsov refused to make a public offer of the post until they were sure of the Prince's dispositions. Russia was chancing no slight to its honor by a public refusal.

What Douglas did not know, being far from court gossip and rumor in Versailles, was that Louis was still greatly displeased with Conti. As early as February the King had instructed Tercier to "speak to me no more of the Prince de Conti." The King told Tercier that he "should write in covert words to the Chevalier Douglas . . . taking back everything which affects the Prince de Conti." [37] Either such instructions were never sent or they were a little too covert. They certainly did not restrain Douglas and D'Éon. When D'Éon arrived in Paris with what he considered wonderful news, the King was

36. Broglie to Louis XV, Apr. 7, 1757: reprinted in Ozanam and Antoine, *op. cit.*, I, 23–25. On Brühl, see Robert L. Koehl, "Heinrich Brühl: A Saxon Politician of the Eighteenth Century," *Journal of Central European Affairs*, XIV (January, 1954).

37. Louis to Tercier, Feb. 13, 1757: reprinted in Boutaric, *op. cit.*, I, 217–18.

pronouncedly unenthusiastic. "Since D'Éon has a mission from Mikhail Vorontsov to see the Prince de Conti, I suppose that he must see him; but he must give you [Tercier] an exact account of Conti's reply." [38]

D'Éon carried his message to Conti, and both proceeded to wait impatiently for the King's decision on the matter. That decision never came. Conti knew that the King's permission was absolutely necessary for his enterprise, but Louis had decided within the confines of the Secret that "if the Empress of Russia truly calls the Prince de Conti to command her armies and wishes to give him Courland while awaiting better things, I will be happy, but for the present I can take no public part except to remain aloof." [39] Louis ordered D'Éon back to Russia, but Conti kept him dallying in Strasbourg for a long time, awaiting a last-minute decision of the King which would permit Conti to accept the Russian offers. "But the King wished to decide nothing," said D'Éon, "even though Conti kept me at Strasbourg awaiting the last courier." [40]

Conti continued to plead with Louis to change his mind, but Louis did nothing and continued effectively to say no. Louis wrote to Tercier:

I am sending you Conti's letter. When I have moral certitude that the Russian Empress really destines the command of her army and Courland to him, I will give all the authorizations and permissions which one asks of me. Until then, the whole thing repels me a good deal, and I will take no false step which will do more harm than good. [41]

The repudiation of the Russian offer to Conti signaled the destruction of many hopes. Certainly the patient aspirations of Conti were finally crushed, and certainly the plans and dreams of the emigré Scot, Douglas, fell with them. Most important of all, Louis had crushed the Russian branch of the Secret.

The King elected to continue the Secret in the interests of the French party in Poland, but if he restored a unity of

38. Louis to Tercier, July 20, 1757: ibid., p. 222.
39. Louis to Tercier, Sept. 15, 1757: ibid., p. 224.
40. D'Éon to Broglie, London, June 12, 1775: ibid., p. 222, note 2.
41. Louis to Tercier, Sept. 21, 1757: ibid.. 224.

command, it was at the price of a much weakened organization. The branch of the Secret in Russia had wavered from
Broglie's idea of its mission, had been cut down, and would
soon be largely removed. Broglie would have no powerful organization in St. Petersburg to defend his interests. Thus, the
aspirations of Conti to mount the Polish throne with Russian
help not only cost him the throne but weakened his organization as well. The King tried to reset the sights of the Secret.
"If it proves impossible to reconcile our considerations for
Russia with the sentiments I have always entertained for Poland, give preference to the interests of the latter." [42] The King
was too confused in threading his way through foreign affairs
and too aware of the independence and responsibility of his
ministers ever to send similar instructions to the Ministry of
Foreign Affairs.

Douglas had few hopes left. He had handled the Russian
accession badly and had seen his efforts on behalf of Conti
repudiated by the King. From May, 1757, he repeatedly requested his recall. Impatiently awaiting the arrival of the
French Ambassador, his time was occupied with the mounting
importance of the Polish question.

Douglas had been giving some thought to the problem of
Poland. He accurately analyzed the point of Austrian and Russian intrigues in Poland to be the establishment of the Prince
Royal of Saxony, Frederick-Christian, eldest son of the present
King Augustus III, as the next King of Poland. He insisted to
the Ministry and to the Secret that Austria and Russia were
agreed and ready to act against French interests. Douglas,
given sometimes to imaginative flights of high diplomacy, felt
that if Austria and Russia were interested in procuring reparations for Saxony from Prussia in the form of the city of Magdeburg, the French might trade that city with a crown thrown
in for the Saxon Elector in exchange for a French candidate in
Poland. [43]

The French Ministry ordered Douglas immediately to

42. Louis to Broglie, 1757: reprinted
in G. P. Gooch, *Louis XV: The Monarchy in Decline* (London: Longmans Green, 1956), p. 206.

43. Douglas to Rouillé, Jan. 15, 1757:
*AMAE CP R* 52, 37.

cease speculation on these topics. An hereditary crown in the Saxon house should never be mentioned. The Ministry was well aware, however, of the justice of the Scot's charges against Austria and Russia in Poland. Their arguments, said the Ministry, that they had business in Poland because they were neighbors only masked their greed. It was up to Douglas and the other French diplomats to be watchful that the influence of the allied courts did not expand in Poland.[44]

The last days of Douglas as chief of the French mission were complicated by the reappearance in St. Petersburg of Stanislas Poniatowsky, this time as Minister of the Polish King. Poniatowsky's past liaison with the Grand Duchess, his ties with the British, and his friendship with Bestuzhev could only mean new plots. It was the well-founded opinion of Douglas that the return of the Pole was the sign of renewed intrigue by Bestuzhev, undertaken because of the rumors of the rapidly failing health of the Empress Elizabeth. "The wavering health of the Empress, in the critical age for her sex, is all important. The impulse given to plots and intrigues by the slightest alteration in her precious health demands the presence of our Ambassador. . . . He could give you a clearer picture of this court, one of the most intriguing, deceptive, and difficult to understand in all Europe." [45] Douglas predicted that the Empress would outlive all the plotters, but the French Ministry doubted his diagnostic art. "It is interesting to think that the Empress will live a long time, but it is nevertheless true that all her authority will be annulled by her death. This will be an epoch of revolution in that empire. It behooves us to prepare in advance." [46]

However, the French Ministry, under the halting and diminishing leadership of Rouillé, was making no preparations either to come to terms with the Russian future or to make decisions in Poland. Rouillé was seriously contemplating his retirement from these confusing events.

If the Ministry of Foreign Affairs was holding back on

44. Rouillé to Douglas No. 12, Feb. 18, 1757: *ibid.* 52, 137.
45. Douglas to Rouillé, Jan. 14, 1757: *ibid.* 52, 39.
46. Ministerial observations, Apr. 6, 1757: *ibid.* 52, 292–295.

commitments to a vacant Polish throne, Broglie and his Secret were not. Broglie, at Versailles in February, had stated firmly that the King must look quickly to his choice to replace Conti or France would be outmaneuvered.[47] When Broglie returned to Poland in March, 1757, Louis had been persuaded to consider specific candidates for the Polish throne. His first thought went to the Infant Don Louis, son of Philip V of Spain, but Louis was not enthusiastic. His second and more solid thought went to Prince Xavier of Saxony, second son of Augustus III and a constant attendant at Versailles. The close attachment of Xavier to his sister, then Dauphine of France, cemented him by preference and by politics to France. Such a candidate would be eminently suitable to offset Austrian support of Xavier's brother, Frederick. France could play on Austrian preference for the Saxon house, use Augustus III's own desire for the continuance of his heirs in Poland, and succeed in placing a Francophile King in Warsaw.[48]

Such plans were really long range. There were much more current affairs upon which the future of the Polish kingdom and French interest depended. The questions for French agents in the field continued to be the Russian troops who were already massed for their march across Poland. Both official and Secret diplomacy in France were busy posing objections to the Russians: the former in the belief that a saturation program of complaints would make the Russians tread ever so lightly in Poland, and the latter in the hope that the march could be detoured or avoided.

The Secret was proposing a series of guarantees to which they wished the Russians to subscribe. These included a declaration from Russia, before entry into Poland, as to the exact time required for passage and a promise never to mingle in the internal affairs of the republic nor to abet a confederation. The fear that this march was the signal for the downfall of Poland was now always foremost in the thoughts of the Secret. Durand even went so far as to charge that the Russians would

---

47. Broglie to Louis XV, Feb. 11, 1757: reprinted in Ozanam and Antoine, *op. cit.*, I, 17–19.

48. Louis to Tercier, Apr. 9, 1757: reprinted in Boutaric, *op. cit.*, I, 220–221.

never undertake the campaign for which they were supposedly gathered: that the war was really only a ruse for the movement on Poland.[49]

The French Ministry was no less active a complainant. Rouillé did not hesitate to tell the Russians that the good conduct of the Tatars, with whom the French maintained excellent financial relations, depended entirely upon Russian behavior in Poland. The same was true for the Turks. Rouillé even contributed a rumor that the British had sent agents into Poland to arouse a confederation against the Russian march, that the French were doing their best to counteract them, but that the Russians had consequently best avoid all cause of offense to the Poles.[50]

The official French diplomacy was aiming simply at getting a public declaration from the Empress promising a quick and harmless passage through Poland. The Russians felt that assurances already given to the Poles were quite sufficient and that further declarations of any kind by the Empress would be "useless, superfluous, and undignified." [51] The French asked Esterhazy for aid in eliciting an open commitment from the Russian Empress, but he refused. The French, already sufficiently annoyed at Austrian machinations against their alliance with Turkey, now felt Vienna to be meddling overmuch in Poland. Rumors that Brühl, Polish Minister, was negotiating secretly with Bestuzhev only frightened the French the more. French interests in Poland were menaced from all sides, and French diplomats evaluating the worth of the Russian ties to date could note only that they were indeed embarked on hazardous times.[52]

In the midst of these war preparations the new Ambassador of His Most Christian Majesty was approaching his post

49. Durand to Douglas, Warsaw, Jan. 22, 1757: *BN SM NAF* 22011, 218–221; Douglas to Durand, Jan. 26, 1757: *BN SM MF* 10661, 113–116; and Durand to Rouillé, May 18, 1757: *AMAE CP R* 52, 408.

50. Rouillé to Douglas, Jan. 21 and Apr. 2, 1757: *AMAE CP R* 52, 67 and 288.

51. Memoir from the Russian Ministry, Mar. 7, 1757: *AMAE CP R* 51, 233.

52. Rouillé to Douglas, Feb. 19, 1757: *AMAE CP R* 52, 142. For copies of intercepted letters between Bestuzhev and Brühl, see *ibid.* 52, 242–244.

near the Empress of Russia. With this approaching relief from responsibilities, the Chevalier Mackenzie Douglas again begged the Ministry for his recall. He was assured of it as soon as he had properly acquainted the new Ambassador with the condition of the Russian court. Douglas was tired, ill, discouraged, and almost completely without funds. The King reluctantly agreed to pay his outstanding debts in St. Petersburg, a sum in excess of twenty-thousand livres. There was little of the honor and glistening fortune which the wandering Scot had envisioned when the adventure began. He was forty-three years old, and he prophesied accurately that his active life was over.

In summary, the outbreak of the Seven Years' War had been the primary motivation for the establishment of Franco-Russian friendship. The war required the union. Douglas had been charged with a double mission: by the Ministry with securing Russian adherence to the Franco-Austrian treaty and by the Secret with securing Russian help for Conti's ambitions in Eastern Europe. Douglas had failed in both missions. The accession of Russia to the treaty had been gained only after an embarrassing and dangerous mistake in signing a secret agreement with Russia against the Turks, into which Douglas had been tricked by Austrian and Russian pressures. The command of the Russian army and the Duchy of Courland were procured for Conti by Douglas, only to have them repudiated by the King of France because of private disagreements between himself and Conti.

The retirement of the Prince de Conti from public affairs not only ended the Secret mission of Douglas in Russia, but transferred the Secret organization into the hands of Broglie. The Count, anti-Austrian and anti-Russian, attacked Douglas and D'Éon as too sympathetic to Russian interests. This sympathy was, of course, the result of Conti's instructions. Conti's division of the Secret thus ended with the destruction of the St. Petersburg branch and the transfer of the mission of the Secret from a dynastic to a national purpose.

It was from these events that the march of Russian troops across Poland emerged as the most significant problem between

France and Russia. The Secret under Broglie was intent on defending the ability of France to name a future candidate for the Polish throne and opposed the entry of Russian troops under any circumstances. The French Ministry of Foreign Affairs, with broader if not necessarily more correct view and aim, sought a quick and victorious war. To this end the Ministry accepted the necessity of a Russian march through Poland if it could be hedged about with guarantees. External pressures would expand this small fissure of difference between Ministry and Secret into the destruction of the Polish republic.

The years 1756 and early 1757, during the time when Douglas was the King's diplomat in Russia, thus served to demonstrate that this new-found alliance, created by impulses from without, was generating more problems than solutions. Russia had begun by tricking and pressuring a French diplomat into betraying his trust and then had tried to push France into accepting that betrayal by repudiating the Ottoman Porte. Furthermore, the Young Court and the Grand Chancellor did not even bother to hide their dissatisfaction with the new French ties. In return, France had repudiated the secret offers of the Empress of Russia for the command of her army. Finally, French interests were attempting to make the Russian march across Poland impossible or as difficult as possible. Against these differences, the two states had still agreed on nothing except that they were both at war with the King of Prussia. As yet these were certainly no marks of mutual trust upon which to project the bright future of this union.

CHAPTER **4**

# Bernis: *The Testing*

THE SECOND MOVEMENT of the Franco-Russian *rapprochement* took place under new French leadership. Rouillé, the Secretary of State for Foreign Affairs under whom the whirling and confusing development of the diplomatic revolution had occurred, felt himself incapable of bearing the burden of foreign affairs that daily grew heavier and more complex. The rupture with Prussia, the British colonial war, the Austrian alliance, the reopening of relations with Russia — all momentous events — had occurred circumstantially and haphazardly during Rouillé's tenure, but he deserved neither praise nor blame for their development.

The man chosen to fill his place was Abbé François Joachim Pierre de Bernis. The Abbé had served in diplomatic posts in Venice, Spain, and Austria and had been the chief negotiator of the Austrian alliance. Small in stature, rotund as a monk should be, Bernis was clever in intrigues but untalented in public affairs. He boasted the diplomatic experience of posts where he had served without distinction, but his real claim to the Ministry of Foreign Affairs rested upon his intimate and carefully cultivated friendship with the Marquise de Pompadour.[1]

Bernis was, under the protection of Pompadour, a chief defender of the Austrian alliance and the leader of the Austrian party at the French court. He was called in to cement the new alliances and to wage the war — or, in short, to give consistency to a badly disarranged foreign policy. If the sympathetic and optimistic Bernis could not draw satisfaction from France's new system, then truly no one could. His lieutenant in the Vienna embassy was now another friend of the new Austrian ties and another great and good friend of Pompadour, the Count de Stainville.

At the same time as these changes in personnel at the French Ministry, the first Ambassador of France to the Empress of Russia in over twelve years was nearing his post. This was Paul François de Galucci, Marquis de Chateauneuf, Marquis de l'Hôpital. A Lieutenant General in the army, L'Hôpital had served as Ambassador in Naples until 1751 and then as Inspector General of Cavalry until his new appointment. The Marquis was nearing sixty years of age when he received his Russian mission. He was robust, charming, and elegant, but shallow, slow of wit, and easily deceived. He was, in all, a perfect French courtier whose likes were often to be seen in the hallways of Versailles. He loved ceremony and precedence, court intrigue, gossip, the appearance of politics, and the accumulation of honors. Despite the forbidding distance and legendary climate involved in his journey, the Marquis de l'Hôpital looked forward with great expectation to a post which would rank him among the most important diplomats in Europe.

L'Hôpital's instructions were issued by the Ministry of Rouillé on December 28, 1756, almost six months before he reached his post. They were simple and general:

1.     To gain the confidence of the Empress and to concili-

---

1. Standard works include *Mémoires et lettres du Cardinal Bernis*, ed. Frédéric Masson (Paris: Plon, 1882), 2 volumes; Frédéric Masson, *Le* *Cardinal de Bernis* (Paris: Plon, 1884). See also the sketch of Bernis in Broglie, *Le secret du roi*, I, 260–64.

ate the Young Court, especially the Grand Duchess Catherine.

2.    To weaken British influence in politics and commerce.

3.    To determine the extent of Russian aims in Poland, Turkey, and Sweden.

4.    To uncover the purposes of Austro-Russian understandings.

5.    To wage the war.

6.    To examine the succession to the Russian throne.[2]

The Ambassador departed Paris in January, 1757, accompanied by a large and imposing entourage of twelve carriages and sixty-five gentlemen and attendants. The European gazettes hailed the passage of the "shining embassy."[3] After a slight delay over protocol at Riga, L'Hôpital entered Russia and was met by the Chevalier Douglas outside the capital on July 2. They arrived in the early evening at the Apraksin Palace, the Ambassador's temporary home. After resting a few days, L'Hôpital received Mikhail Vorontsov as his first caller. The eighth of July was quickly set for the imperial reception, and on that day the Empress of Russia received L'Hôpital with sufficient pomp to delight him and even deigned to speak with him in French. Two days later, on the feast of Peter and Paul, the Ambassador attended a grand ball in his honor and danced the first minuet with the Grand Duchess Catherine, whom he thought he had won entirely.

In Paris, parallel formalities were being accomplished. Mikhail Bestuzhev, brother and enemy of the Russian Chancellor, arrived in Paris on June 21. He was terribly and chronically ill. In view of L'Hôpital's supposed slight at Riga, the King decided to abandon the customary public entrance. Bestuzhev was escorted to his home, where he retired to his bed, from which he was seldom to rise again during a long and inactive embassy.[4]

2. Notes for L'Hôpital, Paris, Dec. 11, 1756: *BN SM NAF* 22011, 177–182; instructions, Dec. 28, 1756, in Rambaud, *op. cit.*, IX, 32–48.

3. *Gazette d'Amsterdam et d'Utrecht*, Dec. 19, 1756.

4. Note to La Tournelle, Versailles, June 21, 1757: *AMAE CP R* 53, 77; Bektiev to Rouillé, June 22, 1757: *ibid.* 53, 81.

In Russia the diplomatic life of the Chevalier Douglas was over. He left Russia on September 1, 1758, after spending a year acquainting the new Ambassador with the tasks of his mission, but in reality his own mission and his significance in affairs ended with the arrival of L'Hôpital. Douglas was allotted an annual pension of 4,000 livres by the King of France. Although he sought new positions of service, among them the official representative of the Jacobites in France, all were refused him. He finally retired to Bourges with his French wife and her wealthy merchant family.

It was, therefore, under the fresh but shaky hand of Abbé Bernis, creator and exponent of the new system which had little popularity at court among the old soldiers, that the Marquis de l'Hôpital undertook to deal with the emerging problems of this hastily created union between France and Russia. The first year and a half of the new French embassy in Russia served as the testing time of the reconciliation. The problems of this period were the standard problems of the union: dominance in Sweden; the conduct of the war and agreement on its consequences; influence in Poland, Danzig, and Courland; relations with the Empress and the Young Court, especially the exchange of Holstein; and the development of commerce. All of these problems had in common the difficulty they posed to a lasting union and future alliance between France and Russia. French policy set out to consider them under the fresh leadership of a Minister and an Ambassador open-minded and even sympathetic to the new dispensation. The question remained: could this hastily contrived *rapprochement* produce results that would make its continuance and development either possible or desirable?

*i.*

## A TRUCE IN SWEDEN

As the war came closer and closer to active operations, it became more and more desirable to bring Sweden into the war on the side of the new alliance. In the light of past Swedish-Russian enmities and the precarious position of French interests, this was a delicate matter. The French Ambassador in Stockholm noted:

Of the two parties which have divided and still divide Sweden, one is that of France, which sustains our close union with Sweden, and the other is that of Russia, which Russia has always regarded as attached to her but which is truly attached to her only accessorily; its true object has been to attach Sweden to England, to give that power dominance here.[5]

France had successfully defended its interests in Sweden over the preceding twenty years, but the diplomatic revolution, here as elsewhere, brought contradictions difficult to resolve. King Adolphus Frederick, formerly regent of Holstein and a relative of the Grand Duke Peter of Russia, was elected to his throne because the aristocratic Diet wished to dominate a weak monarchy and bolster its claims to Holstein. The French had held their place by supporting the aristocratic party against the monarchy. To this end the former Franco-Prussian alliance had engineered the marriage of the sister of Frederick of Prussia to Adolphus Frederick in 1744. Louisa Ulrica, always awake to the interests of her brother, restrained her own absolutist urges in the interests of the French party. But the diplomatic revolution changed all that.

The Queen, the real power behind her weak husband, was now freed by the enmity between France and her brother to pursue her own policies. Desirous of restoring the power of the Swedish monarchy, she became the center of opposition to the French party of aristocratic landowners. France maintained its influence against the Queen's intended coup only by dint of heavy subsidies to its party. Russia gave vocal support to the Queen, but a purge of her supporters at French instigation checked her plans.

Count Horn, representing the Queen of Sweden, arrived

5. Havrincourt to Douglas, Stockholm, Oct. 18, 1756: *AMAE CP S* 176, 46. On Sweden in this period, see R. N. Bain *Gustavus III and His Contemporaries: 1746–1792* (London: Constable, 1897); the first chapter of Erik Amburger, *Russland und Schweden, 1762–1772* (Berlin: Emil Ebering, 1934); and Ragnar Svanström and Carl F. Palmstierna, *A Short History of Sweden* (Oxford: Clarendon Press, 1934).

in Russia in October, 1756, to beg for financial aid for his party against the French or possibly even a Russian troop movement on the Finnish frontier to intimidate the French party among the aristocrats. The Russians were very upset that executions had actually been carried out in repressing the Queen's plans. The disturbance only demonstrated again that France shamed and practically imprisoned a close relative of the Russian imperial house; the Swedish King was related to both the Grand Duke Peter and the Grand Duchess Catherine.

However, despite expressions of Russian sympathy, Count Horn received no aid. The Russians were too fearful of the Prussians and too disgusted with the British to risk offending France openly at this time. However, the shaky condition of French interests in Sweden and the possibilities of Russian gains were not lost on either party. The French party in Sweden and the French Ministry were both frightened to see Russia in a position once again to give them difficulties at Stockholm.[6]

Russian resentment against France in Sweden had to be tabled in view of the impending campaigns. France, Sweden, and Austria signed a treaty of alliance on March 21, 1757. Sweden was persuaded to send a guarantee of the Treaty of Westphalia to the German Diet, and in return France and Austria agreed to guarantee Swedish lands against Prussian invasion. France specifically guaranteed the inviolability of Swedish Pomerania.

The French requested Russian adherence to this treaty, but there was a supplementary treaty of September 22, 1757, which France chose to keep from Russian view. This document "stipulated some additional advantages for Sweden," consisting of parts of Pomerania and East Prussia. France did not want to trigger Russian desires for commitments to their own

6. This section may be followed in Pipin (ed.), *Socheneniia,* XII, 367; Havrincourt to Rouillé, Stockholm, Sept. 24, 1756: *AMAE CP R* 50, 22–34; Horn, *op. cit.,* pp. 245–48; Instructions of the King of Sweden to Count Horn, Jan. 9, 1756: *BN SM NAF* 22010, 111–112; M. S. Anderson, *Europe in the Eighteenth Century* (New York: Holt, Rinehart and Winston, 1961), p. 184.

territorial aggrandizement. France also made immediate plans at Stockholm for the use of Swedish troops in a Pomeranian campaign.[7]

Russia was now faced in its turn by a problem of the diplomatic revolution. Sweden and Russia had been traditional enemies, and Russia had long sought to weaken or to dominate this troublesome neighbor. Now Russia was called upon to sanction and even assist a Swedish war. Russia made the decision to accept Swedish participation in active military operations for two very good reasons. The first was immediate and pressing. The British, inactive to this point, decided to make a threat of intervention to disrupt the rapidly jelling coalition against Frederick. They notified the Russians that an observation fleet was being sent into the Baltic to protect the flow of commerce with Prussia, and they also warned against violating the borders of any German state. The Empress and her ministers were unanimous in their resentment of this unveiled threat. Anglo-Russian relations had never been at such a low ebb.[8]

Russia did not intend to restrict itself to indignation. The Empress ordered her navy to send as many vessels as possible from Prussian blockade duty to Gotland and, if Swedish ships ventured to block the British, to join and assist the Swedes. It was therefore expedient to have a Swedish commitment to the war. It would ensure Swedish assistance against British ventures in the Baltic.[9]

The second reason for Russian acceptance of Swedish military assistance was less immediate. French influence now reigned in Sweden, but Russia saw no reason to renounce fu-

7. Bernis to L'Hôpital, Apr. 21, 1758: *AMAE CP R* 56, 90; Havrincourt to Douglas, June 7, 1757: *ibid.* 51, 309–314.
8. The Russian answer was terse but pointed: "The use of ships to aid land attacks is so customary in wartime as to make useless your comments on the protection of commerce. As to your treaty commitments in Germany, they do not apply, since the King of Prussia began the war and himself violated the peace . . . and England did not stir to prevent him. Russia will continue to distinguish between England and Prussia, but will consider any hindrance to its fleet as a violation of all treaties ever concluded between us." Verbal declaration of Golitsin in London; *AMAE CP R* 53, 144–147; note to L'Hôpital from the Russian Ministry, July 16, 1757: *ibid.* 53, 410–411.
9. Note from the Russian Ministry to L'Hôpital, July 26, 1757: *AMAE CP R* 53, 170–172.

ture hopes. Common sense dictated Russian support for Swedish campaigns. If the war went well for Sweden, then Russia
would benefit militarily and have lost nothing, since France
was already dominant. If, however, the war did not go well
for Sweden, then French interests might well suffer an irre-
trievable loss. Russia could hope to fill such a vacuum. The
Russians and French both saw that the French were risking
their place in Sweden by pushing that government to war.
Swedish successes might be helpful, but Swedish defeats would
be disastrous. The Swedes would remember who had spawned
the idea.[10]

The Empress of Russia adhered to the Swedish treaty on
November 16, 1757, and Russia and Sweden went ahead to
draft joint precautions against British interference in the Baltic.
In October the French-inspired neutrality treaty of 1742 was
renewed. Fifteen Russian ships of the line and four frigates
sailed to join the Swedish fleet off the Sund.

Russia and France, therefore, came to an uneasy truce in
Sweden based upon their mutual desire to press Swedish
troops and ships into the war. Russia was gambling nothing
in Sweden; France owned all the stakes. If the war went well
for Sweden it would assist Russian penetration of Prussia. If
the war went badly for Sweden, it would most certainly endanger and perhaps end the already shaky French influence in
that state. Russia had but to wait. France had its reasons for
suspecting that the new alliances it had assumed might be all
danger and no security.

*ii.*

### THE WAR

Russia and Austria, the members of an offensive alliance,
went to war happily and eagerly, with a sense of something to
be gained. France was dragged into the war as the defensive
ally of Austria. At the outset of hostilities, therefore, France

10. Rouillé to L'Hôpital, June 2,
1757: *ibid.* 53, 65–67; Bernis to
L'Hôpital, May 11, 1758: *ibid.* 56,
157–160; Bernis, *Mémoires* I, 298–99;
Waddington, *La guerre de sept ans*
(Paris: Firmen-Didot, 1890), I, 203–4.

and Russia shared only one common hope and expectation: that the war would be carried to a rapid victory.

What that victory was to bring to either participant had never been discussed, and beneath the first spontaneous aim of the union, quick victory, there lurked basic disagreements. Russia and Austria were waging the war for territorial compensation and the abasement of the Prussian state. France was waging the war half-heartedly, at first in order to maintain its alliances on the Continent and later in hopes of some dynastic gains in the Low Countries and Italy. France's heart would be increasingly in the war with Britain, but France could not risk offending its allies in Europe. The French, as a result, had growing hopes that the Continental war would drive Frederick from the British alliance, fulfill France's obligations to Vienna, and leave Europe in a rearranged balance that would free France to wage war on its primary enemy.

The problem was simple. France was forced to war with Britain, and Russia and Austria chose to war with Prussia. Neither set of allies wished to exchange mutual enemies, and neither had a similar set of war aims. Unfortunately, France had come to overlap the natural positions and was committed with little reason to a war with Prussia. France's task was to get out from under the Continental war quickly without alienating its friends or weakening Prussia overmuch. A quick but inconclusive victory was France's need, but the war was to be neither quick, victorious, nor inconclusive.

The French had been waiting expectantly for a Russian troop movement since early June, 1757. The French expected the Russians to take the pressure off the Rhine, especially after the small but nasty defeat suffered by the French at the hands of Frederick on May 6. Said Bernis, "We see so much slowness in Apraksin's operations that we cannot penetrate its cause and are very worried. The pretext is lack of supplies and the difficulty of establishing warehouses. But these delays certainly have a hidden cause. . . ." The hidden cause, the French Ministry believed, was Grand Chancellor Bestuzhev, who was taking British bribes to impede operations.[11]

11. Bernis to L'Hôpital, July 30,
1757: *AMAE CP R* 53, 234.

There was little substance to this charge, since Bestuzhev was much more of a Prussophobe than many a noble at Versailles. If the Grand Chancellor had any responsibility for the slowness of Apraksin's march, it could only have been based upon his desire for assurances of protection from his allies should Frederick retaliate by an invasion of Russia. Esterhazy and L'Hôpital quickly gave official assurances that Austria and France would live up to the letter of their obligations to Russia in case of a Prussian invasion.[12] Thereafter the French and Austrian ambassadors put increasingly heavy pressures on the Russian court, including undisclosed bribes, to move the Russians to action. The Swedes, upon whom the French had spent considerably more money, were planning to launch a first thrust into Prussian Pomerania and awaited Russian cooperation. Russia agreed to Swedish plans, but seemed reluctant to join the fray.[13]

Then, on August 30, the Russians gave the French a great surprise. They delivered a telling blow to the Prussians under Marshal Lehwald at the Battle of Gross-Jägersdorff. The Empress Elizabeth took this opportunity to make use of her personal correspondence with Louis XV to announce the momentous victory.[14]

The battle, when its first impression had faded, seemed a mixed blessing to the French. "This advantage will certainly change the dispositions of the Russian ministers, who could not have assumed great influence at any congress except in proportion to the part they played in the defeat of the King of Prussia."[15] The battle was a revelation to the French, since it

12. Protocol of conference of Bestuzhev, Vorontsov, Esterhazy, and L'Hôpital, St. Petersburg, Aug. 8, 1757: *AMAE CP R* 53, 311–312. The French did not think that they would ever have to carry out these promises easily given. "We do not feel that the King of Prussia will have time for such adventures. In a case where his Majesty might be obliged to furnish aid, we think that it will have to be in cash because of the distance our 24,000 troops would have to march. We could try to convince them that if Prussia attacks them, our best contribution would be a bigger diversion in Germany to draw them off." Bernis to L'Hôpital, Oct. 8, 1757: *ibid.* 54, 110.

13. L'Hôpital to Bernis, Aug. 22, 1757: *ibid.* 53, 314–321; Havrincourt to Bernis, Stockholm, Sept. 26, 1757: *AMAE CP S* 72, 7–8; and note from the Russian Ministry, *ibid.* 72, 5.

14. Elizabeth to Louis XV, Dec. 4, 1757: *AMAE CP R* 54, 354–58.

15. L'Hôpital to Bernis, Sept. 16, 1757: *ibid.* 54, 42.

clearly exposed their Russian dilemma. Having urged Russia to quick action, they now faced the possibility of dealing with an ally whose total victory might make it the arbiter of the peace and a new force in Germany. Europe might be so unbalanced by Muscovite power that it would require years of war to restore it. Truly France could not win. Overwhelming Russian victories and overwhelming Russian defeats were equally repugnant.

France brightened a bit, however, when lack of news from the Russian army indicated that Apraksin had not followed his victory with a complete rout of the Prussians. Meanwhile, the French were themselves busy. In mid-September they eliminated the Duke of Cumberland from the war — or so they thought — by the Convention of Kloster-Zeven. Then the impossible word arrived from the Russian front. Apraksin had not only failed to follow up his victory, he had gone into full retreat. The Grand Chancellor was stunned, and saw in the retreat only more threats to his difficult position. The Grand Duchess Catherine, at the center of most intrigues, was no less astonished:

No one understood anything of this operation; even his friends did not know how to justify it, and everyone saw in it undercover dealings. Truly, I myself did not know to what to attribute the Marshal's hasty and incoherent retreat, never having seen him again. However, I think the cause of it could have been that Apraksin received from his daughter . . . very precise news of the health of the Empress, who was going from bad to worse.[16]

Many agreed with Catherine that the illness of the Empress had frightened Apraksin: that knowing the sentiments of the Grand Duke Peter for Prussia, he felt that a victory over Frederick would be badly received by the new Emperor. Actually the general inability of eighteenth-century armies to operate for very long at large distances from their stockpiles of supplies was at the root of Apraksin's decision. Nevertheless, everyone took the hasty retreat of the Marshal as proof that the Empress was dying and that the expected reversal of policy

16. Pipin, *op. cit.*, XII, p. 387.

was the result. Unfortunately for Apraksin, the Empress re-
covered once again from her malady, and what seemed a
prudent retreat became now an imprudent treachery.[17]

Everyone was thrown into confusion by the retreat. The
Empress and Chancellor met immediately and ordered Apraksin
back to the front. The French feared that the Russian army
would make their winter quarters in Poland, an impossible
situation. Bestuzhev, knowing that the wrath of the Empress
might well and justly fall on the Young Court as the instiga-
tors of this retreat, counseled his student Catherine to write to
Apraksin urging him to return to the battle. This she did.[18]
Still, Apraksin's army disappeared for over a month. Finally,
two officers were sent into Livonia to find the troops and re-
organize supplies.

The French Ministry, filled with stories of Apraksin's
treachery by Mikhail Bestuzhev, determined to seek Apraksin's
recall as army commander. Wittinghov, French attaché with
the Russian army, was ordered to return to St. Petersburg to
help L'Hôpital build a case against the hapless Marshal. The
French felt that the replacement had to come quickly, since the
Swedes had entered Pomerania in expectation of Russian cover
but were now exposed to Prussian attack. Bernis believed that
the Swedish Queen was impatiently awaiting a Swedish defeat
that would destroy her opposition. A Russian general had to be
found quickly who would save France and Sweden from such a
disaster.[19]

The Russians performed L'Hôpital's task for him. The
temporary Russian explanation for Apraksin's retreat had been
lack of forage, but his retreat into Poland had carried a bad

17. There has been a continuing con-
troversy over the true causes of
Apraksin's retreat. For Russian military
operations, see Alfred Rambaud,
Russes et Prussiens: Guerre de Sept
Ans (Paris: Firmen-Didot, 1895);
and R. E. Masslowski, Der Siebenjahrige Krieg nach Russischer Darstellung (Berlin: R. Eisenschmidt, 1889–
93). A short but comprehensive description of this campaign will be
found in R. N. Bain, The Daughter of

Peter the Great (New York: E. P.
Dutton, 1900), Chapter 9.
18. Pipin, op. cit., p. 388. K. Osipov,
(Alexander Suvarov, translated by E.
Bone [London: Hutchinson, 1941])
represents the wartime Soviet historians who charged that Bestuzhev,
Apraksin, and Catherine were all
"traitors" in the pay of Prussia. See
p. 20.
19. Bernis to L'Hôpital, Oct. 16 and
24, 1757: AMAE CP R 54, 145–176.

thing too far. A ministerial conference on October 20 removed Apraksin and named Count William Fermor as army commander. The Empress finally admitted publicly to her allies that her Marshal had behaved himself abominably.[20] Apraksin was ordered back to St. Petersburg to undergo investigation. No one was happy that such a trial was to be held, neither Chancellor, nor Young Court, nor the court in general. Too much might be uncovered.

Apraksin's retreat had major effects on French policy. The first repercussion was an unavoidable recognition at Versailles that the differences of political opinion between the Empress of Russia and the Young Court made any diplomatic agreements with that state extremely tenuous. The support of the Russian political and military leaders for any program depended almost completely on the prevailing health of the Empress. France had begun to confirm its suspicion that the Russian state could guarantee no continuity of policy beyond the wavering life of the Russian Empress and no firm support for policies already undertaken.

The second result of the retreat was the growing disenchantment of France with Russian military contributions, in part reinforced by the serious military setbacks suffered by the French on the Rhine at the same time. Bernis found no difficulty in ascribing the ill luck of the Prince de Soubise, French military commander against Frederick at Rossbach, to the failure of Apraksin at least to hold firm. The Duke of Cumberland returned to the war and threatened the Duke de Richelieu's rear. Bernis felt that "Marshal Apraksin, by retreating after the battle of August 30, has taken the first step toward the disintegration of a system so well begun." Despair was slowly creeping over the normally ebullient Minister of Foreign Affairs, and he glimpsed the disasters before him:

We are awaiting the news of a battle [between Richelieu and Cumberland] with great impatience. Whatever happens, we do not expect much. If we win we cannot follow up our victory for lack of

20. Notes from the Russian Ministry, Oct. 11 and 25, 1757: *ibid.* 54, 131–136 and 181.

supplies, and if we lose we shall be driven out of Hanover, West-phalia, Hesse, and the Low Countries. . . . Then Frederick will turn on Austria. If he defeats the Swedes, Frederick's sister will foment a revolution against us there. Holland would then enter the war against us, and perhaps even Denmark. The Russians are the cause of our troubles; they must now move rapidly to relieve us.[21]

Ambassador L'Hôpital did nothing to allay the fears of Bernis. His opinion of Russian military operations was that Russia would "simply make manifestations and demonstrations of serving the allies, but would remain a quiet spectator to the war . . . in order to put Russia in the most advantageous posi-tion to follow the flow of events." [22] Bernis and L'Hôpital had, in a few short months, changed their minds radically on Russian military contributions. The change in Bernis was most signifi-cant of all. "The utility of Russia in the alliance is such . . . that it is essential to preserve her therein even if she does nothing for us, in order that she may do nothing against us." [23] That was quite a decline in great expectations. It was also a mistake to assume that Russia was not already in the best position to operate against the interests of France.

The third effect of the Apraksin retreat on French policy was a renewed determination in the French Ministry to avoid discussion of Russian war aims. When the Russian army moved brusquely into Prussia it seemed that their claims might demand immediate attention. Thus, the equally brusque retreat relieved French minds and convinced them that talk of cessions to Russia might well await the final accounting of the war.

France was determined not to communicate to Russia the provisions of the Second Treaty of Versailles, signed between France and Austria on May 1, 1757. This offensive alliance against Prussia had enumerated the increased military commit-ment of France in Germany and had become specific about the territories that France might reasonably expect to obtain in the Low Countries and in Italy. Knowledge of such provisions might inflame Russian desires for specific territorial compensa-

21. Bernis to L'Hôpital, Dec. 31, 1757: *ibid.* 54, 436.
22. L'Hôpital to Bernis, Jan. 7, 1758: *ibid.* 55, 10–11.
23. Bernis to L'Hôpital, Jan. 25, 1758: *ibid.* 55, 90.

tions to be guaranteed to the Russian Empire by the allied powers. France wished to avoid discussing such guarantees. Still, L'Hôpital reported that the Russians learned through their Austrian allies that some sort of supplementary agreements had been reached between Vienna and Versailles.[24]

Bernis was well acquainted with the rumors that Brühl and Bestuzhev desired to cede Courland to Russia in return for the cession of East Prussia, to be taken from Prussia, to a son of the Polish King. Brühl's attempts to aggrandize the Saxon house, his lifelong task, fitted well with Russian plans. The French Ministry interpreted the slow movement of Russian troops in 1757 as partly the result of pressure tactics in favor of these schemes. Bernis believed that the Russians planned to wangle more money from Austria and more specific territorial commitments from both allies in return for a more active war effort. Bernis told L'Hôpital to procrastinate indefinitely if such questions were now raised by the Russians:

If Russia seeks lands in East Prussia, Poland would run terrible risks, for her extended frontiers with the Russian Empire are already too considerable. His Majesty . . . can never consent to the Russians establishing themselves in Pomerania or in Brandenburg. It is extremely important to the King and to the Empress-Queen that the Russians find no means to mingle in the affairs of the Empire or have free entry there. Consequences could be disastrous in case present relations did not remain in their current state.[25]

Even Bernis had a concept of a balance of power which worked to the salvation of the Prussian state. The Abbé instructed L'Hôpital to insinuate to the Russians that France understood Russia's purposes in the war to be aid to her Austrian ally, an end to Prussian ambitions, and glory for the Russian Empire. Surely the Russians expected no recompense beyond the satisfaction of seeing these ends accomplished. Russia ought to concern itself with bringing order to its already large dominions, rather than with adding to them. The most

24. L'Hôpital to Rouillé, July 28, 1757: *ibid.* 53, 234. For a discussion of Austro-French commitments, see Anderson, *op. cit.*, p. 211.

25. Bernis to L'Hôpital, July 31, 1757: *AMAE CP R* 53, 236–237.

significant gain Russia was making from the war, according to Bernis, was security against the Turks. This should be sufficient reward. "Having gambled little and assisted little, they ought to expect little." [26]

Bernis therefore decided to elude any talks with Russia on territorial cessions. He preferred to procrastinate in this, as in all things, hoping that time and changing events would resolve his dilemma. In this resistance to Russian demands it would seem that Bernis showed good sense. A French diplomat still in his right mind could hardly deed away the integrity of Poland, the safety of the Germanic states, the friendship of Turkey, the liberty of Sweden, and the continued existence of Prussia as a power in return for the dubious benefit of having the services of an army in full retreat whose future conduct toward the allies might be rapidly affected by the chaos of politics at home!

The fourth and final consequence of Apraksin's retreat for French policy was the fall and exile of the Grand Chancellor Bestuzhev. The Chancellor had already taken a heavy blow when Britain abandoned him for Frederick of Prussia. His continuation in power even after the substance of his policy had crumbled in his hands was a testimonial both to Bestuzhev's capacity and to his persuasiveness with the Empress Elizabeth. Apraksin's retreat had accentuated the fact that many persons at the Russian court, including Bestuzhev, were preparing for the hasty exit of the Empress. Elizabeth's realization of this fact put Bestuzhev in a bad light with his Empress. He was adapting himself only with the greatest difficulty to the new system and was still intriguing with the Grand Duchess to ensure his continuance in power. Field Marshal Apraksin was his friend and supporter, so the Marshal's conduct reflected clearly on the Grand Chancellor. News of the retreat and then of Apraksin's recall had sent Bestuzhev into one of his renowned "sick spells," by which he removed himself from the center of undesirable affairs.

L'Hôpital caught the atmosphere of tension and began to

26. Bernis to L'Hôpital, Oct. 24, 1757: *ibid.* 54, 167–172.

warn his Ministry in September, 1757, that Bestuzhev was in danger. Bernis, converted to belief in the Grand Chancellor's political immortality by Austrian propaganda, replied that this might be true, but that "we must be careful that the desire of his enemies for his fall does not give the appearance of a nearer fall than there really is." Bernis was so certain of Bestuzhev's durability that he confided to L'Hôpital "that His Majesty has the intention of making an annual present of 10,-000 ducats to the Grand Chancellor Bestuzhev, which you may insinuate to him, on condition that he give attention to the success of His Majesty's views." [27]

L'Hôpital, hearing in all quarters that Bestuzhev was ready to topple, could not bring himself to attempt a bribe of the Grand Chancellor. He feared, properly, that Bestuzhev would use an attempted bribe and his refusal of it to raise himself once more in the esteem of the Empress. L'Hôpital did not want to help the falling foe, and in this the Ambassador was wiser than his Ministry.[28] The trial of Marshal Apraksin for his alleged misconduct of the war was leading to disturbing revelations. Aleksandr Shuvalov, having secretly seized Apraksin's papers, revealed to the Empress that the Grand Duchess Catherine had been in touch with the Marshal by letter through Bestuzhev. Although the letters were harmless, appearances were damning.

As late as February 9 the French Ministry was raging at L'Hôpital for delaying the bribe to Bestuzhev; Bernis ordered L'Hôpital to offer a flat gift of 8,000 ducats and a set of Gobelins tapestries in addition to the annual payments.[29] Before the Ambassador received these orders, he had elected to add his weight against the Chancellor. The impetus for the action of the French party in alliance with the Shuvalovs was the

27. Bernis to L'Hôpital, Sept. 13, and Oct. 16, 1757: *ibid.* 54, 62 and 143.
28. L'Hôpital to Bernis, Nov. 13, 1757: *ibid.* 54, 223. Bernis, however, was thinking ahead to a future dismissal of Bestuzhev and considering eliciting a personal letter from Maria Theresa to that end. Bernis to Stainville, Nov. 8, 1757: Bernis, *op. cit.*, II, 137.

29. Bernis to L'Hôpital, Feb. 9, 1758: *AMAE CP R* 55, 151. Bernis was under heavy pressure to secure Russian military aid. "Russia alone at this moment can restore the balance and give us breathing space." Bernis to Stainville, Jan. 14, 1758, in Bernis, *op. cit.*, II, 165.

report that the new British Ambassador, Robert Keith, was passing Berlin and on his way to St. Petersburg. Fear that renewed British support and subsidies for Bestuzhev would rescue the Grand Chancellor drove the coalition of his enemies to make a final effort to overthrow him.

L'Hôpital's part, and therefore the French role, in the attack on the Chancellor was hardly as great as the Ambassador indicated after the event. L'Hôpital maintained that, hearing that Keith had reached Warsaw, he sought out Vice-Chancellor Vorontsov and told him that the assault on Bestuzhev must come immediately. He supposedly threatened Vorontsov that if he did not press the Empress to remove the Chancellor, the French Ambassador would be forced by his Ministry to act in concert with Bestuzhev and bypass Vorontsov. Then, according to L'Hôpital's version, Vorontsov became alarmed, summoned all his persuasive powers, sought out the Empress, and, as once long ago he had driven her to a throne, drove her now to jettison the Grand Chancellor. The Ambassador's role was much more subsidiary than his own version. The Empress, always slow to act, had finally made a long overdue decision at the urging of the Shuvalovs and Vorontsov. However, L'Hôpital understandably magnified his own part for the consumption of his Ministry.[30]

In any case, the Empress was finally convinced. As Bestuzhev entered the unfinished portals of the Winter Palace to witness the trial of his friend Apraksin, the guard placed him under arrest. He was led home and imprisoned there with his wife and son. Two of the intimate servants of the Grand Duchess were arrested at the same time. The Empress Elizabeth notified her allies that she "finally saw with much regret that she could not trust her Minister Bestuzhev, in view of the

30. L'Hôpital's version was partly corroborated by Keith to the English Ministry, Mar. 30, 1758: reprinted in E. I. Turgenev, *La Russie il y a cent ans: extraits des dépêches des ambassadeurs anglais* (Paris: E. Dentu, 1858), p. 158; and Pipin, *op. cit.*, XII, p. 405. L'Hôpital's version was followed by R. N. Bain, *Daughter of Peter the Great* (New York: E. P. Dutton, 1900), pp. 238–39; and by Jules Fabre, *Stanislas Auguste Poniatowsky et l'Europe des lumières* (Paris: C. Lévy, 1952), p. 222. See Yevgeni N. Shchepkin, "Padenie Kantslera Grafa A. P. Bestuzheva-Riumina," *Zapiski, Imperatorskoe Odesskoe obshchestva istorii i drevnostei* (Odessa, 1901), XXIII, 207–60.

discovery of so many crimes, intrigues, plots, and other black deeds," but that Russia's commitments to her allies were in no way altered by the change in ministers.[31]

British Ambassador Keith, on his arrival, sensed the extent of the allied victory. "I found on my arrival . . . that the French party was in possession of all credit at that court, and that the two ambassadors, Esterhazy and L'Hôpital, give the law to court and city." [32] The friends and minions of the Grand Chancellor were struck down in all quarters. Said the disgruntled Netherlands envoy, "It matters not whether someone be guilty or not, it suffices to have been a friend of the disgraced minister." [33] An attack on the Polish Minister, Brühl, was planned by the French to complete the enemy rout. Stainville in Vienna provided definite information that Brühl had been conspiring with Bestuzhev. Brühl recanted abjectly. Perhaps hearing the cock crow thrice, he denied even having known the Chancellor personally and agreed to purge the Saxon and Polish delegations at St. Petersburg of agents who were *persona non grata* to the French. Recalls were also sought for other friends of Bestuzhev on diplomatic mission in Poland, Sweden, and Vienna, but the Empress, as ever, moved slowly.[34]

The trial of Bestuzhev was a long affair. One of the investigators gave voice to the cynical nature of the undertaking: "We have arrested Bestuzhev and soon we shall seek the reasons why." [35] The French, as many others in St. Petersburg, were fearful that Bestuzhev would escape lightly, since his judges were well aware both that the Young Court was involved and that judges and witnesses might one day repent their actions. Bernis ordered L'Hôpital to "demonstrate no appearance of triumph, nor appear publicly to have had any part in this busi-

31. Elizabeth to L'Hôpital, Feb. 27, 1758: *AMAE CP R* 55, 214; Pipin, *op. cit.*, XII pp. 406, 408, and 474; *Gazette de Saint-Petersbourg*, No. 18, Tuesday, Mar. 3, 1758.
32. Keith to English Ministry, Mar. 14, 1758: reprinted in Turgenev, *op. cit.*, p. 174.
33. Secret letter of Swart, Envoy of the States-General of the Netherlands

in Russia, to his Ministry, Mar. 28, 1758; intercepted by the French: *AMAE CP R* 56, 139.
34. Stainville to L'Hôpital, Vienna, Mar. 14, 1758: *ibid.* 55, 254–256; Brühl to L'Hôpital, Apr. 19, 1758: *AMAE CP Po* 213, 78–83; Pipin, *op. cit.*, XII p. 407.
35. Pipin, *op. cit.*, XII p. 407.

ness. Bestuzhev and his friends could do you harm." [36] The charges against Bestuzhev, however, were declared proven, and he was found guilty of influencing Apraksin to retard military operations. The Empress sentenced Bestuzhev to death, and then, in accord with her abolition of capital punishment, banished him to Siberia.

The immediate French reaction to the fall of Bestuzhev was great joy and a concerted effort to fix the Vice-Chancellor Vorontsov firmly in the French orbit. The furnishings of the Vorontsov Palace, then under construction, were donated by the King of France. The Vice-Chancellor also received a secret gift of 250,000 livres for services rendered. In return the Minister agreed to remove his present secretary and to take one recommended by the French.[37]

However, the feeling of exultation over their victory soon was lost to the French. In believing that only the Grand Chancellor kept Russia mindful of her true interests and in ascribing to him all the intrigues and faults of the Russian court, France had made a serious mistake. The French Ministry soon found reason to agree with the comment of Kaunitz to Stainville that Grand Chancellor Bestuzhev should be handled carefully "for the simple reason that there exists no one of quality to replace him." [38] L'Hôpital was not long in discovering that Bestuzhev's absence had made little change in Russian dispositions. "We have one enemy less here by the disgrace of Bestuzhev . . . but the lack of constancy at this court, the lack of wit of the Vice-Chancellor, the laziness and delays of the Empress, the uncertainties, stupidities, suspicions, and plots of her favorites all remain . . . and leave us no hope of ever making a solid and lasting alliance with Russia." [39]

The Chancellor was gone but nothing had changed. The

36. Bernis to L'Hôpital, Mar. 24, 1758: *AMAE CP R* 55, 331–332.
37. Note in the Ministry of Foreign Affairs, June 11, 1758: *ibid.* 56, 293; Bernis to L'Hôpital, May 30, 1758: *ibid.* 56, 239; Swart to Ministry, Mar. 28, 1758: *ibid.* 56, 139. Bernis said of the Chancellor's disgrace that "this

event in Russia can save our country." Bernis to Stainville, Mar. 24, 1758; in Bernis, *op. cit.*, II, 194.
38. Stainville to L'Hôpital, Vienna, Mar. 14, 1758: *AMAE CP R* 55, 254.
39. L'Hôpital to Bernis, June 2, 1758: *ibid.* 56, 255–256.

arrival of a new and financially fortified British Ambassador threatened the French anew. In the diplomatic corps rumors were rife that Ivan Shuvalov and Mikhail Vorontsov were targets for enormous bribes from the British. The Russian army seemed still determined to remain behind the Vistula, and the French considered it now of little more use than an observation corps. Rumors of secret peace negotiations being carried on by both parties with the enemy only added to the air of suspicion. Even worse for relations, French armies had suffered overwhelming reverses in Germany. The defeat at Rossbach was among the worst in French military history. This disastrous campaign called forth another secret letter from Louis XV to Elizabeth explaining that only lack of supplies had caused the French retreat.[40] Esterhazy's tales to the Russians, however, gave the Russians a different impression. L'Hôpital now feared "that the Russians, learning of our defeat and retreat, will use them as reason to defer crossing the Vistula indefinitely." [41]

The Russian army indeed moved slowly, and Esterhazy and L'Hôpital spent day after day pleading for speed. Bernis was falling more deeply into despair as calamity followed calamity for the French. He insisted that the Russians would have to bring pressure on Frederick immediately or all was lost. "Insinuate to the Russians that all Europe is convinced that Russia wishes to be only a spectator in the present war or at least only a mediator at the peace. If they in turn reproach us, it must fall upon our generals and not upon our sincerity." Another letter from the King was dispatched "to root the Empress from her inactivity." This letter asked for a prompt movement of the Russian army and mutual promises to make no separate peace.[42]

Once again the King's intervention seemed successful. By July the Russians had crossed the Vistula and were on their way to besiege Küstrin. A bit tardily Elizabeth sent word to

40. Louis XV to Elizabeth, Mar. 13, 1758: *ibid.* 55, 246.
41. L'Hôpital to Bernis, Apr. 22, 1758: *ibid.* 56, 99.
42. Louis XV to Elizabeth, June 10, 1758: *ibid.* 56, 278. The King's letter was carried by D'Éon in a volume of *Esprit des lois* which had a false cover. D'Éon to Vergennes, London, May 28, 1776: in Boutaric, *op. cit.*, I, 232, Note 2.

Louis that she would make no separate peace. There was, however, a very large fly in the ointment. In return for doing its duty, Russia wanted French participation in the Austro-Russian treaty of January, 1757, which would have involved France in subsidies to the Russian army and in discussions of postwar concessions. Russia was arranging to send *pleinpouvoirs* to Mikhail Bestuzhev in Paris to begin such negotiations.[43]

The ever-gentle Bernis, overwhelmed by disaster, for once lost his temper. "Never mind arrangments for Bestuzhev to negotiate war results. You tell them that we are in deep troubles, and that they had better get into the war or there will be precious little left to discuss." While putting France's position succinctly, such undiplomatic language obviously had to be rephrased. France would appreciate a more rapid Russian movement on Prussia. As to the Austro-Russian treaty, France could not participate for several reasons:

1. It was based on the treaty of 1746, which was directed against France.

2. It did not except Turkey from its operations.

3. It guaranteed the return of Silesia to Austria, which France did not think practical at the moment.

4. It guaranteed subsidies to Russia that France was in no position to pay.[44]

What the French did offer, equal to nothing, was a public declaration of adherence to the treaty, excepting all its disturbing clauses.[45] This was the most that Russia could elicit. Actually, Bernis had properly asked himself what benefit such participation could possibly have for France. "The Convention promises the very considerable advantage of the recovery of Silesia to the Empress-Queen. It is known that the Empress of Russia has definite concessions in mind. What benefit could possibly be stipulated for the King of France?"[46]

What the King of France needed would not be delivered

43. Elizabeth to Louis XV, Oct. 28, 1758: *AMAE CP R* 58, 157.
44. Bernis to L'Hôpital, June 22 and Oct. 8, 1758: *ibid.* 56, 339; and *ibid.* 58, 47–53.

45. Declaration of the King of France to the Empress of Russia, Oct. 24, 1758: *ibid.* 58, 127–132.
46. Bernis to L'Hôpital, Oct. 8, 1758: *ibid.* 58, 54. In code.

to him by his allies. Cry as the French might for a campaign by the Russian army, it became increasingly clear that what Bernis really wanted from the Russians was precisely what he could not get — peace. Whereas Bernis was attempting to accomplish the possible, to get the Russians to war effectively, he was at the same time hoping for the impossible, the end of the Continental struggle. France had begun the war in the belief that a quick war would ensure the Austrian alliance and free France to fight the British. Two years of warfare, some of the most disastrous France had ever undergone, destroyed that belief. France was being pushed beyond its endurance. The war had to be ended by a quick victory or a quick peace, and as 1758 drew to a close it became clear to Bernis that quick victory was not a prospect. Considered from the French point of view, the Franco-Russian reunion under Austrian auspices had failed to achieve its purposes.

As early as April, 1758, Abbé Bernis had decided that France must find a way out of its dilemma. Such a decision would necessarily change the relationship of France and Russia. It is easy to unite nations in the fervor of war, but more difficult to unite them in the contemplation of peace. Bernis now set out to discover whether the Franco-Russian *rapprochement,* created spontaneously by the diplomatic revolution and the war, could be put to more useful purposes. Bernis wrote a key dispatch to L'Hôpital in April, 1758: "I will end this dispatch on a point more important than any I have yet treated with you; it is the order which His Majesty sends you to sound out the dispositions of Russia with regard to the making of peace." Defeats, demoralization, and overwhelming expenses, said Bernis, forced the King to end the Continental war. Austria, of course, was never to know of these peace overtures to Russia. This expensive war had been undertaken by France for the sake of the Austrian alliance, and there was no point in losing that alliance now that the price had been so painfully paid.[47]

The task proposed to L'Hôpital was one worthy of a diplo-

47. Bernis to L'Hôpital, Apr. 25, 1758: *ibid.* 56, 126. In code.

mat. Bernis did not want Vienna to know of French plans, nor did he want Russia frightened out of the alliance by peace propositions. "All your art must be employed so that the Russians never think that the King desires peace, but so that you leave the impression without ever openly stating it of the King's dispositions for a just peace." Bernis was not averse to making promises that the Russians might redeem much later. "The Empress of Russia ought to feel that the immense expenses of the war do not permit the King of France to do all that he would like for her. It is then at the peace . . . that he will be able to give tangible marks of His esteem for Her." [48] In other words, France, which had been unwilling to pay Russia for the war, now expected to purchase Russian aid for peace with promises.

As 1758 drew to a close the determination of Bernis for peace was strengthened by the mounting defeats of French arms in Europe and abroad. "We must end the war on the Continent so that we can at least make some semblance of fighting abroad. . . . The English have involved us in a war in Germany while we lose our colonies, our commerce, and our life." [49] L'Hôpital tried to fulfill his extremely difficult instructions, but his approaches to the Russians on peace were doomed to failure. Vorontsov, now charged with foreign affairs, answered the Ambassador's discreet inquiries by saying that much as the Russians would like to make peace that winter, the sad state of the allies made it impossible. Russia would not forego the possibility of gains, for which it had paid dearly in blood, for nebulous promises from France. Russia would make peace in its interests when peace could be dictated by the Empress in Berlin. [50]

48. Bernis to L'Hôpital, May 11 and 30, 1758: ibid. 56, 161 and 243–244. See also Bernis, op. cit., II, 44.
49. Bernis to L'Hôpital, Sept. 15, 1758: AMAE CP R 57, 279.
50. Austria was of the same determination, and a struggle was emerging between Kaunitz and Bernis on France's apparent backsliding toward peace. Austrian suspicion of Bernis's determination led to his removal and the choice of Choiseul as seemingly more energetic and devoted to the Continental war. See Waddington, La guerre, I, 734 and 742–43; II, 415–16, 449. Masson collected the documents on these negotiations with Vienna that convinced the French of the necessity of seeking peace through St. Petersburg. See Bernis, op. cit., II, appendix XI.

This was news which Bernis preferred not to hear. It was not some fly-by-night court general that the allies were fighting, it was Frederick of Prussia. To dictate peace terms to him in Berlin would require more years, more blood, and more money than Bernis had courage to imagine. Bernis might well try to remember how France had become entrapped in this unfortunate business. L'Hôpital told the Abbé that France might have better luck with Russia if it spoke of "rectifications" in Poland. Bernis wrestled with the justice or necessity of cutting up Poland, which had no part in the war, and giving Russia a voice in Germany for the sake of Russian aid for peace. Bernis wrestled similarly with the distinct possibility that, making such territorial guarantees to Russia, the Russians would never be content to make peace until the delivery of those territories was assured. Knowing the disposition of Frederick of Prussia for the province of East Prussia, this amounted to there being no peace in the foreseeable future. The problem was basically that Russia intended to make war until its voice could be heard in the peace treaties, whether France acquiesced in its demands or not. This being the case, there was little point in France making any concessions to Russia.[51]

Bernis, at his wits' end, fell back upon his customary waiting policy. He instructed L'Hôpital to continue hinting at peace in hopes of a Russian change of heart, but to preserve Russia in the alliance in hopes of some future advantage. At the same time French military fortunes had fallen to an unbelievable low. The Battle of Krefeld, a new Rossbach, came on June 23. The Austrians were holding in Moravia with great difficulty. France was satisfied if the Russians sat quietly on the Oder, "letting their conservation be their victory."[52] The Russians, however, encountered the Prussians at Zorndorf on August 25 and 26. Fermor retreated once again into Poland; the terrible casualties suffered by the Russians at this supposed victory were reason enough. Thus, the campaigns of 1758 ended in depression and general retreat for the allies. France

51. Bernis to L'Hôpital, Aug. 1, 1758: *AMAE CP R* 57, 82–83.

52. Bernis to L'Hôpital, Sept. 4, 1758: *ibid.* 57, 215.

was defeated in Europe and abroad and was exhausted financially. French commerce had been reduced to a trickle.

Bernis crumbled in the face of the terrible times. Never energetic and never able, he could imagine no way out of the disaster that threatened France. The Russian branch of the alliance had failed him because neither France nor Russia had realized what the other wanted from the war — or, having discovered it, was willing to deliver it. Militarily the Russian ties had been useless to France. Bernis, who had picked up the direction of French foreign affairs as a shiny bauble to decorate his career, was preparing sadly and more wisely to put it down.

*iii.*

### THE POLISH QUESTION

If the administration of Abbé Bernis had been disastrous in the waging of the war, it was no less disastrous in the diplomacy of the Polish question. France had an ancient interest in the Polish state. By alliance with the powers on the border of Europe, France had balanced off her larger European neighbors. In return France supported Poland against the ambitions of its neighbors. Since the early years of the eighteenth century the growing power of Russia had created an unprecedented threat to Poland and to French influence there. Slowly, after 1745, the Secret in Poland had strengthened and enlarged the French party in Poland under the Potocki. The enemy was always Russia, which had a party of its own led by the Czartoryski. The diplomatic revolution, here as elsewhere, wrenched and twisted old policies.

Russian entry into the war as an ally of Austria and France had made likely the march of troops across Poland. During the diplomatic tenure of the Chevalier Douglas, French policy began to show the strains of the new system. Both the Ministry of Foreign Affairs and the Secret were united on the protection of Poland. However, the Ministry, whose aim was a quick end to the Continental war, accepted the march of Russian troops across Poland in the belief that such a move was necessary and that Russian ambitions could be constrained. The Secret, on the other hand, whose aim was the preservation of Poland above all, resisted every Russian intervention as necessarily detrimental to the French cause in Poland. Beneath this seemingly minor disagreement were more serious differences in policy. At the beginning of the new alliances the Ministry under Bernis was prepared to be shown the advantages of the new union. The Secret, however, was convinced that the French attachment to the Austro-Russian alliance was a temporary expedient from which France would have difficulty escaping unscathed. Events in Poland would demonstrate which group had foreseen the future the more clearly.[53]

Broglie in Warsaw opened his correspondence with L'Hôpital in St. Petersburg by requesting an exchange of confidences on Russian affairs and by urging the Ambassador to put more vigor in his complaints to the Russian Ministry about troop movements across Poland. Friction between the two was immediate. L'Hôpital resented the superior attitude of Broglie in presuming to send what sounded very much like orders to an ambassador at a court more elevated than his own. Once again, differences were more deep-seated. In their persons L'Hôpital and Broglie reflected the more serious rift in policy between the Ministry and the Secret. L'Hôpital placed his faith in the new alliances and linked Poland in their future. "The three allies can give the law to Europe in the future, a just and irreproachable law, if they could come to some honest exchange of views on Poland." [54] Broglie entirely disagreed: he could not imagine Russia or Austria being honest about their intentions in Poland. Broglie, learning of L'Hôpital's disturbing senti-

---

53. For general treatments of Poland in this period see Wladyslaw Konopczynski, *Polska w dobnie wojny siedmioletniej* (Krakow and Warsaw: W. L. Anczyca, 1911); Jules Fabre, *op. cit.*; Herbert H. Kaplan, *First partition of Poland* (New York: Columbia University Press, 1962); and L. R. Lewitter, "Poland Under the Saxon Kings," *New Cambridge Modern History* (1959), VII, 365–90. Also useful

is claude Carloman de Rulhière, *Histoire de l'anarchie de Pologne et du démembrement de cette republique* (Paris: Desenne, 1807). See also W. F. Reddaway *et al.*, *Cambridge History of Poland* (Cambridge: Cambridge University Press, 1941–50), II, Chap. 1 and 2.

54. L'Hôpital to Bernis, Aug. 13, 1757: *AMAE CP R* 53, 277.

ments from Tercier, attempted to convert the Ambassador to Russia to views more acceptable to the Secret:

After this presentation . . . you may judge if I think that it is to the interest or dignity of the King to sacrifice any liaison, however slight, to new ties which would acquire a certain force only with extreme difficulty. It seems to me that what was most to be desired of this union with Russia is already gained: it removes from England and Prussia a possible phantom alliance which might have convinced other powers to follow the same road. . . .

I agree that Poland may seem at first glance, weak and divided as it is, to be a liability to us. However, this view is taken only by persons who have not been able to see the service we draw from Poland while it remains free. . . . Poland can only, it is true, be considered as a liaison between the Porte and the north which alone is not solid, but which acquires strength by the interest which we give to it. . . . I am even tempted to believe that with care and money one will find in Poland alone the means to guard against the ambitions of the Russians. I think it is clear that if we had at all wished it, the Poles would have proven as much during the passage of Russian troops. We must always consider that we can give to this Republic another form than the one in which it now languishes and make Poland a successful member of the other strong powers who will always be attached to us.[55]

Broglie and the Secret were on their way into deep trouble. The Ambassador in Russia, a man unacquainted with the Secret and unsympathetic to its aims, was replacing the Secret's agent, Douglas. The only operative of the Secret left in Russia was the Chevalier d'Eon, an unstable personality whose subordinate position as embassy secretary required him to be extremely careful about communicating affairs to Broglie. Then Abbé Bernis came to the direction of Foreign Affairs in August, 1757, and Broglie's distaste for Pompadour and his independent manner had erected a strong personal animosity between him and his new Minister. Further, Broglie knew the attitude of Bernis toward the new alliances. Bernis and L'Hôpital promised to be a formidable obstruction to the Secret program.

55. Broglie to L'Hôpital, Aug. 18,
1757: *ibid.* Suppl. 9, 96.

L'Hôpital, offended by the continuing advice from Broglie, made his position clear. He would not endanger Franco-Russian cooperation by continuing to carp incessantly to the Russians about minor infractions in Poland. Broglie then replied sharply:

The principle of the court where you are is to act with Poland as if it were a province of the Russian Empire. . . . If this Russian desire to dominate . . . is allowed to become a major motive of Russian policy, it will be for the King's Council to decide if it is advantageous to abandon the protection which France has always extended to the Poles. This is a subject upon which I do not pronounce. I content myself to conform . . . carefully to my instructions to hear the complaints of the Polish nation, to appease them as much as possible, and to accord to the Poles our support and prestige in representations to the Russian Ministry.[56]

Broglie believed that any concessions to Russia in Poland would only lead to more, until Russian ambitions became too powerful to stop. Therefore, the Russians had to be checked at every minor point, lest their small offenses grow to great ones. What worried Broglie, far more than lack of enthusiasm on the part of L'Hôpital in delivering Polish complaints, was the rumor that the Polish succession was becoming a matter of general discussion at the Russian Ministry.

I think the Polish crown is already being negotiated between Saxony and Russia for the Prince Royal of Saxony. . . . If you want the Prince Xaxier, we can, I think, succeed in his behalf. . . . The Poles have also shown interest in Prince Edward [Charles Edward Stuart], whom they think you favor.[57]

To make matters worse, Broglie learned from D'Éon that L'Hôpital and Brühl, the Polish Minister, had the topic under discussion by letter.[58] Broglie ordered L'Hôpital to stop such talk immediately and rained reproaches upon him. Douglas,

56. Broglie to L'Hôpital, Sept. 1, 1757: *ibid.* Suppl. 9, 119–120.
57. Broglie to Louis XV, Sept. 5, 1757: in Ozanam and Antoine, *op. cit.*, I, 35–37. See A. Thevenot (ed.)
*Correspondance du Prince François-Xavier de Saxe* (Paris: Plon, 1874).
58. D'Éon to Broglie, Nov. 14, 1757: *AMAE CP R*, Suppl. 9, 244.

stopping for talks with Broglie on his return to France, corroborated that L'Hôpital was speaking loosely about the future of Poland.[59] The noise of the dispute soon reached Versailles. Bernis was unhappy with both parties, and L'Hôpital was first to feel his wrath. "His Majesty and Council are amazed . . . to see evident traces of a secret negotiation which you hold with Brühl on the Polish succession. Your instructions never order you to speak of such an important affair with the minister of a court to which you are not accredited, and which could have results opposed to the King's interests." [60] Broglie escaped more lightly. Although Bernis was upset with the policy and recalcitrance of Broglie, he could not find him at fault in this case. "The general activities of Broglie afflict me by the bad results which may follow. No one is more displeased with the relations of Broglie to the Russians than I; but, taking into account the prejudices and well-known system of this Ambassador, there remain many facts about which he is quite correct. Therefore, I cannot find fault with his opinion in this case, although I reject its consequences." [61]

The affair created a deep rift between L'Hôpital and Broglie. The rupture was aggravated even further by Broglie's desire to remove Poniatowsky from his ministerial post in St. Petersburg. In November, Broglie finally convinced Brühl to bring this about and Poniatowsky received his recall to Warsaw. Although L'Hôpital desired this recall, he was still smarting over the affair of the Polish crown and charged that Broglie's action infringed on his embassy and did irreparable damage to French influence with the Grand Duchess. "Broglie acts more like a Foreign Minister with me than a fellow ambassador. . . . You will find some means in the future, I hope, to spare me the great displeasure of treating of affairs of state

59. Broglie to L'Hôpital, Sept. 27, 1757: *ibid.* Suppl. 9, 124–125; Broglie to L'Hôpital, Sept. 7, 1757: *ibid.* Suppl. 10, 119. See also letters from Broglie to L'Hôpital, from December, 1757, to February, 1758: *AMAE CP Po 277*, 22–144.

60. Bernis to L'Hôpital, Sept. 24, 1757: *AMAE CP R* 54, 87.
61. Bernis to Stainville, Oct. 8, 1757: *AMAE MD F* 571, 36; see also Bernis, *op. cit.*, II, 126.

with Broglie. I can henceforth have no confidence in him whatever." [62]

Bernis this time agreed with the Ambassador that the
matter had been handled with "too much heat and precipitance." [63] The Minister was becoming increasingly offended at
the independent air of authority which the Count de Broglie
seemed often to assume in Eastern Europe. Broglie, feeling the
pressures of opposition beginning to mount against him, tried
to formulate a program which he hoped would remove the
growing differences between the official and the Secret diplomacy. He sent his plan to the King, with the intention of having
it passed on to Bernis. Broglie recalled this plan much later
for Louis XVI:

> The danger was that Russia might use the pretext of the war . . .
> to move in force on Polish territory. . . . In permitting them to do
> this . . . we would free this vast country to the Russian generals,
> to the despotism of the Russian court, and to all the future projects
> of usurpation to which they would be tempted. To protect against
> this, France could have . . . demanded that all requests and requi-
> sitions that the Empress of Russia might make in Poland be first
> communicated to Versailles for our approval. These requests could
> then have been carried under French auspices to a *senatus consul-
> tum* or even an extraordinary diet of the Polish state. . . . France
> would thus have assisted and protected her ally, at the same time
> being the guarantor of Russian behavior. The Republic of Poland
> would, thus, have ceded only to the preponderance of this crown.[64]

Bernis rejected this proposal from the King as too provoking to the allies and too time-consuming. France had no time
for negotiating subtleties. The failures of the war thus far made
it clear to him that this was no military exercise. France was
fighting for its life. In such a situation Bernis had neither the
fortitude nor the means to take the initiative in Poland. A
defensive posture by France in Poland would have to suffice.

Broglie considered a defensive role in Poland as completely

---

62. L'Hôpital to Bernis, Nov. 18,
1757: *AMAE CP R* 54, 235; Vandal,
*op. cit.*, p. 318; Pipin, *op. cit.*, XII
p. 399–400.

63. Bernis to L'Hôpital, Dec. 30,
1757: *AMAE CP R* 54, 430.
64. Memoir proposed in September,
1757, Broglie to Louis XV, Apr. 16,
1773: in Boutaric, *op. cit.*, II, 11–13.

unsatisfactory. The moment when Russian ambitions were rising was the moment when French influence should be strengthened to resist them. Broglie again carried his pleas back to the King through the Secret, charging that Bernis was content to let Polish affairs stand idle while the war was waged. This, complained Broglie, would permit the Polish crown to slip through France's fingers. It was the last possible moment, he said, to protect Poland and declare for the Prince Xavier. Louis sent no reply. Truly, he did not know what to say. His determination to defend Poland had never changed, but he had also determined never to interfere with the officials of his Ministry in the performance of their duties — except to remove them. He was not considering removing Bernis. He was a spectator to this struggle between Ministry and Secret.[65]

Broglie and Durand finally came under open fire from the Russians for their consistent opposition to Russian interests. With satisfaction and even enthusiasm, L'Hôpital declared to Bernis that Bestuzhev was lodging official complaint "because Broglie and Durand are energetic and bitter against Russia. The Grand Chancellor insists that if the King does not contain them, the relations between our courts will be affected." [66] Very probably L'Hôpital's arguments with Broglie had come to Russian attention, perhaps through L'Hôpital himself. This would explain the timing of an imperial note which stated that "in the interests of good relations, Her Imperial Majesty of Russia must complain bitterly of the Count de Broglie and the Sieur Durand. Some badly intentioned persons had the malice and effrontery to circulate copies of a false declaration by Apraksin in Poland." [67]

Broglie felt the attack mounting from all quarters. He reported to the King that he was opposed by the French Ministry on one side and the Russian Ministry on the other and

65. Broglie to Louis XV, Oct. 30, 1757: in Ozanam and Antoine, *op. cit.*, I, 39.
66. L'Hôpital to Bernis, Nov. 3, 1757: *AMAE CP R* 54, 202.
67. Imperial Rescript to L'Hôpital, Nov. 18, 1757: *ibid.* 54, 256; Waddington, *La guerre*, I, 114. Durand

was proposing a project to mobilize all the French tutors in Poland to propagandize their pupils against Brühl and against the Russians. Fabre, *op. cit.*, p. 102; Broglie to Durand, Jan. 21, 1756, and Durand to Broglie, May 14, 1756; *AMAE CP Po* 248, 111 and 114.

that he could not face such formidable opposition without the King's help. Broglie begged the King to "come to my aid and let me know your will. This secret project of five years is not mine in concept. I pursue it because you have wished it." Broglie insisted that he could not continue with never a word of encouragement from the King. "I know how simple it would be to live easily with Brühl . . . [and] to receive the approprobation of the allied courts. . . . I know well enough that I make myself disagreeable by always proposing difficulties for the present system, but I am obliged to execute your orders. . . ." [68] He warned the King that the affairs of Poland demanded some immediate and organized French response. "I have already subordinated the affairs of Poland to the needs of Russia even beyond the bounds of your orders. . . . Naturally, this does not satisfy them. The Russians simply wish us to abandon Poland. This is an aim in which they succeed only too well." [69]

The King pulled himself together and contrived an answer to the beleaguered Count, but his instructions were no help. He repeated his fondness for Broglie, his desire to continue the Secret, and his interest in the preservation of Poland, but insisted he could do nothing with the Ministry of Foreign Affairs. The advice of Louis to Broglie: continue at your post and weather the storm. [70]

Louis XV, however, took no steps to make even this last order possible. On February 1, 1758, Bernis recalled Broglie from his embassy. Broglie thought at first that this action meant Bernis had discovered the Secret, but no such discovery had occurred. The recall of Broglie was simply the attempt of Bernis to root out opposition and stubbornness among his subordinates and to expunge a cause of severe irritation to the allies. Broglie's report to the King on his return was despondent.

68. Broglie to Louis XV, Dec. 2, 1757: Ozanam and Antoine, *op. cit.*, I, 43–44. See also letter of Nov. 25: *ibid.*, p. 41.

69. Broglie to Louis XV, Dec. 20, 1757: *ibid.*, p. 45. Kaunitz, too, was inclined to give the Russians wide latitude in Poland and to discount Polish complaints. He joined the attack on Broglie, maintaining that the Count was provoking the Russians and thus injuring Austria. Waddington, *La guerre*, I, 596 and 601–2.

70. Broglie to Louis XV, Jan. 3, 1758: in Ozanam and Antoine, *op. cit.*, I, 47.

I see with much distaste that Bernis has decided to count the affairs of Poland for nothing and to sacrifice them to the two imperial courts. He did not hide from me that he cannot conceive of any advantages to be gained in Poland. . . . He is trying to cut me off from the French party in Poland. He says that I may not see . . . letters from Durand and L'Hôpital.[71]

The King was thrown into confusion by Broglie's removal. He begged Broglie not to enter the army, as the Count planned, but to wait for the King to consider the matter.[72] Broglie's recall had far-reaching effects. It practically cut off the French party in Poland from funds, direction, and encouragement. It terribly complicated the workings of the Secret if it were to be continued.

The months that Broglie spent at Versailles plunged him into despair. Durand, the only Secret agent left in Poland, felt Polish resistance to Russia disintegrating around him and thought that the King "had abandoned everything." Tercier was no less troubled. "It gives him the greatest chagrin to see daily the loss of a work whose usefulness is known to all of us." Broglie's proposals for the future, which Louis accepted, were poor replacements for the former Secret organization. Broglie and Tercier were again charged with the Secret's direction, but now Tercier was clearly the key man. He alone had access to official policy. Broglie was in fact relegated to an advisory role: his enthusiastic role in the field was over.[73]

These changes bore immediate and bitter fruit in Poland. Pillage, confiscations, and disorders began to spread like wildfire along the Russian supply lines. The Russian army settled comfortably in Poland for the first time in many years. The illness of the Polish King created the strong possibility of a Diet and election in August, and there were 30,000 Russian troops in Poland to intimidate them. Now even Brühl was openly dealing with the Russians about the future of the crown. Brühl's conviction that intrigues were no longer necessary was

71. Broglie to Louis XV, Mar. 24, 1758: *ibid.*, p. 55–56. See also Bernis to Stainville, Mar. 31, 1758: in Bernis, *op. cit.*, II, 199–200.
72. Louis to Broglie, Apr. 25, 1758: in Boutaric, *op. cit.*, I, 228–229; also letter of May 21, 1758: *ibid.*, p. 229.
73. Broglie to Louis XV, May, 17 and 29 and July 31, 1758: in Ozanam and Antoine, *op. cit.*, I, 64, 72 and 79–81.

a striking indication of the state into which French power had fallen.[74] The members of the Secret were witnessing, reluctantly and with horror, the loss of Poland to Russia. The "absolute" monarch Louis XV seemed powerless to halt the flow of events. Even Bernis, who was intellectually convinced that Poland ought not to be abandoned, was shocked by the discovery that such a process was already far underway.[75]

The best proofs of the decline of French influence were events in Danzig and Courland. As early as December, 1756, the Russians were upset by the failure of Danzig to prepare defenses against the Prussians and had sent out a Resident to urge them on. The Russians were determined never to allow Frederick to take the city peaceably. The French Ministry received this threat to Danzig with great calm. Russian statements that they would occupy the city only with Polish assistance placated the increasingly gullible L'Hôpital. This Ambassador went so far as to write to the Grand General of Poland to allay his fears for the city. Even Bernis allowed the possibility that Danzig might have to be delivered into Russian hands. He sent orders to Durand which must have been bitter indeed for a Secret agent to receive: "Though the liberty of Danzig is, of course, imperative . . . if a lost battle or some other emergency makes it necessary, we must not impede the entrance of Russian troops into Danzig." [76]

Broglie, chafing among the pleasures of Versailles, was

74. Grand-General of Poland to L'Hôpital, Mar. 16, 1758: *AMAE CP R* 55, 257; Wittinghof and Menager to L'Hôpital, at Posen with the Russian army, July 9, 1758: *ibid.* 57, 24–28; Bernis to L'Hôpital, Aug. 1, 1758: *ibid.* 57, 84–85; Kasimir Waliszewski, *Potoccy i Czartoryski: Walka stronnictw i programow politycznych przed upadkiem Rzptej 1734–1763* (Krakow, 1887), II, p. 371.

75. Bernis to L'Hôpital, May 23, 1758: *AMAE CP R* 56, 200. See also Broglie, *Le secret du Roi*, p. 279 ff. "The Russians make nothing but a pretext of action against Prussia while they seize control of Poland and Danzig, from which they draw immense resources": Bernis to Choiseul, Apr. 7, 1758: in Bernis, *op. cit.,* II, 202.

76. Bernis to L'Hôpital, Apr. 5, 1758: *AMAE CP R* 56, 21; Douglas to Durand, Dec. 21, 1756, and note from the Russian Ministry to Douglas, Jan. 5, 1757: *BN SM MF* 10661, 101 and 162; L'Hôpital to Bernis, Mar. 10, 1758: *AMAE CP R* 55, 226; L'Hôpital to Branicki, Apr. 2, 1758: *ibid.* 56, 2–5. "Thus I order our ministers in Poland and Danzig to favor the Russian plans. This may possibly cause an uproar in Poland, but we are in a crisis;" Bernis to Stainville, Apr. 16, 1758: in Bernis, *op. cit.,* II, 205–206.

furious. To state any conditions under which the occupation of Danzig would be permitted seemed to him equivalent to an invitation. Broglie could imagine no act so likely to terrify the Poles and give Russia a foothold in Poland as the occupation of Danzig. Yet he was powerless to prevent it.[77]

Bernis had badly misjudged the reaction of the Poles to Danzig. A Russian announcement that Danzig had agreed to a Russian occupation proved false, and Poland erupted in fury. Bernis was rudely awakened. "The precipitance of this Danzig affair comes close to wrecking us in Poland. . . . We will support the Russians there, but the Russians must come at all speed to the aid of the Swedes in Pomerania or all is lost for us in Sweden also." [78] Bernis was caught between his ill-defined desire to protect Poland and his need for Russian aid to the Swedes to protect French interests in Stockholm. The Russians were playing upon the sort of dilemma which plagued France constantly in the war. If Bernis voted to protect Poland, he might hinder the Russian attack, lose Sweden, and perhaps forego a chance to end the war. If he voted to sacrifice Danzig and Poland in the face of increased pressures, he might well lose them both and gain nothing. It was a terrible choice for a weak-willed man. To the impassioned pleas of the burghers of Danzig to save their city from Russian occupation, Bernis sent what he himself called "an equivocal reply." [79]

Fortified by French indecision, the Russians grew bolder. An imperial conference was held in which Pëtr Shuvalov insisted that the Danzigers must cease their resistance. A substantial threat or even a slight bombardment might serve to convince them. In answer the citizens of Danzig chose a commander to organize the city to resist attacks from any quarter. These developments shook the French King and Council. Resistance was far too late, since French commitments to the idea of an occupation had already been given. The future of Danzig had passed from French hands.[80]

77. Broglie to Louis XV, Apr. 22, 1758: in Ozanam and Antoine, op. cit., I, 58.
78. Bernis to L'Hôpital, May 11, 1758: AMAE CP R 56, 157.
79. Corporation of the burghers of Danzig to Louis XV, June 6, 1758: ibid. 56, 271; Bernis to L'Hôpital, June 6, 1758: ibid. 56, 273.
80. Bernis to L'Hôpital, Nov. 19, 1758: ibid. 58, 229.

The Duchy of Courland went the same way. This Duchy, with its capital at Mitau, consisted of the broad peninsula jutting into the Baltic west of the Western Dvina River. Courland was under the vague suzerainty of Poland, which had the right to appoint its duke, but the years had brought a significant Russian influence. Poland had been persuaded by the Empress Anne of Russia, once married to the last Kettler Duke of Courland, to invest her favorite, Biron, with the Duchy. The Empress Elizabeth had exiled Biron in 1741, and since then the Duchy had been dukeless. Russia's interest in this strategic area was well known.

The Russians used the excuse of military operations to fortify Kovno, the town commanding the entrance from Lithuania to Courland. At that time France had discovered the discussions of Brühl and Bestuzhev on the cession of Courland to Russia for the attachment of East Prussia to the Saxon house. The disgrace of Bestuzhev postponed Russian plans momentarily, but the Ministry soon took them up again. France was given more proof that the fall of their enemy meant little change in Russia's pursuit of its best interests. The journey of Prince Charles of Saxony, third son of Augustus III, to St. Petersburg in April, ostensibly to fight in the Russian army, was actually to receive the approval of the Empress as next Duke of Courland. Russia arranged for a deputation from Courland to visit the Empress Elizabeth and have her declare the dukedom vacant. The Empress announced publicly the deposition of Biron and recommended Prince Charles as the next duke.[81]

What was significant about this whole affair was that it had been carried on from beginning to end without reference to the French by either Poland or Russia. The French did not resent Prince Charles, who was at best nonpartisan, and might even have approved him under different circumstances. The disturbing fact was that it had not been necessary even to approach France on the decision. Bernis complained that

81. Bernis to L'Hôpital, Sept. 24 and Oct. 8, 1757: *ibid.* 54, 84 and 117; Pipin, *op. cit.*, XII p. 391; Imperial declaration delivered by Gross to the Grand Chancellor of Poland, Oct. 23, 1758: *AMAE MD F 6*, 32–33; *Waliszewski, La dernière des Romanov*, p. 469; Solov'ëv, *op. cit.*, XXIV, 222.

"Brühl has told us nothing of his moves at Petersburg or at Mitau to secure the election of Charles of Saxony. We do not think we would be opposed, but why have we not been consulted?" [82] Charles was confirmed as Duke by his father in November, with eternal promises of friendship and aid to the Empress of Russia. Meanwhile, Louis XV came late to the party. "It seems that Prince Charles is going to be Duke of Courland. . . . Surely before the end of the year we will be able to see the issues more clearly and will be able to take a position." [83] The matter was already concluded. The Secret had indeed fallen on evil days.

As Bernis prepared to put down the burden of foreign affairs in the last months of 1758, French interests in Poland were in a shambles. The Count de Broglie watched tiredly from the sidelines: "I warned of what is happening . . . but to no avail. Our ministers satisfied themselves with saying that Poland was a country of savages whose affairs were not necessary to consider, and which we could always have time to repair." [84]

Broglie was a trifle harsh in his judgment of Bernis and his cohorts. They did not forsake Poland out of pleasure or out of malice. Broglie and his Secret had only one small area to consider in their work, the preservation of Poland. Bernis bore responsibility for all of France and all French interests. The year 1758, plagued by French defeats and bankruptcy, had driven Bernis into a great retrenchment and reevaluation. What Bernis had done was neither malicious nor stupid. Although he may well be blamed for leading France into the war, he cannot easily be blamed for trying to lead France out again. The Secret was badly wounded because of Bernis's ignorance of it and because the Minister desired unanimity among his subordinates and cooperation among his allies. These hurts notwithstanding, there was cause to believe the Secret was to die in any case. France was being bled to death. Cash and men were

82. Bernis to L'Hôpital, Nov. 11, 1758: *AMAE CP R* 58, 210.
83. Louis to Tercier, Oct. 26, 1758: in Boutaric, *op. cit.*, I, 234; Memoir

on Courland, Nov. 30, 1758: *AMAE CP R* 58, 281–283.
84. Broglie to Louis XV, Aug. 12, 1758: in Ozanam and Antoine, *op. cit.*, I, 82.

no longer available for Polish adventures. If the question was the salvation of France, then Poland could be counted as of little consequence.

What is important to note is that France retired, reluctantly but effectively, from Polish affairs. Less than five years later Poland would have a Russian-dictated king, and in less than fifteen years Poland would fall shattered before the former allies of France. If one must seek the causes of the failure of French policy in Poland, one must seek beyond the duality of French diplomacy in Poland, which worked well enough when victories were won and the coffers were full. The fall of Poland rests at the feet of everyone and everything that drew France into this two-front war and all those who failed to wage the war well. France could learn one lesson in Poland: that France and Russia were involved in a greater struggle during their *rapprochement* than they ever were in their time of greatest opposition — and France was suffering all the losses.

*iv.*

### THE YOUNG COURT AND THE EMPRESS

The French learned quickly that their new ties with Russia were under the constant threat of the Young Court:

Thus, it is evident that these facts, the sickness and the indolence of the Empress, being known to all Russia, there must necessarily and invariably result in all the actions of the generals and ministers, the courtiers and the favorites, a fear of opposing the leanings, tastes and passions of the heirs presumptive . . . whose party can do naught else but grow daily.[85]

The Young Court — the Grand Duke Peter and the Grand Duchess Catherine with their followers — complicated life at St. Petersburg almost beyond endurance. They represented con-

85. L'Hôpital to Bernis, Aug. 16, 1758: *AMAE CP R* 57, 146. There is no good summary of the role of the Young Court; see, among others, Alexander Brückner, *Istoriia Ekateriny Vtoroi* (St. Petersburg: A. S. Suvorina, 1885); Pipin, *op. cit.*, R. N. Bain, *Peter III: Emperor of Russia* (New York: E. P. Dutton, 1902); Dominique Maroger (ed.), *Memoirs of Catherine the Great* (New York: Collier Books, 1961); Kasimir Waliszewski, *The Romances of an Empress* (New York: Appleton, 1905), and other works; Ilchester, *op. cit.*; and Pëtr Karlovich Shchebalskii, *Politicheskaia sistema Petra III* (Moscow: Moscow University Press, 1870).

stant opposition to the programs and wishes of the Empress Elizabeth. The Grand Duke was a lover of Prussia, a Lutheran and a German at heart and a hater of most things Russian. The Grand Duchess, neither loving her husband nor loved by him, was the willing ally of the British, a constant intriguer under the tutelage of Bestuzhev, and another staunch enemy of the French *rapprochement*.

The significance and the influence of this opposition changed from day to day and from event to event, dependent largely upon the health of the Empress Elizabeth. Official St. Petersburg was always in the process of arranging itself for shifts of fortune, and in this game of prophecy Field Marshal Apraksin had been one of the unfortunate losers. A partial explanation of the terrible indolence of the Russian court and Ministry in all affairs was their conviction that it was better to do nothing than to offend the Empress now or risk the displeasure of the heirs later. Intrigues sprouted like hydra's heads around the Young Court, and Catherine testified in her *Mémoires* how carefully each action of the imperial couple was scrutinized for its meaning. Count de Broglie observed from Warsaw that "the Young Court renders Russia completely untrustworthy, and its favorites make it rotten." [86]

The French Ministry was soon well aware that any future for the Franco-Russian ties depended in large measure, if not completely, on French ability to influence the Young Court to new feelings and new policies. Unfortunately for them, the French never carried any weight with the Young Court. L'Hôpital, always convinced of his own irresistible charm, thought that he had won the affection of the Grand Duchess Catherine, but he was never more mistaken. The French Ambassador was so appalled at the peculiar nature of the Grand Duke that he chose to ignore him altogether. "I avow, Sir, that his ideas are so singular and his prejudices so strange that I restrict myself to the respects which are due him. . . . He is crude, and hated by the priests and courtiers. . . . He has neither judgment nor good sense." [87]

86. Broglie to L'Hôpital, Aug. 18, 1757: *AMAE CP R*, Suppl. 9, 96.

87. L'Hôpital to Bernis, Nov. 1, 1757: *ibid.* 53, 324.

In view of the importance of the Young Court to the future of the war and the Russian ties, and in view of the great uncertainty as to when they might ascend the throne of the Tsars, France had to attempt something. Bernis knew "well enough how dangerous it will be to form bonds with the Young Court that will displease the Empress, and how much at the same time we must avoid giving the Young Court reason to think we neglect them." Some decisive steps had to be taken, and Bernis knew that "we must follow this, since it involves not simply the fate of the Young Court, but the succession to the throne and future relations." [88]

The French first considered the possibility of taking over the heavy financial obligations of the Young Court — in short, a bribe. The Austrians had evolved an interesting method, arranging a treaty with the Grand Duke Peter that took into Austrian pay all the Holsteiners that the Grand Duke could provide, at an annual subsidy of 100,000 florins. It was the unpopularity of this Austrian scheme with the Russian Empress that determined the French to avoid the direct financial approach.[89]

If the French would not immediately bring money to bear on their Imperial Highnesses, they could at least begin by the removal of baneful influences. The French Ambassador debated with himself at length as to the best and most harmless means of removing the British-sponsored lover of the Grand Duchess, Stanislas Poniatowsky. The decision was removed from his hands when the Pole was abruptly recalled to Warsaw through the influence of Broglie. Despite the ensuing argument between Broglie and L'Hôpital as to their respective sovereignties, Poniatowsky was finally removed. L'Hôpital predicted dire consequences for French influences with the Young Court, but he was mistaken. Catherine had already tired of the handsome Pole and saw his departure with some relief.

The French could not be satisfied with such negative approaches to the Young Court. If it was not advisable to make

88. Bernis to L'Hôpital, Sept. 13, 1757: *ibid*. 54, 57; and letter of Sept. 19, 1757: *ibid*. 54, 65.

89. Convention, July 26, 1757: *ibid*. 53, 168–169; L'Hôpital to Rouillé, July 28, 1757: *ibid*. 53, 213 (in code).

financial overtures, some more devious influence would have to be arranged. As early as February, 1757, L'Hôpital had, while passing Vienna, written to his Ministry to urge consideration of the Princess of Zerbst. Johanna Elisabeth, Princess of Zerbst, was the mother of the Grand Duchess Catherine of Russia. She had accompanied her daughter to Russia in 1744, and had been expelled by the Empress Elizabeth, who detested her, for her excessive intrigues on behalf of Catherine. L'Hôpital was informed by an unidentified friend in Vienna that the Princess of Zerbst still exercised great influence with her daughter and that it might be useful to bring the Princess into the French camp. Rouillé had thought the idea worth investigating when the Ambassador reached his post.[90]

Bernis, on assuming direction of the Ministry, decided to pursue the scheme vigorously. "His Majesty, in order to break all bonds which attach Russia to England, has decided to send the Marquis de Fraignes to Zerbst to inspire the Princess of Zerbst, mother of the Grand Duchess, to attach her daughter to French interests." Jean Jacques Gilbert, Marquis de Fraignes, chosen for the task, had been serving at minor diplomatic posts in Hanover and in Berlin. He was sent to Zerbst despite warnings from the Ambassador in St. Petersburg that the Princess retained no influence whatever with her daughter. These reports were true: there was little love lost between these two ambitious but eternally antagonistic females. Still, the French Ministry persisted in deluding itself into the belief that the Princess or Zerbst could be useful.[91]

The Marquis de Fraignes, journeying to Zerbst, met Sergei Saltykov, then serving as Russian Minister in Hamburg. Saltykov had been the lover of the Grand Duchess, and quite probably he was the father of the future Tsar Paul. He was in Hamburg to remove the embarrassment of his presence at court. Saltykov told the French agent that the Princess of Zerbst would one day play a great role in Russian affairs due to the

---

90. Rouillé to L'Hôpital, Apr. 2, 1757: *ibid.* 52, 286; L'Hôpital to Bernis, Feb. 27, 1757: *ibid.* 52, 190; Fabre, *op. cit.*, pp. 221–22; Broglie, *Le secret du roi,* I, 275–276.

91. Bernis to L'Hôpital, Aug. 21, 1757: *AMAE CP R* 53, 288; *AMAE Pers* 31, *Fraignes.*

affection of the Young Court for her. He also confided the existence of a secret correspondence between mother and daughter which passed through him. The first allegation was untrue: Catherine did not want her mother's advice or presence under any conditions, while Peter cordially detested his mother-in-law. The second comment on a correspondence, however, may well have been true. Later French assistance to such correspondence testified to its existence. Saltykov was no doubt in the market for a bribe and hoped to pique French interest.[92]

Only once did the French attempt to utilize their new contacts with Zerbst. During the attack on Bestuzhev, Ambassador L'Hôpital tried to convince Fraignes to acquire some incriminating document from the Princess that would guarantee the disgrace of the Grand Chancellor. No assistance from the Princess was forthcoming, although she extended her good wishes to the French at every opportunity.[93]

The mission of the Marquis de Fraignes to Zerbst ended as abruptly as it had begun. On January 19, 1758, a detachment of Prussians invaded Zerbst, arriving at the palace at midnight. Frederick of Prussia had somehow become informed of the presence of the French agent. Fraignes barricaded himself in his room and in the ensuing scuffle shot one of his attackers. The Duke of Zerbst arrived on the scene, only to be handed a writ for Fraignes's arrest signed by Frederick. However, with the aid of the Princess, Fraignes escaped and was hidden. The King of Prussia tried again within the week, this time with an artillery company under his brother, Prince Henry. The Prussians threatened the castle of Zerbst with destruction, and the Marquis de Fraignes surrendered rather than bring grief to his hosts. The poor Marquis spent the next five years cruelly imprisoned at Magdeburg.[94]

92. Bernis to Douglas, Nov. 29, 1757: *AMAE CP R* 54, 313.
93. L'Hôpital to Bernis, Dec. 11, 1757: *ibid.* 54, 369.
94. *AMAE Pers* 31, *Fraignes*, 435; Bernis provided a version of the Fraignes mission in *Mémoires*, II, 1–8; editor Frédéric Masson compiled the pertinent documents and instruc-tions in Appendix VIII, Volume II, 375–406. For Frederick of Prussia's version see Frederick II, "Histoire de la guerre de Sept Ans, *Oeuvres* (Berlin: Prussian State Archives, 1846–56), IV, p. 157. Bernis to L'Hôpital, Feb. 18 and Mar. 17, 1758: *AMAE CP R* 55, 183–186 and 284–287.

The Fraignes mission had no good and some unfortunate results. Bernis hoped that the Grand Duchess would be won over to the French cause by the insult which the Prussians had inflicted on the family of Zerbst. Catherine was unconcerned. The affair had quite undesirable results with the Empress Elizabeth, who had nurtured her hatred of the Princess of Zerbst over the years. When news of the French mission was made public by the Prussians, the Empress was extremely annoyed that the French had bothered to court the favor of this Princess. Continued use of the Princess of Zerbst to influence Catherine only aggravated matters. Letters from mother to daughter now came enclosed in official French dispatches. Catherine was still unmoved.[95]

News that the Princess of Zerbst, in self-imposed exile from her estates, was journeying to Paris finally reached the Empress of Russia. The French tried desperately to stop her from coming to Versailles until they could calm the Russian Empress, but the Princess would not wait. When the gazettes announced the plans of the Princess, the Empress Elizabeth flew into a rage. She could not bear any indication that people were favoring the Young Court in anticipation of her departure. The French tried to repair the damage by having the Princess write an explanatory letter to the Empress, asking her permission to reside in France. The letter did no good. The French reluctantly ceased further letters from mother to daughter, lest the Empress discover them and become more enraged.[96]

France's first devious attempt to influence the Young Court had won no one and offended everyone. The Grand Duchess was upset that her mother was creating threats to her already precarious position with the Empress. The Grand Duke was repelled by thoughts of his mother-in-law. The Empress was annoyed with the French for conniving behind her back in expectation of her demise. The mission had been a total loss.

France's second attempt to come to terms with the Young Court was less imaginative but more important. In the inter-

95. For example, Bernis to L'Hôpital, dispatches of Apr. 21, May 6 and 23, 1758: *ibid.* 56, 84, 146, and 209.

96. L'Hôpital to Bernis, Oct. 31, 1758: *ibid.* 58, 187.

ests of the war, France became involved in the Holstein question. The provinces of Schleswig-Holstein had long been a thorn in the side of Europe. The claims and counterclaims to these duchies, which sat astride the peninsula between Denmark and Germany, were badly complicated. Sweden, Denmark, Russia, and Prussia all had claims to the area. Of these states, Sweden had accumulated the most obvious claims, and Denmark had the most to fear: the idea of Denmark being thus surrounded by her northern neighbor was a frightening one.

The situation was further complicated and worsened by the fact that the Grand Duke Peter of Russia was, in addition to being heir to the Russian throne, the former heir to the Swedish crown and the reigning Duke of Holstein. Sweden had come to agreements with Denmark in 1749 for the exchange of Schleswig and parts of Holstein for the counties of Oldenburg and Delmenhorst. The accession of Peter to his majority as Duke of Holstein ended negotiations over ducal Holstein, which was still reserved by treaty to his family. Peter loved his Duchy and refused any talks of an exchange with Denmark for less provocative territories. In fact, Peter persisted in considering the cession of Schleswig to Denmark as illegal, thus keeping alive a good cause for war.[97]

France was dragged into this business because of French interest in, and fear of, Denmark. The reconciliation of Sweden and Denmark, prevention of Denmark's entry into the war on the side of Prussia, and the eventual assistance of Denmark against Prussia were all much desired by France. Opposition to the entrance of a British fleet into the Baltic, for example, would be far more successful if Denmark could be persuaded to join Sweden and Russia in active preparations for resistance. Consequently, France was disposed to assist Denmark in any legitimate desires in return for Danish aid in the war. France had also to prevent a falling out between Russia and Denmark that might easily drive Denmark into the enemy camp.[98]

97. See memoir on the Treaty of 1749 between Denmark and Sweden, Dec. 20, 1756: *BN SM NAF* 22011, 166–169.

98. Bernis to L'Hôpital, July 30, 1757: *AMAE CP R* 53, 234.

The French position was not an easy one. Denmark absolutely required that the Russian Grand Duke guarantee the cession of Schleswig and begin negotiations with Denmark for the exchange of Holstein. This the Grand Duke Peter refused to do, and the Empress Elizabeth was determined not to pressure him in any way. Douglas reported to his Ministry that "the Empress refuses to involve herself in the affairs of Denmark and the Grand Duke because of his formal refusal to listen to such propositions and because she thinks it unjust to despoil the patrimony of their house for motives of convenience." [99] Bernis procrastinated for many months, fearing to offend by his interference either Denmark or the Young Court — or both. The affair of Zerbst had taught him to tread warily with the Young Court. The Austrian Ambassador, Esterhazy, continued to ask L'Hôpital to begin negotiations with the Grand Duke on the exchange, but Bernis was afraid. "I am hindered by the apparent distaste of the Empress of Russia for this negotiation." [100]

Once again Bernis was prompted to act by an external stimulant. The habitual procrastination of the Minister seemed to make him always the plaything of events. Denmark was organizing its army, and such an assembly behind French lines frightened Bernis, who noted that the Danes were in excellent position to get what they wanted from the French. The Danes were active diplomatically, also. They let slip to the Russian envoy in Copenhagen that Denmark was aware of allied promises to return Silesia to Austria and Pomerania to Sweden and liked these plans very little. "The King of Prussia might still find friends." [101] France took these threats as they were intended and undertook to use its influence on the exchange of Holstein.

The French began quietly by approaching the Grand Duke Peter's minister for Holstein, who was easily bribed but consistently useless. At the same time the French promised the immediate disarmament of Holstein and French help in an ex-

99. Douglas to Rouillé, Apr. 21, 1757: *ibid.* 52, 316.
100. Bernis to L'Hôpital, Sept. 21, 1757: *ibid.* 54, 74.
101. Bernstorff to Korff, Dec. 19, 1757: *AMAE CP D* 162, 366.

change if the Danes would immediately sign a convention aligning Denmark against Prussia. However, Denmark was to be bought with results, not promises. The most the Danes would offer was an uncertain neutrality until France produced some signs of success in Russia. The fall of Bestuzhev encouraged the French, and Bernis finally agreed on action: "Since Denmark has served us well, His Majesty wishes the Ambassador L'Hôpital to serve them. You are ordered to assist the Danish envoy with the exchange of Holstein, so that Denmark is convinced that they owe their success in this matter to us. Be very careful of the feelings of the Empress and the Grand Duke." [102]

Danish pressures for a successful negotiation became oppressive in October, when the Danes massed troops in Schleswig. The Russians complained bitterly that these troops menaced ducal Holstein. Bernis instructed L'Hôpital to restrain the Russians from reprisals at all costs and to proceed with the exchange of the troublesome duchy as quickly as possible. Unfortunately, an official demand from the Russians for a Danish guarantee of the inviolability of the duchy had already been fired off to Copenhagen. Vorontsov blamed this move on the Grand Duke. The demand set Denmark and Russia in belligerent moods, as the Grand Duke no doubt planned, and ensured that the exchange would never occur. [103]

It became increasingly clear that the Grand Duke Peter, while often appearing to yield on the future of his native duchy, would never really do so. Whatever the reputation of the Grand Duke Peter for weakness and vacillation in other affairs, his determination to hold his beloved territory was unshakable. The sad state of the Holstein affair was another demonstration of French inability to deal with the Young Court. French approaches to the Grand Duke and Grand

102. Bernis to L'Hôpital, Oct. 8, 1758: *AMAE CP R* 58, 69–71; see also letters between Danish and French Ministries, Sept. 16, 1758: *AMAE CP D* 163, 72–73. Bernis was working with Stainville on a project to have Austria cede East Frisia to Denmark, which could in turn exchange it for Holstein. Austria refused to cooperate. See Bernis to Stainville, Nov. 29, 1757, and Jan. 30, 1758: in Bernis, *op. cit.*, II, 165 and 180.

103. Bernis to L'Hôpital, Oct. 29, 1758, and L'Hôpital to Bernis, Nov. 30, 1758: *AMAE CP R* 58, 184 and 270.

Duchess had proved not only fruitless but often disastrous: they had brought the imperial heirs no nearer to France, they had angered the Empress, and they had offended Denmark by their failure. Even in the interests of binding Denmark to the allied cause the French had found the Young Court exasperating. The threat of the hostility and intracability of the Young Court to French interests was one very solid reason why France could never chance a thorough commitment to a Russian alliance. Such a commitment might easily be abused or repudiated at any moment, since the Empress lived in constant ill health.

It was not strange, therefore, that the French should have been preoccupied with the life and death of the Empress of Russia. Bernis saw so little hope for France in the Russian succession that he ordered his Ambassador to retire to his country house if the Empress should sicken and die and there await events. Bernis frankly admitted to L'Hôpital that on the succession "we do not know what order to give you." [104] The French were coming more and more to realize that the wartime union with Russian was valid only while the Empress remained alive and amicable. Whether it was the Grand Duke Peter with his Prussian devotions or the Grand Duchess Catherine with her British allies, the French would find themselves openly betrayed by any succession or revolution. Bernis expressed the fervent French hope, hardly the sturdy base of a health policy, "that Her Imperial Majesty would live long enough to see the war ended." [105] France, as a result, placed its interest in keeping the Empress Elizabeth alive and satisfied with France.

The French decided that the first way to ensure the continuing good will of the Empress was to bribe her friends, confidantes, and favorites. L'Hôpital's first request for 200,000 livres for secret expenses was granted. Vice-Chancellor Vorontsov was naturally at the head of the list of those receiving favors, since the Empress clearly intended the post of Chan-

---

104. Bernis to L'Hôpital, Mar. 17, 1758: *ibid.* 55, 278.

105. L'Hôpital to Bernis, Nov. 1, 1757: *ibid.* 54, 199; also letter of Apr. 16, 1758: *ibid.* 56, 65.

cellor to be his after Bestuzhev's fall. Ivan Shuvalov, favorite of the Empress, was included for an undisclosed bribe, although he was "weak, uncertain in principles, badly intentioned, and surrounded by ignorant people." Alsuviev, newly appointed secretary for the College of Foreign Affairs and private secretary to the Empress, was on the list for 5,000 livres because "he speaks the best French, translates all documents, is active in the private office of the Empress. In this way we will follow all that occurs very carefully." At least eight other people in St. Petersburg were paid for secret services near the Empress, including a French actor in Elizabeth's theater company, the French governor of the Dolgorukii children, certain gentlemen named Martin and Moremberg, and the Hetman Razumovskii's secretary.[106]

The inability of Louis XV to command the least of his subjects in a simple matter prevented the French from gratifying an urgent wish of the Empress Elizabeth and thus winning her devotion. The Empress loved the French theater and requested that Louis XV send her some of the great names of the Paris stage, above all Kaint and Clairon. Louis, answering honestly, said that he had approached the actors and actresses but that they had refused to make the long journey. Louis complained that he could not order his subjects to perform against their will and that, seeing their popularity, he could not risk offending their vast audience. Louis noted that he had already sent the famous Tocqué to paint the Empress and even volunteered to work for Spanish recognition of the Russian imperial title in order to repair Elizabeth's disappointment.[107]

Such minor concessions and such undercover financial transactions with the Russian court only provided some needed assistance in keeping the Empress well disposed to the French, but they did not ensure her life. The course of the Seven Years'

106. L'Hôpital to Rouillé, July 29, 1757: *ibid.* 53, 202–205; notes at the Ministry, June 11, 1758: *ibid.* 56, 293; list of furniture sent to Vorontsov, Oct. 1, 1758: *ibid.* 58, 8–9; L'Hôpital to Bernis, dispatches of May 24, 1758, Sept. 15, 1757, and Aug. 13, 1757: *ibid.* 58, 37; 54, 15; and 53, 268. See also notes of Douglas, Aug. 30, 1757: *ibid.*, Suppl. 5, 172.

107. Vandal, *op. cit.*, pp. 333–34; Bartenev, *op. cit.*, II, 344.

War found Elizabeth in constant danger of death from a variety of undiagnosed ailments. Hardly a political or military crisis was not retarded in its solution by some indisposition of the Empress. Despite her illnesses, the Empress pursued her pleasures and her religious exercises with all her accustomed enthusiasm. L'Hôpital fearfully reported that she "never slept at regular hours, dined at midnight, arose at four in the morning, ate voraciously at some times and fasted for weeks at others. Recently she fell into such rigorous devotions that it seemed more idolatry than religion." [108] The life of the Empress abounded in fainting spells and seeming apoplectic fits.

L'Hôpital's response to these dangerous threats to the life of the Russian Empress was to notify the French Ministry of a friend of his family, François Poissonnier, an "expert in women's diseases." Poissonnier was then serving as Doctor in Chief of the French Army, and L'Hôpital requested that he be sent on special mission to assist the Empress. Bernis was very receptive to the idea of sending a French doctor into Russia. Henceforth, the Poissonnier affair was referred to in the Ministry codes as the "secret of sixty-one," after the number of the dispatch in which the idea had been broached.

Bernis ordered Poissonnier to appear at Versailles in December, 1757, but the Doctor's difficulties in finding a replacement for himself at the front delayed him. Poissonnier was only notified of his proposed mission when he appeared at a private audience with the King in March, 1758, and was unable to leave for Russia until early in June. His journey and his mission were described as "an impenetrable secret, known only to the King, Bernis, and L'Hôpital." For his trouble Poissonnier was to receive 20,000 livres for his trip, 24,000 for each year away, and 20,000 upon his return.[109]

Meanwhile, the Russian Empress, who had a deep-seated fear of doctors, of illness, and of the very idea of death, had finally been persuaded to convoke an assembly of doctors to consult on her case. It was a measure of her illness that she

108. L'Hôpital to Rouillé, Dec. 23, 1756: *AMAE CP R* 54, 407.
109. Memoir, 1761: *AMAE Pers* 58, *Poissonnier;* L'Hôpital to Bernis, dispatches of Nov. 18 and 19, 1757: *AMAE CP R* 54, 243 and 265; Waliszewski, *La dernière des Romanov*, p. 471.

permitted such a consultation. The French Ambassador was so frightened for her life that he adjourned to his country residence and commuted daily to the capital, an expedient reserved in his orders for an imminent change of rulers. The doctors who surrounded the Empress, largely Italians and Dutchmen, could decide on no cure for her. On September 8 the Empress, emerging from a religious exercise in the chapel at Tsarskoe Selo, had a terrible seizure and lay for a long time surrounded by an awe-struck crowd that dared not touch her. Recovering slowly from this attack, Elizabeth withdrew the more from court life. Such a retirement was almost as frightening as death to the French. The Empress grew melancholy, feared constantly that she would suffer another seizure, and immersed herself in an excess of devotion.[110]

The French doctor, Poissonnier, arrived in St. Petersburg on October 20, but was unable to see the Empress immediately because of her passion for secrecy and the return of her distaste for medical discussions. The regular doctors of the Empress, ignorant of his mission, were suspicious of this visitor and refused to consult with him because of his insufficient court rank. L'Hôpital begged the French Ministry to make Poissonnier a Counselor of State in secret at Versailles so that he could use the title at St. Petersburg. "Everything here is prestige and smoke. Ranks are virtues. But the essential point is to conserve the precious days of the Empress and to render P's voyage efficacious." [111] The Ministry refused, stating that the doctor's superior talents should be enough for the Russian court.

The resistance of the other doctors to Poissonnier in defense of their monopoly, and the return of a measure of health and confidence to the Empress kept the French doctor at a distance for a long period. From his distant observations Poissonnier found that Elizabeth had a convulsive and habitual cough. She suffered from spasmodic flickering of the eyelids, trembling of the arms and legs, and periodic attacks of general weakness. Poissonnier ventured a diagnosis of some form of

---

110. There is an excellent description of this event by Catherine in *Pipin, op. cit.,* XII, p. 397.

111. L'Hôpital to Bernis, Oct. 27, 1758: *AMAE CP R* 58, 144.

lung congestion, but was unable to reach the Empress to pre-scribe diet or medication.[112]

To the problems posed for France by the illness of the Empress and the unsatisfactory nature of the Russian succession, the ministrations of a French doctor, even had they been carried out, were hardly dependable and well-organized answers. France had failed to influence the Young Court, and was reduced to the rather ineffectual role of supporting with every possible resource the waning life of the Empress of Russia. Such a ridiculous pastime was a clear measure of the value and future promise of the Franco-Russian *rapprochement*. If such a likely and unmanageable event as the death of Elizabeth could throw the relationship into chaos, that relationship was surely ill founded and surely temporary.

*v.*

COMMERCE

The *rapprochement* between France and Russia was failing militarily and politically. Forces within each state had been working against the union even as it was being born. In short, the war-inspired ties of France and Russia on behalf of Austria had elicited warm response in neither Versailles nor St. Petersburg. Because the alliance was thus proving itself secondhand, frail, and tenuous, the French felt that special care was needed to strengthen French influence in Russian affairs. The Duke de Choiseul, while Ambassador at Vienna, had seen that hopes for mutual usefulness or future friendship of the new allies would depend in some measure on the development of close economic ties such as then bound Russia so tightly to Great Britain.

Without entering into a discussion of the reasons that could make us fear or desire that Russia return into the state where it languished before Peter, our whole object ought to be to draw from Russia all possible assistance for the present moment and to try to establish a commerce with Russia. . . . The position of Russia

112. Poissonnier to Bernis, Nov. 30, 1758: *ibid.* 58, 289–295.

ought always to render our political relations with the Russians
subordinate to the more lasting bonds of commerce, as much from
a consideration of our real interests in the north as because it is
commerce which enables the English to engage the Russians to participate in political affairs. . . . The English method ought to inspire our own. . . . This, of course, is not the work of a day.[113]

Choiseul was quite correct: the building of commercial
ties between Russia and France was not the work of a day.
Commerce between the two states had never been strong prior
to the eighteenth century. French reports summarized that "in
the sixteenth century the French traded in Muscovy, but the
frequent wars and revolutions in each country ruined and destroyed that commerce." [114] Negotiations between the govern-
ments of Louis XIII and Louis XIV and the Russian state had
been opened several times but always broken off. At the beginning of the eighteenth century a bad situation became even
worse. The French Ministry of the Marine recorded that "before the year 1724 French commerce in Russia was onerous to
the point where the French could not continue without en-
countering certain losses. In that year, 1724, an exorbitant

113. Stainville to L'Hôpital, Vienna,
Sept. 16, 1758: *AMAE CP R*, Suppl.
10, 105. On commercial negotiations
between France and Russia the most
recent contribution is Walter Kirchner, "Relations économiques entre la
France et la Russie au XVIIIe siècle,"
*Revue d'histoire économique et so-
ciale*, XXXIX (1961) No. 2, pp. 158–
97. A survey of materials useful in
this neglected area will be found in
Douglas K. Reading, *The Anglo-Russian Commercial Treaty of 1734*
(New Haven: Yale University Press,
1938). Useful or suggestive are S.
Rojdestvensky and I. Lubimenko,
"Contributions à l'histoire des relations commerciales franco-russes au
XVIIIe siècle," *Revue d'histoire
économique et sociale*, XVII (1929),
pp. 363–402; Henri Sée, "Les relations commerciales et maritimes entre

la France et les pays du nord au
XVIIIe siècle," *Revue maritime*, New
Series, No. 71 (November, 1925);
Max Gideonese, "Dutch Baltic Trade
in the Eighteenth Century," unpublished Ph.D. dissertation, Harvard
University, 1932; P. W. Bamford,
*Forests and French Sea Power 1660–
1789* (Toronto, 1956); and Clifford
Foust, "Sino-Russian Trade Relations
from 1727 to the End of the Eighteenth Century," unpublished Ph.D.
dissertation, University of Chicago,
1957. Russian statistics will be found
in Mikhail Chulkov, *Istoricheskoe
opisanie rossiiskoi kommertsii pri
vsekh portakh i granitsakh ot drevnikh
vremën do nyne nastoiashchego* (St.
Petersburg, 1781–88).
114. Memoir on Muscovite commerce, Dec. 31, 1721: *AMAE MD
R* 3, 29.

tariff on all merchandises of wool, cotton, and silk determined the French to renounce absolutely the Russian trade." [115]

At the same time Russian favoritism for the British and Dutch was combined with a French ignorance and scorn of Russian commerce.[116] The early years of the reign of the Empress Elizabeth saw no change in these conditions. Cardinal Fleury's plans to restore this trade in some measure failed due to the frictions of the wars of the Polish and Austrian succession.[117] The few ships leaving the Baltic bound for French ports in the years from 1735 to 1748 were scarcely worth noting.[118]

It was certainly not the lack of Russian interest in French manufactures that hindered commerce between the two. The heavy majority of cargoes carried into Russia by British, Dutch, and Hanse ships were French items: a great array of wines, *eau de vie*, liqueurs, oils and olives, anchovies, dried fruits, confiture, coffee, indigo, furniture of all description, tapestries, ribbons, chocolate, fine hats and clothes, laces, and all manner of rich cloths. Similarly, most of the furs, caviar, copper, potash, sailcloth, naval stores, and rough uniform material used in France were carried from Russian ports by the ships of other states. This was the ironic note in the Franco-Russian commercial relationship, or lack of it: that although the French and Russians shared a rather extensive and expensive interest in each other's manufactures, all the handling, shipping, and profits were in the hands of the British, the Dutch, and the north German cities.[119]

One key to this situation was the unpreparedness of the French for a Baltic commerce and their unwillingness to en-

115. Memoir adapted from that of 1728, Versailles, 1756: AN AE B III, 432. See also Georges de Saint-Pret, Notes on Treaties, 1702: AMAE MD R 3, 21.

116. Kirchner, op. cit., p. 167.

117. Rojdestvensky and Lubimenko, op. cit., pp. 389 and 401. See also Arthur M. Wilson, *French Foreign Policy During the Administration of Cardinal Fleury, 1726–1743* (Cambridge: Harvard University Press, 1936), pp. 313–14.

118. Nina Ellinger Bang and Knud Korst, *Tabeller over Skibsfart og Varentransport gennem oresund 1661–1783* (Copenhagen: Lars Schmidt, 1930), pp. 56–84.

119. Villardeau (Consul in Russia), Memoirs on French commerce in Russia, St. Petersburg, 1728: BN NAF 22010, 163–180

gage in one. French merchant ships were constructed for a crew of from fifty to sixty men, while equivalent Baltic merchantmen from Britain, Holland, and the Hanse cities had crews of sixteen or less. Thus, cost of shipment in French bottoms was excessive. In addition, French vessels had too deep a draft to be practical for the Baltic. The French were not interested in building the new fleet necessary to make them competitive in the Baltic trade. Further, the French refused to accustom themselves to Russian trade practices and necessities. They rejected the Russian custom of extending cargo payments over one year's time. Neither would they arrange in advance for return cargo from Russia in order to complete the hazardous round-trip voyage within the year, the only system under which a decent profit could be expected. The heavy Russian tariff of 1724 only added to French difficulties; it did not create them.[120]

Statistics from the Russian customs houses at St. Petersburg and Riga bore out the contention that, although French goods were popular in Russia, the French gained none of the advantage of their delivery to the high-priced Russian market. French merchandise was bought by Dutch traders at Western prices and reshipped by Dutch and British ships from the Netherlands to Russia at large profits. Reports on merchandise arriving in St. Petersburg in 1754 revealed that well over half the volume of goods — and by far the most valuable segment — was in French items passed by Dutch and British companies. In that year the British carrying trade was almost ten times the value of the French; the Netherlands, over three times. The French carrying trade was matched or exceeded by that of Denmark and Lübeck.[121]

The reopening of diplomatic relations between France and Russia in 1756 brought this commercial situation sharply to the attention of the Ministry of the Marine, which reported

120. *Ibid.* 22010, 175; see also Memoir on commerce, 1756: *ibid.* 22010, 204.

121. Statistics of Russian customs houses for 1754: *AN AE* B III, 432. See also specifications of the Ministry of the Marine for merchandise arriving and departing St. Petersburg in 1756, Dec. 15, 1757: *ibid.*, B III, 432. For a summary of British commercial policy in Russia, see Reading, *op. cit.*, pp. 295–301.

to the King that France was providing northern Europe with most of its needs, while the profits went into British and Dutch pockets.[122] Reports from the newly arrived French diplomats in St. Petersburg testified that French merchandise entering that port in 1756 had a total value of 2,000,000 rubles (10,000,-000 livres). France in turn received 1,600,000 rubles (8,000,000 livres) worth of exports from Russia.[123] Yet 90 percent of those imports and exports were carried in foreign bottoms.[124] Observers in St. Petersburg were astonished: "The Petersburg agency would suffice to support twenty French companies." [125]

France had allowed Great Britain to gain a stranglehold on Russian commerce. It was difficult to persuade the Russians that France was the most significant element in the Russian trade while French ships and French companies were plainly absent. The French representatives in Russia noted that "it is apparent to all here that of the fifteen hundred ships which frequent the ports of the Baltic every year, one sees hardly five or six that are French." [126] The absence of Franco-Russian contacts was also obvious on the French side. From 1755 through 1757, during the years of friendliest relations between the two states in the century, of almost fifty thousand vessels entering French ports, only three were Russian.[127]

As a result of these conditions there were "no French merchants at Saint Petersburg, but only a number of ragged peddlers without credit or reputation who were never concerned with real commercial operations." [128] The merchants who composed that report, Beaujon and Goosens of Paris and Raimbert and Michel of St. Petersburg, evidently did not consider themselves part of the motley band they described. These gentlemen represented the small band of French merchants with a

122. Memoir in the Ministry of the Marine, May, 1756: *AMAE CP R,* Suppl. 8, 250–262.

123. Memoir, 1757: *ibid.,* Suppl. 9, 214.

124. Official reports on the value of direct French commerce in 1756 at St. Petersburg (imports: 962,623 livres; exports: 378,353 livres) are provided in Kirchner, *op. cit.,* p. 187.

125. Memoir, 1757: *AMAE CP R,* Suppl. 9, 214. See also Memoir by Godin, Dec. 15, 1757: *AN AE B III* 432.

126. Memoir, 1757: *AMAE CP R,* Suppl. 9, 214.

127. French and foreign vessels entering the ports of France 1755, 1756, and 1757: *AMAE MD F* 2016, 4.

128. Memoir by Michel, Beaujon, Raimbert, and Goosens, St. Petersburg, Jan. 1757: *AN AE B* III, 432.

continuing interest in Russian commerce. Michel, long active as
Vorontsov's secretary and as a link between the French party
in Russia and Versailles, had formed a commercial operation
in Russia with an associate in 1747. The venture had failed of
its own weight and because of the diplomatic break between
France and Russia in the same year. Michel had remained impatiently in Russia from 1747 to 1756, hopefully awaiting the
restoration of diplomatic relations and the reestablishment of
his fortunes. The expectation of a major role in any Franco-
Russian commerce was assuredly Michel's motive in his secret
work between the two states. In 1756 Michel had come into
contact with Godin and Company of Rouen, Nicholas Baudouin of Rouen, Beaujon and Goosens of Paris, and Joseph
Raimbert. Raimbert joined him in St. Petersburg.

These gentlemen now proposed to form a company in
Russia to serve as the base of future French commerce. They
requested precisely what Colbert had recommended a century
earlier for just such an establishment: permission to admit foreigners and noblemen to the company; government subsidies
to cover losses for the first year; exemption from tariffs and
internal duties in France; a monopoly for the supply of naval
stores to the French fleet; and a twenty-year exclusive right to
Russian commerce. Their arguments were persuasive:

In the north our products and manufactures are in general consumption. . . . They enjoy a preference which facilitates and aug-
ments their flow. We think that there is now sold in Russia about
100 million livres worth of French merchandise every year. The
English provide only a tenth of that. On the other side, France ab-
sorbs nearly 30 million livres of Russian goods every year. Yet both
sides of this commerce are made indirectly, by other states, against
French interest. We think we can assume this commerce. Here
France will find sailcloth, saltpeter, candles, anchors, cordage, can-
nons, powder, salt meat, and tobacco which it buys elsewhere at
double the price.[129]

129. Memoir on establishment of new
commercial house in Russia, St. Petersburg, 1756: *AMAE MD R*, 7, 58–
59; Memoir from the King's Council,
1756: *ibid.*, Suppl. 8, 131–132; Michel
and Raimbert to L'Hôpital, Aug. 8,
1758: *ibid.*, Suppl. 10, 92.

The French merchants presented a good case. The need for temporary subsidies was explained away by the observation that "France has the advantage that any power that allies with it adopts French tastes and styles, and we have no doubt that the Russians will do the same." They also argued the case against British influence, informing France that the British merchants in Russia, in order to frighten the Russians at the time of the *rapprochement* with France, had cut off purchases in 1756 and early 1757 to demonstrate their power over the Russian market. Michel and his colleagues saw a French opportunity and urged the King and Council to decree immediately that no orders for Russian materials pass through any but approved French houses.[130]

The French Ministry preferred more objective judgments on the matter of Russian trade and withheld comment while it sent a new consul into Russia. Jean-Baptiste de Cury de Saint-Sauveur, former Consul in Russia from 1743 to 1748 and subsequently Commissioner of the Marine at Amsterdam, went back to his post at St. Petersburg. The new Consul seemed to recognize that the omens for a renewed French commerce in Russia were propitious; the Anglo-Russian commercial treaty of 1734 was due for renewal and political conditions led Russia to be noncommital. Saint-Sauveur and Douglas agreed that France should take advantage of this rift between Russia and Britain by establishing in Russia the same commercial institutions as the British had set up. Douglas sent home a copy of the Anglo-Russian treaty, recommending it as the best model for French emulation.[131]

The hopes of the French merchants were also raised by Russian intentions to request freedom for Russian trade on the Black Sea from the Ottoman Empire. To this end, the Russians were establishing a new company, at Timernick on the Don,

130. Memoir, St. Petersburg, September, 1756: *BN SM NAF* 22010, 211–212; Michel to Tercier, with copy to Keeper of the Seals, Dec. 18, 1756: *ibid.* 22009, 106–109.
131. *AMAE Pers.* 62, 325–327, Saint-Sauveur; notes by Saint-Sauveur: *AN*

MM C 7, 296; letters of Saint-Sauveur and Rouillé, Aug. 3–16, 1756: *BN SM NAF* 22009, 209–213; Saint-Sauveur to Louis XV, Amsterdam, Dec. 21, 1756: *AN AE* B I 987: Douglas to Rouillé, Sept. 24, 1756: *AMAE CP R* 51, 26.

to build merchant vessels and to process and manufacture cloth and furs. The French in Russia, realizing that trade in that area of the world was in the hands of Greeks and Armenians, felt that France might well exploit an opportunity to introduce themselves into this hitherto closed commerce — and perhaps even establish new commercial ties with Persia.[132]

It was the Count de Broglie, Secret chief and natural enemy of any Russian scheme to abuse Turkish prerogatives, who sounded the alarm on this project:

Many diverse ambitions found themselves united for Russia in its views on Black Sea commerce. . . . The Russians sought to preface commercial negotiations with France by insinuating to us that we could establish a considerable branch of our trade with the southern provinces of Russia by way of Constantinople. The consent of the Porte for Russian naval activity on the Black Sea was necessary, and *it was up to France to get it*. This Russian proposition was a trap: if France succeeded against all odds it would have been a Russian success. Russia was only seeking a means to accustom the Turks to seeing a strange flag pass and repass the straits. Under pretext of a commerce with France, it was its own commerce that Russia would have established on that sea. If, on the contrary, the Porte had refused the French request, as we have every reason to believe they would, France would have suffered an overwhelming loss at the Porte by having taken a step which the Turks would have considered proof of French partiality for Russia and French connivance in Russian schemes for the Black Sea.[133]

The French Ministry of the Marine agreed with Broglie that aiding Russia on the Black Sea might well destroy French influence with the Turks. Although commerce through the Black Sea might possibly eliminate some of the problems of Baltic trade, Turkish resentment against French and Russian unity would overweigh any possible gains. At the same time, the French Ministry was not sure it could find any French merchants interested in pursuing the government's initiative. On the contrary, the city of Marseilles greatly feared that gambles in the Black Sea would raise costs and duties. The

132. Douglas to Tercier, May 22, 1757: *AMAE CP R* 52, 432.

133. Broglie to Louis XV, Apr. 16, 1773: reprinted in Boutaric, *op. cit.*, II, 53–54.

French decided to await further developments before committing themselves in this area.[134]

The Ministry of the Marine was given further pause in its plans for Russia by the developments in Russian tariff policy. The tariff of April 2, 1757, was Grand Chancellor Bestuzhev's last major effort to make the Russian *rapprochement* offensive to France. In addition, the tariff was one answer to Russia's pressing need for revenues to wage the war. The effects of the Russian tariff were felt immediately among French manufacturers. Already stung by British sea power, they were struck deeply by any decrease in Dutch purchases. Tariffs on French luxury goods in Russia went up as much as 164 percent. Since the increases were designed to affect expensive goods most heavily, the fine products of France suffered most, while cheaper British products underwent a mean rise of only about 50 percent. France demanded an immediate return to the tariff rates of 1754 until commercial talks between Russia and France could begin, on the grounds that the new rates could only prejudice negotiations. Russia refused.[135]

Saint-Sauveur, the new Consul, arrived in St. Petersburg in early November, 1757. Ambassador L'Hôpital was extremely suspicious of the new arrival and tender about the amorphous relationship of the Ministry of the Marine and the Ministry of Foreign Affairs in the field. Bernis assured the Ambassador that the Consul had orders to subordinate himself to L'Hôpital and treat all affairs through him, but actually the Minister had instructed Saint-Sauveur to investigate the possibilities of peace at St. Petersburg and to pass such information to Bernis be-

134. Moras, Minister of the Marine, to Bernis, July 18, 1757: *AMAE CP R* 53, 166–167. On the problems of Black Sea commerce the only work is Paul Masson, *Histoire du commerce français dans le Levant au XVIIIe siècle* (Paris: Hachette, 1911). On the relations of southern France and the Baltic, see the general survey of Oscar Albert Johnsen, "Le commerce entre la France meridionale et les pays du nord sous l'ancien regime," *Revue d'histoire moderne*, II (1927), 81–98.

135. Walther Mediger, *Moskaus Weg nach Europa* (Braunschweig: G. Westermann, 1952), pp. 617–627; merchants of Lyon to the Director of Commerce, Aug. 20, 1757: *AMAE CP R* 53, 281–283; memoir by the manufacturers of Marseilles; *AN AE* B III, 432; Russian tariff of 1757: *ibid.* B III, 76 pages; comments on tariff of 1757: *AN AE* B I 907; Bernis to L'Hôpital, Sept. 20, 1757: *AMAE CP R* 54, 66.

hind the back of his Ambassador.[136] L'Hôpital was rapidly losing the confidence of his Minister, and Bernis preferred to have others handling the difficult matter of commerce. "L'Hôpital gives us great hopes for our commerce in Russia. We will see. This alliance with Russia is costing us dearly enough. We have a right to hope that it will be useful at least in this regard." [137]

The Russians to whom Saint-Sauveur and the French merchants were obliged to address themselves on these commercial problems were Pëtr Shuvalov and Mikhail Vorontsov. Shuvalov, cousin of the imperial favorite, had acquired through imperial donation the monopolies for the sale of tobacco, vodka, furs, and other commodities, which made him the most important merchant in the empire. His ambitions seemed boundless.[138] Vorontsov, the Vice-Chancellor and later Chancellor, held the right of exportation of all sorts of grains from St. Petersburg and Riga on a seven-year grant from the Empress.

Actually, the French government immediately refused an offer from the pro-French Vorontsov to take the major portion of his grain exports, on the grounds of "exorbitant cost and doubtful usefulness." [139] The only means available to the French Consul and merchants to break into the Russian carrying trade was the purchase of tobacco. In January, 1758, negotiations were begun between Pëtr Shuvalov and Michel and Raimbert for a treaty on the provision of Ukrainian tobaccos to France. The treaty was signed on March 23, 1758, and provided for the delivery of 300,000 *puds* (approximately 10,000,000 pounds) of tobacco a year. Ambassador L'Hôpital was jubilant, convinced that "this first project is an affair of state and the basis of all our commercial operations." [140] Bes-

136. Saint-Sauveur to Bernis, Elsinore, Sept. 14, 1757: *AMAE CP R* 54, 11; Saint-Sauveur to Ministry of the Marine, Nov. 19, 1757: *AN AE* B I 987, 72; Bernis to Saint-Sauveur, Dec. 31, 1757: *ibid.* B I, 987, 72.
137. Bernis to Stainville, Sept. 27, 1757: *AMAE MD F* 571, 67.
138. On Pëtr Shuvalov's role in Russian economic development, see Roger Portal, *L'Oural au XVIIIe siècle*

(Paris: Institut d'Etudes Slaves, 1950), p. 140–141.
139. Bernis to L'Hôpital, Sept. 21, 1757: *AMAE CP R* 54, 74.
140. L'Hôpital to Bernis, Mar. 25, 1758: *ibid.* 55, 361. For the origins of tobacco enterprises in Russia, see Jacob M. Price, *The Tobacco Adventure to Russia* (American Philosophical Society Transactions, March, 1961), Vol. 51, Part 1.

tuzhev's fall from power at this time no doubt had much to do with Shuvalov's decision to cooperate with the French.

Unfortunately, French enthusiasm in Russia for this "affair of state" was not reciprocated in Paris. The Farmers-General had been obliged to seek out 2,000,000 pounds of tobacco quickly in February when the war cut off supplies from the New World. In April, however, shipments of tobacco again reached France. With a good supply in hand, the Farmers-General changed their minds and instructed the French merchants in Russia to postpone their scheme for Russian tobacco. Michel, Raimbert, and their associates were outraged. Repudiation of the treaty with Shuvalov by the Farmers would destroy the foundation of future commerce in Russia and do irreparable damage to French prestige there. The Farmers answered the arguments from the St. Petersburg merchants by demanding prolonged new samples and tests for the Ukrainian tobaccos.[141] The two groups had arrived at an impasse.

Michel made a flying trip to Versailles to present the complaints of the merchants in Russia to the King's Council. Realization of the importance of the treaty decided Louis XV to intervene. "His Majesty has decided in Council that the propositions Michel has brought here will be accepted by the Farmers-General despite their reasons for demanding new samples." [142] The reasons for the King's actions were simple: "Although it might appear at first glance that the tobacco treaty concerns only commerce, the present condition of Europe makes it of the greatest political interest. The success of all our Russian projects may well depend upon it." [143] The King promised the Farmers-General that the state would cover any losses suffered by the Farmers as a result of British attacks on these tobacco deliveries. The French in Russia were notified that all difficulties had been cleared, and Michel prepared to leave Paris in late July with the treaty in his care. Everything

141. Roslin,   Farmer-General,   to   L'Hôpital, Mar. 28, 1758: *AMAE CP R* Suppl. 10, 51–52; Raimbert to Ministry of the Marine, May 3, 1758: *ibid.* Suppl. 10, 53.

142. Bernis to Saint-Sauveur, J̶ ̶e 10, 1758: *ibid.* Suppl. 10, 65.
143. Bernis   to   Controller-General, June 11, 1758: *ibid.* Suppl. 10, 56.

seemed completed for the beginning of the Franco-Russian carrying trade.[144]

However, Louis XV was no absolute monarch, at least not absolute enough to tell the Farmers-General how and when money was to be made or lost. The Farmers, after much discussion, notified the Controller General that they had decided that they could not subscribe to the King's orders. Russian tobacco promised to be more expensive than American tobacco, it was of uncertain quality, and its transport was much too risky in wartime. The Farmers made a counterproposal that would limit the convention with Shuvalov to two years, at a test delivery of one million pounds a year. That was the Farmer's final offer. The merchants in Russia were shocked. They would be hard put to notify Pëtr Shuvalov that they could buy only one of the ten million pounds of tobacco that he handled each year. After all, Shuvalov well knew that France consumed fifteen million pounds annually.[145]

Louis, faced with two groups of brawling subjects, backed down before the more influential. Bernis told L'Hôpital that he knew Pëtr Shuvalov was waiting impatiently for the ratification of the tobacco treaty and that the reduction of the terms from ten to one million pounds might well drive the Russian merchant back to the British to get rid of his surplus. However, "His Majesty cannot order the Farmers-General to sell tobacco to which the French people are not accustomed. The King might well lose a fortune and destroy the Farmers. One must follow first the tastes of the public, for whom the King cannot order what it will find good or pleasing." [146] Pëtr Shuvalov did not understand this reversal. Angrily he signed a new agreement for the much smaller delivery of tobacco to France over only two years, but no one was optimistic enough to think that the matter pleased him or promised future bene-

144. Bernis to L'Hôpital, July 15, 1758: *ibid.* 57, 50–53; Michel to Bernis, July 22, 1758: *ibid.* 57, 67. 145. Memoir of Michel to Tercier, Paris, Aug. 8, 1758: *ibid.* Suppl. 10, 101–102.

146. Bernis to L'Hôpital, Aug. 8, 1758: *ibid.* 57, 92. For general observations, see Kirchner, *op. cit.*, p. 194.

fits. Shuvalov had been persuaded to sign only by promise of immediate rather than deferred payment.[147]

In short, the tobacco treaty failed miserably to satisfy either economic or political ends. The agreement was useless in terms of its contribution to a sizable commerce upon which to erect French carrying companies, and it served only to disgust Pëtr Shuvalov with dealing with indecisive Frenchmen. Three British houses waited to pick up the bulk of his tobaccos, and Shuvalov did business.[148] Finally, the convention greatly discouraged the long-suffering French merchants in Russia. Raimbert, disgusted, thought of leaving Russia. From the general resentment the French Consul felt that when Raimbert left the other French merchants, including Michel, would be close behind him.[149]

The failure of the French and Russians to come to any agreement in their period of *rapprochement* was thus reflected again in the condition of their commercial ties. The administration of Bernis had confirmed that the Russians were satisfied with their present commercial arrangements with Britain and Holland, and that the French were really indifferent toward any major attempts to alter the old order. A time of war, with its destruction of French commerce, was certainly a difficult time to attempt to build substantial trade agreements between France and Russia. Yet, without the temporary cohesion of the wartime ties between the two, there was even less chance of binding them together. The period of the Seven Years' War, in other words, was the most opportune time in the century for the development of commercial ties between France and Russia, ties that might promise well for the future. No such ties were developed. Choiseul's feeling that the future of Franco-Russian commercial negotiations would in part mirror the future of the alliance was correct. Two states that invested no effort in developing mutual interests in time of war were cer-

147. Raimbert to L'Hôpital, Sept. 28, 1758: *AMAE CP R* Suppl. 10, 116–117. See also Treaty for 60,000 puds of tobacco, Sept. 26, 1758: *ibid.* Suppl. 11, 106–107.

148. The British houses were Gomm, Reynold, and Thomson and Peters.

149. Saint-Sauveur to Bernis, Oct. 10, 1758: *AMAE CP R* 58, 78–79.

tainly not much concerned with the distant relationships of peace.

*vi.*

SUMMARY

The end of the year 1758 brought an end also to the Foreign Ministry of Abbé Bernis. France had been plunged by its two-front war and more especially by its defeats into the most disastrous condition the nation had ever experienced in its long and not always fortunate history. Bernis wrote to his successor in tones of desperation:

I have stopped depicting our violent condition to myself; no more commerce, as a result no more money and no more purchases; no more navy, and as a result no more resources to resist England. The navy has no more sailors, the army has no more soldiers, the treasury has no more cash. . . . We may await, therefore, only the aid of heaven.[150]

Thus far the Austro-Russian union had gained France nothing and cost France much. The primary aim of the union, the waging of war, had gone poorly for all parties: a quick victory had not been won, and although France wanted and desperately needed an end to the Continental war, Russia and Austria persisted in their pursuit of territorial rewards. France had been unable to preserve its influence in Poland in the face of mounting expenses and the need for unity in the alliances. The King's Secret had been undermined and ruined, but France had received nothing in return for the diminution of its influence in the republic. Russia followed behind the retreating French defenses in Poland, picking up the pieces at no cost. Sweden also stood exposed to Prussian soldiers and Russian agents, and French influence here, too, was in danger and on the wane. In Russia itself the Young Court stood as an unveiled threat to the present and the future of Franco-Russian cooperation. French attempts to approach the imperial heirs had failed miserably, and French intervention in the exchange

150. Bernis to Choiseul, Aug. 26, 1758: *AMAE MD F* 571, 189.

of Holstein had been a failure. Finally, no foundations for Franco-Russian commerce had been developed.

The Ministry of Abbé Bernis had been the testing time for the Franco-Russian *rapprochement,* the period in which the problems between the two countries had emerged for most careful examination. That examination had been neither pleasant nor rewarding for France. The Ministry of Bernis not only demonstrated that the *rapprochement* between France and Russia was, first, faulty, then dangerous, and finally, destructive, but that France had more pressing business than the repair of the *rapprochement.* While the structure of the French state itself prepared to tumble, France had little time, money, or energy to devote to a union that had proved so treacherous. The question for French policy was now not the future of diplomatic "systems" but the present salvation of France.

CHAPTER **5**

# Choiseul: *The Disintegration*

THE MAN into whose hands the sad state of French diplomacy was delivered on December 3, 1758, was the Duke de Choiseul. Étienne François de Stainville, Duke de Choiseul, held the rank of Lieutenant General in the army and had served as Ambassador in Rome (1753–57) and in Vienna (1757–58). Choiseul had been the protégé of the Abbé Bernis, but more importantly had tied himself to the good will of the Marquise de Pompadour. The esteem of the Marquise was no hindrance to a diplomatic career. As the stanchest remaining friend of the Austrian alliance and the most experienced negotiator at Vienna, Choiseul was called to the Ministry to bring peace to France and to save the alliance. Bernis tersely summed up the instructions of the King to his new Secretary of State for Foreign Affairs: "You see the destruction with which we are now menaced. Peace is the only remedy. That is your task." [1]

When, therefore, Choiseul turned to a consideration of the

1. Bernis to Choiseul, Aug. 20, 1758: *AMAE MD* 571, 189. It is an interesting comment on eighteenth-century research that the Duke de Choiseul still awaits a decent biography. Documents available include the sketchy and unreliable *Mémoires du Duc de Choiseul 1719–1789* (Paris: Plon-Nourrit, 1904); and Maurice Boutry, *Choiseul à Rome 1754–1757: lettres et mémoires inedits* (Paris: Emile Paul, 1895). General works on Choiseul include Gaston Maugras, *Le Duc et la Duchesse de Choiseul* (Paris: Plon-Nourrit, 1902); Alfred Bourget, *Etudes sur la politique étrangère du*

state of relations with Russia, it was with far less freedom of choice than Bernis had exercised a year and a half earlier. Choiseul's task was not to cement or to overthrow systems nor to build or reject alliances, as might have been that of a minister in more tranquil times. Choiseul's task was to save France. All relations and all projects were to be judged in the light of that momentous task.

*i.*

## THE WAR

As the Russian army slipped back toward the Vistula and as the winter of 1758–59 approached, Choiseul was outlining his decisions as to the aim and worth of the war:

The only war which interests us directly is the one that we must sustain against England. That war has for its purpose the defense of our colonies and our commerce. . . . All of our efforts in Germany, even supposing them successful, can be useful only to our allies. We exhaust ourselves for our allies; they profit from our services and can render us no return service of any benefit. To continue the war in Germany will never lead us to the source of the evils which surround us. The weakening of the King of Prussia . . . will produce only indirectly and imperfectly the fall of England. . . . This viewpoint is the only one possible in our relations with Russia. Peace is less obvious but more real than any military assistances. . . . The experience of the last two years has made clear to us that we must not count upon the Russians. It is necessary, then, to use them and to draw from them all that we can for immediate operations against England . . . which will bring us peace, re-establish our commerce, and repair the immense losses which our past beliefs have occasioned.[2]

Duc de Choiseul (Paris, 1907); and Roger Soltau, *The Duke de Choiseul; The Lothian Essay, 1908* (Oxford: B. H. Blackwell, 1909). The only monographs on the Duke's foreign policy center on the period after 1763: John Fraser Ramsey, *Anglo-French Relations: 1763–1770: A Study of Choiseul's Foreign Policy* (University of California Publications in History, Vol. XVII, No. 3 [Berkeley: University of California Press, 1935]); and Francis X. Lambert, "The Foreign Policy of the Duke de Choiseul 1763–1770," Unpublished Ph.D. dissertation, Harvard University, 1952.

2. Memoir of Choiseul to L'Hôpital, Jan. 19, 1759: *AMAE CP R* 59, 119–123. For a more outspoken criticism of the policy of Bernis written by the Duke in retrospect, see Memoir of 1765 in Duc de Choiseul, *Mémoires*, p. 383.

Choiseul came into office charged with hope and conviction that determined French action could reverse the downward trend of French fortunes. Seeing that the Continental war sapped France of all resources without resolving anything, he determined to seize the offensive and carry the war to the real enemy — Great Britain. Choiseul therefore produced a new view of French policy in Russia. Knowing that the Franco-Russian union had failed to accomplish its aims in the Continental war, Choiseul determined to test the worth of the peculiar alliance elsewhere. Choiseul's first projects for Russia were based on the principle that since France could benefit in no way from the Continental war, all assistance possible must be secured from Russia as quickly as possible, and brought to bear on the British war. Therefore, Choiseul began his Russian program by aiming at the extreme: the acquisition of outright Russian military aid against the British. Reasoning that the best way to end the Continental war was to end the British war, Choiseul concluded that a concerted campaign against Britain itself had to be waged. To that end, all possible resources had to be organized by France. Russia was one of those resources.

Choiseul's program required a state of war between Russia and Great Britain. To bring about this desirable condition, Choiseul planned to use the idea of a maritime union against Britain. The suggestion of a league of armed neutrality to protect shipping in the Baltic and North seas from British attacks had first been formulated by L'Hôpital in March, 1758, and proposed to Bernis. The Ambassador had reasoned that the rallying cry of the powers against Louis XIV had been the balance of power on the Continent. He further reasoned that Britain was presently engaged in destroying the balance of power on the seas. It should be a simple matter to convince the northern courts of the obvious dangers of British dominance. An offensive and defensive alliance stipulating mutual naval aid could then be arranged to counterbalance British power. Bernis, during his Ministry, had agreed that the British were "in the process of controlling universal commerce, from which they will proceed to dominate the continent." He proposed that the existing naval agreements between Russia and Sweden might serve as the basis for a maritime league to which Holland, Denmark, France, and even Spain might ultimately be attached. The treaty for the defense of the Baltic against British intrusions might then be rewritten and extended to broaden its scope of operations.[3]

Choiseul picked up the threads of this theoretical maritime league as an instrument of his policy for Russia. Choiseul saw, however, as L'Hôpital and Bernis had not, that the actual creation of such a league was virtually impossible. The reality of any such league would frighten states like Denmark, the Netherlands, and Spain, which would properly fear that such an instrument created ostensibly to restore naval balance would become in turn an instrument for world domination by the three allies. Further, uniting these diverse and often suspicious states would be the task of many years, and financing such a project was an impossibility for France. Denmark alone posed insuperable problems, owing to the antagonism between the Danes and Russians over the exchange of Holstein. Choiseul had no time for such long and devious projects; his use of the idea of a maritime league was to be more immediate.[4]

When Choiseul broached his plans for Russian aid against Britain to L'Hôpital in St. Petersburg, the Ambassador replied that such schemes were impossible and that a Russian war against Britain was inconceivable. It was to create that war that Choiseul intended to use the maritime scheme. He planned to have at least Russia and the Netherlands, with Swedish cooperation, come to terms on the rights of neutrals on the high seas. He knew that Russia was extremely sensitive on this point because of British threats in 1757. Choiseul then believed that Holland could "lead Russia little by little into an open break with the English, because of Holland's tremen-

3. L'Hôpital to Bernis, Nov. 27, 1758: *AMAE CP R* 58, 241; Bernis to L'Hôpital, Oct. 19, 1758: *ibid.* 58, 117; L'Hôpital to Choiseul, Mar. 12, 1759: *ibid.* 59, 370.
4. Choiseul to L'Hôpital, Jan. 9, 1759 and Apr. 10, 1759: *AMAE CP R* 59, 51–55 and 60, 22–23. For Choiseul's ideas on the maritime balance of power and the popularity of a maritime league in the Netherlands and Denmark, see Anderson, *op. cit.,* p. 165–166.

dous trade in the Baltic." [5] Simply by the rumor and first steps of such a northern league, Choiseul hoped to provoke the British to send a fleet into the Baltic to end it. Such a move would, as even Vorontsov allowed, bring a Russian declaration of war against Britain. "A single cannon shot by a Russian subject against an Englishman will occasion a declaration of war and put the Empress in necessity of waging it." [6]

Tricking Britain into acting in the Baltic to end a germinating maritime league and thus driving Russia and Britain to war were merely the first steps in Choiseul's plan. What the French Minister proposed next was daring and impossible. "We wish to effect a descent of Russian and Swedish troops from Göteborg into Scotland, preferably ten to twelve thousand men, while French troops land in either southern England or Ireland. England will be forced to peace, and Prussia will be abandoned. This will bring us what we desperately need: peace." L'Hôpital was instructed to approach the Russians cautiously on these matters, insinuating delicately "that the most sure means to remove Prussia from the war is to attack England. . . . A just peace, so difficult to obtain, necessitates an attack directly on the instigator of the war." Choiseul wished the Russian Empress and her ministers to be deeply impressed with the fact that "peace with England will lead to peace on the Continent." [7]

The best-laid plans can go astray; hastily projected dreams are even less likely to come to fruition. There was never the slightest chance that Choiseul's fanciful schemes for an Anglo-Russian war and a Russian invasion of Britain would ever come to pass. Russia agreed on the desirability of a maritime union, but took no steps to initiate it or to join it. Russia had no intention of being led into a war with Britain, with whom it carried on its most active commerce. Russia could gain nothing from an invasion of Britain that Russia was not already receiving. Bankrupt France could not pay a satisfactory price for Russian aid, for all France's desirable resources were being

---

5. Choiseul to L'Hôpital, Feb. 12, 1759: *AMAE CP R* 59, 210.
6. *Ibid.* 59, 210.

7. Choiseul to L'Hôpital, Jan. 19, 1759: *ibid.* 60, 30.

collected by the Russians already. The Russians persisted in making no answer to Choiseul's projects. As the months went by without result, Choiseul, losing his imaginative energy in the face of the ruin he had inherited, finally lost also his hopes for Russian war projects. "I admit that the success of this project grows every day more doubtful, but no one can reproach us for not having tried." [8] The Minister was coming finally to realize that Russia had even less interest in a war with Britain than France had in a war with Prussia. The difference, of course, was that Russia still had a choice, whereas France had none, and Russia chose to reject French requests for aid against Britain. Vorontsov, speaking for the Russian War Conference, informed the French that there was small cause to hope for success in these wild plans. [9]

Choiseul did not take his disappointment by the Russians gracefully.

Either the Court of Saint Petersburg is in bad faith and never wishes to use its army, or the ministers and military experts of Russia are without ability. In either case, what aid to the common cause do the Russians propose to offer? I swear to you that up to the present moment I have still seen no very beneficial effect from our alliance with those Russians or what the true object of that alliance is. [10]

The idea of a maritime league was hereafter abandoned in favor of the more practical agreement already in effect between Russia and Sweden to guarantee the Baltic for the duration of the war. This idea of an armed league of neutrality would be resurrected by Catherine II, who had no doubt followed its fortunes closely while Grand Duchess.

The proposal and failure of this fanciful scheme for the invasion of Britain served one useful purpose for French policy. Henceforth, France's only interest in the Russian military cam-

8. Choiseul to L'Hôpital, Mar. 24, 1759: *ibid.* 60, 275.
9. L'Hôpital to Choiseul, Mar. 24, 1759: *ibid.* 59, 414.
10. Choiseul to L'Hôpital, Apr. 22, 1759: *ibid.* 60, 56–57. Choiseul did attempt to organize a military descent on Britain without Russian or Swedish help, but it was destroyed by British naval action before it was ever properly prepared; see Pierre Gaxotte, *Louis XV and His Times* (Philadelphia: Lippincott, 1934), p. 251; and Vandal, *op. cit.*, p. 356.

paigns was for the safety of the Swedish army. Otherwise, Choiseul wished only that the Russians preserve themselves quietly along the Prussian front while France sought means for peace. To this end Choiseul urged the Russians to lay siege to Stettin rather than push on to more active operations in Silesia. Choiseul wanted neither Russian victories, which would persuade the Russians to prolong the war, nor Russian defeats, which would persuade the Prussians to prolong the war. What Choiseul desired was that the Russians rest quietly, look as menacing as possible, and merely by threat of their strength force Prussia to a compromise peace.[11]

As a result, the decision of the Russians to march straight on Brandenburg during the next campaign was as distasteful to Choiseul as news that the Russians would not march at all.[12] Failure to wage an offensive war on Britain and fear that Russia would carry on the war indefinitely by its victories or end the war disastrously by its defeats convinced Choiseul that peace was the immediate need on the Continent and abroad. After the failure of Choiseul's war plans for Russia, therefore, military operations became secondary for France and peace negotiations became paramount.

*ii.*

PEACE

Choiseul took up Bernis's original search for peace with great care. The French Minister did not want to frighten either Russia or Austria into a separate peace that would leave France isolated and vulnerable. Britain's public disavowal of the Danish peace mediation sought by Bernis in December, 1758, had badly embarrassed France with its allies. Peace on the Continent had to be a general peace mutually created. Choiseul knew that his allies had him badly hemmed in, and he meant to give them no excuse to abandon him outright.[13]

11. Choiseul to L'Hôpital, dispatches of Dec. 12, 1758, Feb. 19, 1759, and Apr. 22, 1759: *AMAE CP R* 58, 333; 59, 116; and 60, 56.
12. Note from the Russian Imperial Conference of Mar. 7: *AMAE CP R* 59, 310–347.
13. Choiseul to L'Hôpital, Dec. 22, 1758: *ibid.* 58, 397–400.

Acquiring Russian help in making peace in Europe had already proved an impossible business. Yet Choiseul was driven by the extent of French misery to try again. As usual, his first plan was ambitious.

The great difficulties that will occur at the peace do not stem from our particular war with England. I think that it would be possible to end the war honorably and promptly if we were not engaged, England and ourselves, in the quarrels of our allies. However, our engagements are different from those of the English, since England may leave its allies as they were before, whereas we are engaged with our allies to procure them reparations and conquests. We must convince Vienna to abandon ideas of conquest, Saxony to abandon ideas of reparations, or effect a compromise between those states and Prussia. Our attempts at peace in Vienna and Petersburg last year were useless. By our treaties we are trapped in this war as long as Russia and Austria wish to match Prussia in the field. Yet we are obliged carefully to fulfill our commitments to them. Our alliance with Austria is paramount. That alliance has cost so many men and so much gold and can only be useful to France if it is solid and durable at the peace. We know that the King of Prussia will die and with him his power. The Austrian power will not be extinguished, and if we do not arrange the peace carefully, Austria could again revive its old ambitions and again become our cruel enemy. Russia has no inconveniences to fear. Austria is entirely subordinate to Russia and the reason is simple: Austria must depend upon Russia for protection against the Porte, while Russia has nothing to fear of Austria. That is why Russia can undertake a mediation between Austria and Prussia. Russia can make known her feelings for peace without fear, as we cannot. If the Grand Chancellor Vorontsov really wants to create for himself an imposing reputation in Europe as the minister of a great power, he ought to seize this idea with enthusiasm and join thereto a great generosity by returning to Prussia, if Russia should hold it, East Prussia without recompense.[14]

Choiseul's plan was based upon some false propositions, but is clearly presented his problems. His recently concluded Third Treaty of Versailles with Vienna in May, 1758, had re-

14. Choiseul to L'Hôpital, July 8, 1759: *ibid.* 60, 275; see also Choi-seul's Memoir of 1765 in *Mémoires*, p. 385.

duced French commitments to Austria, and Choiseul greatly feared to displease or alienate Vienna further by proposing a peace by which Maria Theresa could never hope to recover Silesia. France needed a scapegoat to propose the peace and bear the Austrian resentment, but a scapegoat strong enough to be listened to in Vienna. It was up to Russia, according to Choiseul, to serve France in this way. Russia could propose the mediation of the war with Prussia and the compromise of war claims and then show the way by foregoing Russian demands on Prussian territory. Thus, peace could be obtained without France bearing the blame for the war's lack of result. Choiseul depended upon Austria's need of Russian assistance to make Russia the unassailable mediator.

Choiseul's plan required (1) that Russia be disposed to peace, which it was not; (2) that Russia feel secure enough in its alliance to push Austria to a repugnant renunciation of Silesia, which it did not; and (3) that Russia itself forego its war claims, which it would not. Despite these absolute obstacles to Choiseul's program for Russia, it was a more immediate event which sabotaged the plan. Any possibility that Russia might have been won for the role of mediator in the war was destroyed, as Choiseul had feared, by a series of Russian victories. The Russians encountered the Prussians and defeated them handily at Züllichau on July 23, 1759. The Russians then routed Frederick himself at Kunersdorf on August 13. By August 26, Russian troops had occupied Frankfort on the Oder. These victories occasioned two more personal letters from the Empress Elizabeth to Louis XV proudly announcing Russian accomplishments, both delivered by the secret method arranged between the two sovereigns.[15]

These victories disturbed Choiseul in two ways. First, they left the Swedes unprotected in the north at the moment the

15. Elizabeth to Louis XV, letters of Aug. 2 and 29, 1759: *AMAE CP R* 60, 322–323 and 389. For a summary of the Third Treaty of Versailles, see Henri Carré, *La regne de Louis XV* (*Histoire de France*, edited by E. Lavisse, Vol. IV [Paris: Hachette, 1911]), p. 269. The cession of the Low Countries to France was dropped, which in the opinion of Carré removed "the only reason which justified French intervention in the continental war." For the same opinion see Waddington, *op. cit.*, III, 453–54.

Estates of Sweden were preparing to meet. A Prussian attack on the outnumbered Swedish army would bring the French party in Sweden tumbling down. Second, the victories seemed to end the hopes that the Russians might consent to leave the war without new properties. L'Hôpital reported "that any peace mediation will be terribly difficult here now. Even the secret of it would be impossible to keep, since the Empress tells Shuvalov everything." [16] L'Hôpital's fears were corroborated when Vorontsov approached the French Ambassador to resurrect negotiations regarding the long-tabled Russian desires for rectifications of the Polish border.

Russia suddenly grew imperious. It was now the Russians who could complain bitterly that the Austrians were giving them little support in the campaigns; that perhaps "Vienna wished to chance nothing as long as it might expose the Russian army to the greatest dangers." The Russians would be put off no longer on secret Austro-French engagements. They wished to see the new treaty of 1758 between Vienna and Versailles, which was duly sent. [17]

French attempts to turn these new Russian military successes into the end of the war without definite territorial commitments to Russia—the only conditions under which Frederick of Prussia would negotiate — naturally ended in failure. Choiseul hoped publicly that the Russian victories were simply intended to restore the *status quo* in Europe, but he did not really believe it. [18] Louis XV was once more rung in to dash off another personal letter to the Empress of Russia congratulating her on her victories and hoping that the result "would procure for the allies a quick, just and honorable peace. . . . I will concur heartily in all dispositions for peace which your Majesty thinks best." [19] The Empress was no doubt growing more blasé about personal messages from His Most Christian Majesty, especially since Russia had emerged as a full-fledged power. This time Louis received no answer.

Choiseul could not afford the luxury of despair. He was

16. L'Hôpital to Choiseul, Aug. 18, 1759: *AMAE CP R* 60, 350.
17. Choiseul to L'Hôpital, Aug. 21, 1759: *ibid.* 60, 399–400.
18. Choiseul to L'Hôpital, Sept. 9, 1759: *ibid.* 61, 23–24.
19. Louis XV to Elizabeth, Sept. 15, 1759: *ibid.* 61, 33.

still intent on finding a way to acquire Russian aid for peace. Frustrated by setbacks to his policy on every hand and unwilling to concede that it had no real chance of success, Choiseul sought a scapegoat: his Ambassador at St. Petersburg might have something to do with the lack of success thus far. L'Hôpital began to receive withering dispatches.

You have, I think, understood my system for peace, which you have not served to any great profit up to the present, my dear Marquis. Apparently you have not been able, although of course you ought, to tell me to just what extent you understand the orders of His Majesty on a project as delicate as it is necessary. . . . Our alliance with Vienna is solid, intimate, and as desirable as it is useful to the two crowns. At the same time, we do not pretend to adopt the whole of the Austrian system. Yet we must never appear to contradict Vienna at Saint Petersburg. . . . Despite this, you persist in treating with Vorontsov directly, without reference to Austria. The more we desire that Russia bring us peace this winter between Austria and Prussia, the more you ought to pretend to show Vienna that we second the Austrian actions in Russia with energy, and the less you ought to confide to Vienna our real views on peace. Therefore, get closer to Esterhazy, whose confidence I think you have lost. . . . In case Russia decides to help us toward peace, you will find yourself the mediator between the two imperial courts to arrive at this desirable end. That, my dear Marquis, is the only aim of your embassy, any other which you envision is so much myth and wind. . . . You tell me often enough that you wish to be made a Duke. . . . I tell you plainly that there are only two ways to attain that honor: fulfill my desires for peace or return to France and seek it by some other means. I strongly recommend that you undertake the former.[20]

Choiseul was blaming L'Hôpital for the impossibility of maneuvering Russia into accepting responsibility for bringing peace. Choiseul should have known better, and no doubt did. L'Hôpital was a shallow and unenterprising Ambassador, but the task was beyond the strength of even the most talented diplomat. The Empress of Russia and her ministers had formed no plans for peace because no one had yet guaranteed their

20. Choiseul to L'Hôpital, Oct. 2, 1759: *ibid.* 61, 103–106.

price, and because East Prussia was not yet securely in Russian hands. The Austrians, in turn, were unlikely to be receptive to plans for peace until prospects for control of at least part of Silesia were much more real than at present. France, as Choiseul well understood, was doomed to ineffectuality by its own fear of destroying its European system — and thereby plunging France into even a worse state than now prevailed.

Emboldened by the increasingly obvious decline in French ability to resist, Russia stated its case baldly in October, 1759. Russian participation in a Danish treaty or in the Third Treaty of Versailles would have to wait until arrangements were made among the allies for territorial cessions to Russia at war's end. The Empress of Russia was determined to wage the war on the Continent with several more campaigns, if necessary, and to wage it so victoriously that the allies would be forced to negotiate on Russia's terms. Nothing could have been more contrary to what Choiseul wished to hear. L'Hôpital's observations on the impossibility of discussing peace with the Russians, though obviously correct, were bound to infuriate his harried Minister.

I see very little appearance of following with safety or with success the object of your letters. . . . In reflecting how measured my steps should be, I have been fearful of hazarding anything. The least indiscretion by the Russian Ministry or the slightest suspicion on the part of Esterhazy would produce disastrous results. I wish, therefore, to let time pass and hope that the fate of the Russian and Austrian armies will change the conditions under which I labor. Vorontsov told me that dreaming of peace was impractical. The Empress-Queen will give up no claims on Silesia; the King of Poland must have reparations; the Empress of Russia, today almost mistress of East Prussia, will give it up only very reluctantly. . . . I asked Vorontsov if the Empress did not greatly desire peace. Yes, he said, but she is so personally engaged against the King of Prussia that she suppresses her normally peaceful heart. If one does not overthrow Frederick completely, says Vorontsov, how can the allied powers be content? [21]

21. L'Hôpital to Choiseul, Nov. 1,
1759: *ibid.* 61, 218–220.

L'Hôpital's horrifying analysis was supported by the appearance of a Russian note to the French which took as its topic "that all the participating powers in the present war ought to expect some particular recompense." The note said that Austria expected and ought to receive Silesia and Glatz; that France was being paid in Italy and the Low Countries; and that Poland, Sweden, and Russia had a right to expect the same kind of compensation. The Russians insisted that 1] all these plans were useless unless Frederick of Prussia were beaten, 2] no permanency for such a settlement could be assured if Prussia were left strong in any way, and 3] efforts for the coming campaigns, therefore, had to be redoubled in preparation for a long and bloody war.

The Russian's went on to complain that the end of the war on the Continent would leave Russia stranded with great problems and no rewards. All the allies would be guaranteed in their states, while the Russian Empire, primarily responsible for all this happiness, would have nothing except an army far from home. The Russian army returning across Poland might well tempt the Turks to declare war on Russia, and Russia did not even have commitments from its allies if such a war should occur.

The Russians then proposed their own answer to their alleged plight. Russia formally requested that "the province of East Prussia, which is already occupied in large part by the armies of Her Imperial Majesty . . . be ceded to Russia by Prussia and that Prussia renounce it entirely, and that France and Austria give their guarantees for this province in favor of the Empress of Russia." The Russians could foresee no difficulties for this plan. The province they desired was not a part of the Holy Roman Empire and had not always belonged to the Hohenzollerns. As to allied fears for the encirclement of Poland, Russia promised to make no threats of war and to guarantee the constitution of that republic.[22]

L'Hôpital, this document in hand, could only repeat to Choiseul that the present situation in Russia did not permit him to think of peace negotiations. Pëtr Shuvalov let slip to

22. Memoir from the Russian Ministry, Nov. 6, 1759: *ibid.* 61, 232–248.

the French that the Russians desired to use part of their Prussian acquisitions to buy a border alteration in the Ukraine. Shuvalov also implied that until the Prussian province was ceded to Russia, the exchange of Holstein would not occur. Russia, fortified by victory, spoke its mind.[23]

Choiseul took these developments very badly. He resented being led by the nose into Russian plans while his own wasted away. His immediate reaction to the Russian note was to emphasize that France and Russia were merely auxiliaries of Austria in the war and that Russia would have to treat first with Austria on reparations. Further, the Ottoman Porte could never be the object of a French guarantee such as Russia hinted might be useful. Upon some reflection, Choiseul also decided that he wanted no part of the vague promises which Austria recommended that France and Austria make jointly to Russia. "If such vague promises discontent the Russians, Vienna will throw all the blame for them upon us. . . . We wish to mingle in no way in Russian demands." [24]

L'Hôpital proceeded to make himself completely odious to Choiseul by advocating the cession of East Prussia to Russia. It was the Ambassador's opinion that the probable weakness of Russia when the Grand Duke would come to the throne at some future date would allow France to take these gains away from Russia. Choiseul was angry. Apparently this Ambassador would never learn that Prussia would never surrender its province without suffering total defeat and that inflicting that defeat would prolong the war indefinitely! Choiseul did not want to prolong the war. Furthermore, such a Russian aggrandizement, the rumor of which was already spread, would drive Denmark to the enemy and completely wreck chances for peace.[25]

23. L'Hôpital to Choiseul, Nov. 10, 1759: *ibid.* 61, 274.
24. Choiseul to Count de Choiseul-Praslin, French Ambassador to Austria, Dec. 25, 1759: *ibid.* 61, 409–410.
25. Choiseul to L'Hôpital, Mar. 1, 1760: *ibid.* 64, 159–160. It was at this time that the Russian Ambassador to France, Mikhail Bestuzhev,

died in Paris. His absence would hardly be noticed. Said Choiseul, "there will certainly be no obvious vacancy in this embassy, since from the day that I took office I have seen Bestuzhev only on extremely rare occasions. . . . He never appeared to be instructed on the affairs of his court, nor did he ever have any order to discuss with me." *Ibid.* 60, 64.

France consulted Austria on its opinions of the Russian territorial demands, but Austria replied in the vaguest terms. Austria hoped, as Choiseul understood, that the French response would guide them. Neither Kaunitz nor Choiseul wished to be the author of the answer to the Russians. Choiseul persisted in telling the Austrians that the matter of reparations was between Vienna and St. Petersburg. When such matters had been arranged between the two, France would be glad to consider accession. "The Austrian Ambassador has been unable to make me come forth from this circular answer. At the same time, I have told Choiseul [Count de Choiseul-Praslin, French Ambassador at Vienna] that it would be contrary to our political interests in the north to give East Prussia to Russia. This would make Russia the mistress of the Baltic. Fears of such an event are pronounced in Sweden and Denmark, our true allies." [26]

France's official reply to the Russian note demanding discussion of Russian war gains was very brief. Choiseul was careful to distinguish the Continental war from the French war with Britain, the latter being the concern only of France. In the Continental war, France held, only Austria was a direct party to the war, France and Russia being merely auxiliaries by treaty. Thus, France reserved the right to make peace with Britain on its terms and in its own time and to discuss the accession of France to any agreement that Russia might make with Vienna. The most important and dangerous conclusion of the French note stated that Russian proposals for territorial gains were more than an enlargement of previous treaties and accessions. These war aims constituted a new treaty that could be arranged only between principal and auxiliary, that is, between Russia and Austria. Only then could France state its position. [27]

This note from the French Ministry, despite France's real desire to prevent Russian expansion, effectively abdicated

26. Choiseul to L'Hôpital, Apr. 3, 1760: *ibid.* 64, 239.

27. Response of the King of France to Russian note of Nov. 6, 1759; Feb. 1, 1760: *ibid.* 64, 122–130.

French interests in Eastern Europe. The dilemma for France had been painful: either France acquiesced in Russian territorial demands and offended Turkey, Sweden, Denmark, and Poland or France refused Russian demands and offended Russia and perhaps Austria. Choiseul had chosen what seemed to him a middle way, by informing Russia that its claims would have to be agreed upon with Vienna before France could act. This position supposedly removed France from any responsibility for Russian expansion and saved French face in Turkey, Denmark, Sweden, and Poland. Actually it was no middle way at all. France's position actually left the whole future of Eastern Europe to be decided between St. Petersburg and Vienna, with a carte blanche from Versailles. Once Austria and Russia came to terms, it would be well nigh impossible for French to resist or alter their decisions.

The Russians were quite content to concern themselves only with Vienna. Austria needed Russia and Russia knew it. Austrian interests in another campaign in Silesia left them open to Russian pressures, and Austria and Russia shared the same attitudes toward the seizure of Prussian territories. The Russians now refused to discuss military operations with the Austrian Ambassador, Esterhazy, until the Austrians agreed to Russian territorial claims. Esterhazy had no instructions on the matter of cessions, but he was under strong pressure from Vienna to conclude plans for Russian cooperation in the next military campaign. Esterhazy, driven to desperation, finally consented to draft a treaty of concessions to the Russians *sub spe rati,* that is, with ratification reserved to his government, always a dangerous arrangement. The draft treaty guaranteed East Prussia to Russia, without Vienna yet knowing that such concrete agreements were being negotiated. Esterhazy's predicament radiated poetic justice: it was precisely the same kind of dilemma and solution into which Esterhazy had forced Chevalier Douglas when Douglas signed the secret act for French aid against the Turks in 1756.[28]

28. L'Hôpital to Choiseul, Apr. 2,
1760: *ibid.* 64, 227–235.

Esterhazy had put the Austrian government in a very difficult position by his hasty commitments. Kaunitz would be
hard put to avoid accepting the terms without offending the
Russians openly and equally hard put to explain the treaty to
his French ally. France notified Austria that there would be no
French adherence for such an agreement and listed three good
reasons: that it did not except the Ottoman Porte, that it
guaranteed nothing to France, and that the cession of East
Prussia to Russia was contrary to the best interest of the allies.
Seeing Austria trapped and embarrassed, Choiseul resolved to
make the best of it for peace. The Minister ordered his representatives to insinuate to Kaunitz in the most devious way that
the Austro-Russian treaty could only be made acceptable to
France if Russia guaranteed Glatz but not Silesia to Austria,
cash payments to Poland, assistance for a peace between Britain
and France, and subsidies to Sweden. Thus, France would be
willing to accept inevitable Russian expansion into Europe in
return for the elimination of Silesia as a war aim and the assistance of Russia in negotiating a peace with Britain. France proposed these new conditions in order to draw the best results
from Austro-Russian agreements. Peace might yet be assured.[29]

France calculated badly. Austria dragged its feet on rati-
fying the cessions to Russia and blamed the French for the
obstruction, while the fact that the treaty had been drafted
made peace an even more difficult matter to handle with the
Russians. L'Hôpital told Choiseul that he could guarantee no
success on peace because the Russians had no need to consider
French demands or pressures counter to their own. It was
Austria that needed Russian troops and Austria that would
agree to pay Russia's territorial price. France had already
agreed to, in fact had insisted upon, such Austro-Russian
negotiations. Russia had no need to buy French acceptance of
any agreements. If France did not agree with the results of

29. Choiseul to L'Hôpital, May 3,
1760: *ibid.* 64, 281. Despite French
resistance, Austria ultimately signed a
secret agreement with Russia on May
21, 1760, which specified territorial
compensations (East Prussia) for
Russia on condition of Austrian recovery of Silesia and Glatz; see Bain,
*Daughter of Peter the Great*, p. 291.

Austro-Russian talks, there was nothing that France could do about it.[30]

The Russians effectively delivered their response to French requests for peace by their negative attitude toward the calling of a general congress of belligerents to discuss the ending of the war. The Duke of Brunswick had forwarded an Anglo-Prussian proposal for such a congress to the allied ambassadors at The Hague in late November, 1759. The French were delighted with this proposition. Choiseul considered it possible and even likely that in a general European conference the inexperienced Russians might be tricked into foregoing their demands and persuaded into accepting peace. He also hoped that cessation of hostilities on the continent for one year might accompany such a Congress. A note from the Russians soon disabused Choiseul of both ideas. Russia held that the invitation to a congress was simply intended by the enemy to tempt one or more of the allies to defect from the alliance. Russia insisted that the alliance would have been created for nothing if its aims were not achieved and that peace was not desirable for the allies if it were a premature peace. To the congress proposal the Russians suggested an answer which would indicate that the allies would be happy to send envoys "when precise explanations as to how a solid peace is to be obtained" were forthcoming. While waiting, the Russians continued, the allies ought to agree on compensations and prepare another vigorous campaign.[31]

The French were truly shocked. They were growing accustomed to Russian passivity in helping them find peace, but now Russia was actively obstructing and attacking its possibility. To have the long-awaited chance for peace snatched from their grasp by the precocious Russians was humiliating for the French. French fortunes had fallen so far as to be in the hands of these disturbing newcomers to the European scene! Months of fruitless negotiations among the allies over the wording of the response to the Anglo-Prussian offer were driving Choiseul

30. L'Hôpital to Choiseul, May 28, 1760: AMAE CP R 64, 337.
31. Note from Russian Ministry, Dec. 12, 1759: ibid. 61, 353–358. On the Congress proposals, see Waddington, La guerre, III, 478 and 485–89.

frantic. Russia continued to slow down negotiations on the affair by arguing endlessly over wordings and minute shadings of meaning. Choiseul was frustrated by this attempt of Russia to demonstrate its imposing position in the alliance. "It is absolutely necessary for our financial stability that we send our response to The Hague immediately and that we avoid giving the French public reason to believe that the King's Ministry is opposed to peace." [32] France had no control over its own future — Austria and Russia were in control. Vorontsov spoke bluntly: "The success of Russian demands in Europe will decide the position that the Empress of Russia will take toward the calling of any congress." [33] The question of a peace congress reverberated hollowly through the diplomatic correspondence of 1760. The dispositions of Russia seemed clear to all Europe, even to British Ambassador Keith:

> All hopes of peace which the Russian Ministry offers and all their words add up to nothing. The Empress of Russia . . . says that although she is very slow to make a resolution, once making it she holds firmly to it; and that she has resolved to pursue this war in any and all events in concert with her allies, even if she be forced to sell all her robes and jewels to do it.[34]

France had secured from her allies neither the war that France had originally planned, nor the peace that France currently demanded. In the agonizing search for the one and then the other, French interests had come crashing down in Europe and around the world. The Russian-French union was no alliance: it was a trap in which France blithely ensnared itself, and from which France struggled to escape through years of growing weakness and paralysing frustration.

---

32. Choiseul to L'Hôpital, Feb. 15, 1760: *AMAE CP R* 64, 94; note from Russian Ministry, Jan. 4, 1760: *ibid.* 64, 4–5; note from Swedish Ministry, Jan. 4, 1760: *ibid.* 64, 9–16. Neither Kaunitz nor the Russians wanted the Congress. They saw it as an attempt to remove France, whom they already suspected of wavering, from the war.

Waddington, *La guerre,* III, 493–94.
33. L'Hôpital to Choiseul, Feb. 18, 1760: *AMAE CP R* 64, 114.
34. Keith to British Ministry, Jan. 1, 1760, reprinted in Turgenev, *op. cit.,* p. 162; on Elizabeth's determination, see also R. N. Bain, *Slavonic Europe* (Cambridge: Cambridge University Press, 1908), p. 376.

*iii.*

## THE POLISH QUESTION

Choiseul carried on — and intensified — the abandonment of Poland. This was not done as an attempt to unify the coalition, as Bernis had first begun it, but out of sheer necessity. There was neither the money, the interest, nor the time to be occupied with the present and future of that country.

The Count de Broglie, the director of the Secret now removed from Poland by Bernis, at first thought that the arrival of Choiseul promised better treatment for French interests in Poland. "I desire strongly, Sire, that the Duke de Choiseul can repair all the checks which Your Majesty's system has suffered in that country. . . . The affair of Courland . . . [is] difficult to repair. God grant these are the last such setbacks." There was every indication that Louis XV also expected Choiseul to be active in the defense of French influence in Poland.[35] The blow, therefore, fell unexpectedly. Choiseul, warned by Bernis of some suspicious activities among subordinates in the foreign office, removed Tercier from his post on February 27, 1759.

Jean Pierre Tercier was removed from the post of *premier commis* on the pretext that he passed, as official censor, the work of Helvetius, *De l'esprit*. Pompadour was the willing servant of Choiseul in this case and pleaded with Louis for his acquiescence in Tercier's dismissal. Since Louis made it an unbreakable rule never to interfere with his ministers, the faithful and devoted servant of the Secret was dismissed.[36] The loss of Tercier struck nearly the final blow at the King's undercover activities in Poland. The removal of Broglie as Ambassador during the preceding year had left field activities in the hands of untalented subordinates, but at least information from the Ministry continued to flow through Tercier. Now that pivot was

35. Broglie to Louis XV, Jan. 10, 1759, reprinted in Ozanam and Antoine, *op. cit.*, I, 88; see also Broglie to Louis, Feb. 3, 1759: *ibid.*, p. 89–90.

36. See Didier Ozanam, "La disgrace d'un premier commis: Tercier et l'affaire de l'Esprit, 1758–59," *Bibliothèque de l'Ecole des Chartes* (CXIII), 1955.

removed and the Secret was denied access to official policy and dispatches. Broglie wrote to the King: "I avow, Sire, that I do not know how we can continue after this dismissal. . . . This act, added to what Choiseul told me yesterday about the necessity of abandoning Polish affairs, makes me suspect strongly that the Secret has been discovered, and that to destroy it they have removed its central instrument." [37]

The Secret was not yet finished nor was it discovered, but its activities in Eastern Europe were henceforth severely hampered. The Secret was impeded, first, by the official policy of Choiseul, which could not countenance further aid to the French party, and, second, by the intricate arrangements that the removal of Tercier made necessary. Louis decided to carry on the Secret as best he could and left Broglie and Tercier in charge, although both were now without official positions. It was necessary, as a consequence, to have many more ministers, consuls, and embassy secretaries initiated into the Secret so that copies of dispatches could be sent from diplomatic posts to the Secret headquarters. For example, Broglie's private secretary, Jean Drouet, was assigned as embassy secretary in Warsaw through the King's influence. [38] Choiseul's plans thus came to the attention of the Secret only at third hand and often too late to be of any use.

In Poland, French influence was truly on the wane. L'Hôpital saw "Russian troops on the Vistula from Thorn to Danzig; they choke Poland to death." [39] Prussia was bringing similar pressures to bear against the hapless Polish King, Augustus III, threatening the destruction of his beloved Saxony if the Poles did not immediately demand the withdrawal of Russian troops. [40] Against these rising threats from Poland's neighbors, the effects of softening French diplomacy and France's powerful protection were no longer felt. Prince Adam Casimir Czartoryski made a tourist's visit to St. Petersburg, presumably representing "the Family" in discussions of the future disposi-

37. Broglie to Louis, Feb. 28, 1759, reprinted in Ozanam and Antoine, *op. cit.*, I, 93.
38. Broglie to Louis, Mar. 6, 1759: *ibid.*, p. 93.

39. L'Hôpital to Choiseul, Jan. 1, 1759: *AMAE CP R* 59, 1.
40. Prasse to Russian Ministry, Jan. 20, 1759: *ibid.* 59, 26; Brühl to Prasse, Jan. 30, 1759: *ibid.* 59, 27.

tion of the Polish throne, but the French could discover nothing. Brühl's contacts with the Russian ministers, broken by the overthrow of Grand Chancellor Bestuzhev, were now reestablished. Durand's complaints against Russian activities and Brühl's intrigues in Poland now went unheeded.[41] It was no longer to France that former Polish friends turned to regulate the problems of future peace. The Primate of Poland sent a special commission to the Empress of Russia to discuss reparations to be paid to Poland by Prussia. France was passed by in these talks and notified long after the fact.[42] It was clear that Choiseul did not like the turn of events, but that he now felt the chaotic affairs of Poland to be outside the "defense perimeter" of French activities:

I must tell you . . . that despite knowing as we do the character of Brühl, which for reasons we have never understood but could easily prove has always tried to raise disagreements with the King's ministers in Poland and remove all influence from them in the republic, we now take the position of forming no more direct complaints or projects against the things which he says or does.[43]

Such an abject retreat signaled the end of French influence in Poland and, in a very real way, the beginning of the dismemberment of that state. Danzig, the key to Russian control of Poland, was also surrendered without a struggle. Danzig fitted well in to Pëtr Shuvalov's new-found interest in commerce. Control of Danzig would make him one of the strongest merchants on the Baltic. Choiseul replied to a request for aid from Danzig that "Danzig would certainly help the cause if they admitted Russian troops" and restricted himself to opposing the destruction of the city. He reasoned correctly that any violence against Danzig would drive the Poles into opposition, frighten Sweden out of the war, and no doubt arouse the Turks. These were further complications that France did not need.[44]

41. Choiseul to L'Hôpital, May 22, 1759: ibid. 60, 159.
42. Lubienski, Primate of Poland, to L'Hôpital, Oct. 27, 1759: ibid. 61, 202.
43. Choiseul to L'Hôpital, Dec. 22, 1758: ibid. 58, 395. Choiseul's withdrawal from Polish affairs dominated his future attitudes: see Kaplan, op. cit., p. 18.
44. Choiseul to L'Hôpital, Dec. 13, 1758: AMAE CP R 58, 338.

The French thus exerted some pressure against an open attack on the city, but their concern was with the continued pacification of the Turks rather than with the freedom of Poland. The continued operation of the war was much to be preferred to the explosion of the alliance over Poland. Choiseul added to his instructions in February, 1759: "We have already ordered Durand to join the Russian Resident in urging the Danzigers to cooperate with the Russians." Russian influence in Danzig increased as French interest in protection decreased, and Danzig was, henceforth, left to the dictates of the Russian Empire.[45]

Courland suffered the same fate. Choiseul found that the Russians and Brühl had consigned the duchy to Prince Charles of Saxony without even a notification to France. He thought that Russia was intent on ending the feudal relationship between Courland and Poland and annexing the former to Russia. To oppose these plans would be expensive and complicated for the French. Any help to the present Duke against Russian encroachments, for example, would be very likely to offend the next ruling family of Poland. Whereas Choiseul hoped that Prince Charles would give none of the guarantees demanded by the Empress of Russia for the future of Courland's affairs, which would "make him absolutely dependent upon the Russians," he could think of no possible way to assist the young Prince nor was he interested in doing so. The guarantees given included the freedom of the Russian Orthodox Church, free passage of Russian troops through Courland, and free entry for Russian ships of war into Courland's ports.[46]

French influence was being retracted from Poland, and Russia was quietly and efficiently filling the void. Choiseul was forced into paying a heavy price for a Russian *rapprochement*. Poland was deeded away for the simple maintenance of Russia among the allies, not for services of real benefit to France.

45. Memoir from L'Hôpital, Jan. 30, 1759: *ibid.* 59, 159; Choiseul to L'Hôpital, Feb. 12, 1759: *ibid.* 59, 218.
46. Choiseul's Memoir on Courland, last months of 1758: *BN SM MF*

10661, 22–31; Choiseul to L'Hôpital, Jan. 9, 1759: *AMAE CP R* 59, 60; conditions with which the Empress of Russia lifted the sequester of Courland, Mar. 26, 1759: *ibid.* 59, 411.

Choiseul himself had decided to abandon Polish affairs as too chaotic, too costly, and too unrewarding. The Minister might well complain that he had yet to see the benefits of this new understanding with Russia. France, writhing on the prongs of a disastrous two-front war, saw its interests being picked to pieces by enemy and ally alike. There was, unfortunately, no solution.

*iv.*

## THE YOUNG COURT AND THE EMPRESS

Choiseul's concern for Russian assistance, first to make war on England and then to mediate a Continental peace, was sufficient for him to make one last attempt to reconcile the Young Court to French interests. It was Choiseul's original confidence and egotism that led him to retrace in part the bitter experiences of Bernis, to discover whether it was truly Russian obstruction or the Abbé's incapacity which was at the root of French misfortune. Choiseul made the same investigation of the dispositions of the Young Court and reached the same ultimate evaluation as had Bernis.

Choiseul was particularly enamored of the idea of winning over the Grand Duchess, but he absolutely vetoed the use of the only persuasion likely to make even a temporary impression on the extravagant young lady. French diplomats had been reduced by the war to the role of niggardly penny-watchers in a world accustomed to the generous dispersal of cash, and the Foreign Minister cut L'Hôpital's public and secret expenses to almost nothing. L'Hôpital complained loudly, pointing out that his secret expenses were well distributed in the household of the Empress, the court of the imperial heirs, and the members of the College of Foreign Affairs. The Ambassador was forced to reduce payments to a list of distinguished personalities that now included Alsuviev, secretary to the Empress; Volkov, secretary of the War Conference; Countess Romansov, friend of the Empress; Mme. Buturlin, sister of the Grand Duke's mistress; Mme. Vorontsov, wife of the Grand Chancellor; Countess Bruce, intimate friend of the Grand

Duchess; and Brockdorff, minister of the Grand Duke for Holstein. Choiseul was adamant: France had no money to spend on such trivialities as card games and gossip in the Russian capital.[47]

In the fertile mind of the French Foreign Minister was germinating an idea obviously implanted by years of reports on the character and inclinations of the Grand Duchess Catherine. It might be possible, he conjectured, to play upon her fondness for young men much as the British had done and to eliminate the baneful influence of Poniatowsky by "giving him a successor in the heart of this Princess." [48] Such a project appealed to Choiseul precisely because it cost little. He resolved to consider the plan and to cast about for a worthy choice.

As to the Grand Duke Peter, France had lost all hope of drawing near to this simple and obdurate little man. Almost daily the Grand Duke was declaring publicly that he loved the King of Prussia and would be honored to wage a campaign under his orders — and that he eagerly awaited the day when he, Peter, would be master in Russia. Choiseul had only "scorn for the affections or the hatreds of this Prince." [49] Most French observers agreed with Duclos that the Grand Duke was little better than a traitor to his country and to the allies. "The Grand Duke was instructing the King of Prussia of all the Tsarina's measures, and since the allies sent all their respective plans to her, the King of Prussia learned them through this prince." [50]

With the Grand Duke Peter finally placed in his proper perspective for French policy, the French intervention in the exchange of Holstein became not a service to the Young Court but an attempt to manage the friendship and future of Denmark. Choiseul summarized the Holstein situation on his assumption of the Ministry:

The King of Denmark desires to exchange the Duchy of Holstein possessed by the Grand Duke of Russia for other lands more convenient to this Prince. Denmark solicited Bernis to broach this topic

47. Choiseul to L'Hôpital, dispatches of Dec. 13 and 29, 1758: *ibid.* 58, 338 and 407; L'Hôpital to Choiseul, Feb. 8, 1759: *ibid.* 62, 11–18.

48. Choiseul to L'Hôpital, Jan. 9, 1759: *ibid.* 59, 60.

49. Choiseul to L'Hôpital, June 17, 1759: *ibid.* 60, 223.

50. Duclos, *op. cit.*, II, 513.

to the Grand Duke, to help him forget a little country so far from his new interests. Bernis wrote to L'Hôpital telling him to concern himself with this exchange . . . and to give Denmark the impression that they owed France everything in this affair. . . . It is a favorable time. If we wait for peace or for the death of the Empress, things will go hard for our interests. We must remove Russia from Germany. The King's agreements with Denmark . . . call for benefits to the Danish King, and it is difficult to find a better solution than this exchange which costs us nothing. If the exchange does not take place, the Grand Duke may become Tsar and a war will result between the two states, since the Grand Duke will no doubt march on Schleswig. To do this he would ally with Prussia in order to pass troops to his duchy. If the Russian Tsar had strong establishments on both sides of the Baltic it would cause great threats to the liberty of Germany and Sweden.[51]

The disagreement over the concentration of Danish troops in Schleswig still rankled between Denmark and Russia. France thought that perhaps the communication of the secret treaty of May 4, 1758, signed between France and Denmark and guaranteeing Danish neutrality for certain compensations, might put the Russians at ease and convince them to join also in managing Denmark by some sacrifice. Such was not the case. No amount of pressure from the French and Austrian ambassadors could move the Grand Duke. What Choiseul had to learn, as painfully as Bernis before him, was that the Grand Duke was simply not interested in the exchange. This German-bred Prince loved Holstein above all other things and could exercise undreamed-of cleverness in manufacturing excuses to avoid the exchange. Said L'Hôpital, "the Grand Duke is light and variable on everything in the world except the exchange of Holstein; there he is forever intractable." [52]

L'Hôpital's reiteration of this indisposition of the Grand Duke to the exchange was only one more reason for Choiseul to generate antipathy for the unfortunate Ambassador. The Minister's dispatches became more and more impatient and chiding as the year went on. Denmark's growing insistence made some

51. Choiseul's Memoir on Holstein, Dec. 15, 1758: *AMAE CP R* 58, 351–356.

52. L'Hôpital to Choiseul, Jan. 29, 1759: *ibid.* 59, 142.

French action imperative. It was L'Hôpital's misfortune that no action was possible. The attachment of Denmark to the naval agreements between Sweden and Russia — and, thus, the assurance that Denmark would remain at least neutral in the war — hung on the outcome of the exchange. Neither could be brought to pass.[53]

France was reduced to the unenviable position of trying to satisfy both parties but being unable to satisfy either. Denmark, for example, sent orders to its envoy in St. Petersburg to offer to sign a naval convention with Russia with the exchange included as a *sine qua non*. France intercepted the envoy and prevented the delivery of any such straightforward alternatives, and was then forced to explain this action to Denmark. France had the task of preventing the head-on collision of two states determined to disagree. In one sense France did its work well, since Denmark did not join the enemy. In another sense Choiseul learned that in this, as in all other matters, it was Russia that stood in the way of an easy accommodation of Denmark to the war. Small wonder, then, that Choiseul had little confidence in an alliance with a state over which this stubborn Prince would no doubt one day come to rule.[54]

Choiseul's first year of office continued to be occupied with eruptions over Holstein. The Grand Duke, continually obstructing negotiations, complained that the Danes were building forts at Friedrichsort. The Empress backed his demand for demolition of these works. The Danes immediately replied with nasty comments that "Her Imperial Majesty declares that she never wishes to meddle in her nephew's affairs, which she proves by refusing to help in the exchange of Holstein, but which she belies by listening to his complaints about his duchy."[55] France was busy throughout the year smoothing over such eruptions. No sooner was one put to rest than another arose. The Grand Duke demanded that his claims to Schleswig be included in the treaties of peace at the con-

53. Choiseul to L'Hôpital, dispatches of Mar. 19, May 22, June 11, and June 24, 1759: *ibid.* 59, 383–384; 60, 159–161; 60, 212–213; and 60, 234.

54. Choiseul to L'Hôpital, July 24, 1759: *ibid.* 60, 316.

55. Bernstorff to Choiseul, July 28, 1759: *ibid.* 60, 336–337.

clusion of the war, and Brockdorff, the Grand Duke's minister for Holstein, assured L'Hôpital that the Grand Duke would never be satisfied until that duchy was in his family once again. When the Empress finally did decide to try to convince Peter of the necessity of the exchange, he retired to Oranienbaum struck down with illness and stated his intention of going home to Holstein. The Empress dismissed his petition impatiently as "emanating from a sick brain," but pressed him no further.[56]

The wrangling over Holstein proceeded apace into 1760, Choiseul attempting to prevent the stubbornness of the Grand Duke and his warlike pretentions from causing more mischief to the alliance than they had already done. Choiseul was forming another idea. Perhaps it would be wise, in the light of L'Hôpital's obvious incapacity with the Young Court, to think of attaching a new French Minister Plenipotentiary to the Grand Duke. Such an individual might be better able to handle matters with this avowed enemy more delicately and more successfully. Since Choiseul had already formed the idea of charming the Grand Duchess Catherine with a new lover, the two missions might well be combined. The Minister of Foreign Affairs now had a young man in mind.[57]

As to the Empress, Choiseul was coming to see in her life the only link in this Franco-Russian union. The presence in St. Petersburg of Poissonnier, the French doctor, at least regularized the life of the Empress to some degree. However, her cough remained and her fainting spells continued. The opposition of Elizabeth's favorites and of her regular doctors had prevented Poissonnier from making a complete examination of the Empress. His diagnoses continued to be made from afar. "Her main problem is an irresolution which prevents her from deciding on the use of indispensable remedies. . . . As her maladies leave her free to emerge often in public with the appearance of good health, she undoubtedly deceives herself on the danger." Her cough, frequent hemorrhages, and spots on her arms and legs convinced Poissonnier that the Empress suffered from a long-standing affliction of the womb and pos-

56. L'Hôpital to Choiseul, Oct. 27, 1759: *ibid.* 61, 192.

57. Choiseul to L'Hôpital, Oct. 2, 1759: *ibid.* 61, 99.

sibly a stomach ulcer, about which he could determine little at such a distance.[58]

Choiseul, ever concious of the costs involved and wary of expending talent and money where they were unneeded or unappreciated while France went begging for services, was angry. Poissonnier had been sent as an experienced and able doctor, but had not been able to approach the Empress nor assist her to repair her health for over five months. "There is an appearance that there has never been a serious question of employing his talents." If Poissonnier was not given charge of the health of the Empress by the end of April, he was ordered to return to France.[59] The threat worked; Poissonnier reached the Empress in early July and began to prescribe a diet and a remedy for her hysterical faintings. The doctor found her blood "heavy and scorbutic." [60]

By October, Poissonnier declared the Empress to be improving rapidly, but he could not persuade her to give up her shut-in life. "Poissonnier has pierced the passions of this Princess and those which arise from her palace, which is a kind of seraglio whose head is woman. There reign there factions, hatreds, and the ambitious views of favorites in place of pleasures. The Empress never emerges from it, and her health and her mind suffer from it." [61] Poissonnier decided that he had done all that was possible and asked for his recall. "The health of the Empress is repaired in as much as this is possible here; her troubles are her favorites who keep her imprisoned. I cannot cure her dissipations." [62] Treatments for the ailing L'Hôpital and for other members of the Russian court kept Poissonnier in Russia until December, 1760. His greatest problem with the Empress was her strict fast during the holy seasons, when "having a horror of fish, she lives on bread, confiture, kvass, and strong beer." Otherwise he found her much improved.[63]

58. Poissonnier to Choiseul, Feb. 28, 1759: *ibid.* 59, 280.
59. Choiseul to L'Hôpital, Mar. 19, 1759: *ibid.* 59, 385.
60. Poissonnier to Choiseul, dispatches of Sept. 17 and 24, 1759: *ibid.* 61, 38–39 and 63.
61. L'Hôpital to Choiseul, Dec. 11, 1759: *ibid.* 61, 341; see also Poissonnier to Choiseul, Oct. 27, 1759: *ibid.* 61, 187–191.
62. Poissonnier to Choiseul, Dec. 11, 1759: *ibid.* 61, 345.
63. Poissonnier to Choiseul, dispatches of Jan. 24 and Mar. 24, 1760: *ibid.* 64, 58–59 and 214.

The improved health of the Empress Elizabeth was the only bright spot in French relations with the Russian Court during Choiseul's first year at the helm of foreign affairs, and that was a true measure of the emptiness of the union. The Young Court was an obdurate enemy whose present obstructed legitimate aims of French policy and whose future threatened disaster. Only the weak buttress of Elizabeth's life held up the shaky union.

*v.*

## COMMERCE

Choiseul, on assuming his new post, found the conditions of a proposed commerce in Russia in a shambles. French agents in Russia were dealing secretly with Razumovskii, Hetman of the Ukraine who had been left out of Shuvalov's tobacco monopoly, in hopes that the Hetman might have the upper hand there someday and wish to do business. Outside this feeble intrigue the only activity related to commerce then underway was an open rift between the French Consul, Saint-Sauveur, and Ambassador L'Hôpital. Saint-Sauveur reported to his Ministry:

My reports would be more interesting sometimes if I dared make them so, but I have to deal with an Ambassador jealous of his shadow and worried about the slightest rumor of freedom on my part. . . . He has made life a living hell for me. . . . I have been warned that L'Hôpital wishes to establish a Vice-Consul here who would ultimately replace me. The man, Lacey, is well known as a French agent among the Tatars and is odious to the Russians.[64]

Choiseul tried to calm L'Hôpital, who had finally discovered that Saint-Sauveur had been provided by Bernis with a code for correspondence with the Ministry of Foreign Affairs. According to Choiseul's explanations, this code was intended only for emergencies.[65] L'Hôpital was not mollified and accused Saint-Sauveur of neglecting the aims of his mission. It was the

64. Saint-Sauveur to Ministry of the Marine, Mar. 23, 1759: *AN AE B I* 989. In code.

65. Choiseul to L'Hôpital, Apr. 10, 1759: *AMAE CP R* 60, 26.

fault of the Consul, said the Ambassador, that commercial developments were nonexistent.

Choiseul, after a rapid examination of the topic, discovered that the blame did not really rest with the Consul. He himself could not immediately find a plan to draw the commercial situation in Russia from its moribund state. "Although the King be of the intention to help his subjects share the commerce of the Russian Empire, I think it will be extremely difficult ever to succeed in this project, above all if the tobacco agreement is too weak to become the principal branch of our trade in Russia." [66]

L'Hôpital advocated that the French consider attempts at negotiating with the Russians a general commercial treaty which might serve the ends pursued through the tobacco agreements. The Ambassador was of the opinion that a well-defined situation between the two states might better serve to entice French merchants into running the risks of a Russian trade and might convince the Russians to withdraw their restrictive tariffs. [67]

Choiseul, meanwhile, had been running straight against the Russian resistance to his new policies. Those disappointments severely altered his views of Russian commercial negotiations for the remainder of the *rapprochement*. The Minister now insisted that his attitude on a general treaty of commerce with Russia was always to be subordinate to his desire for the pacification of Europe. If the former contributed to the latter, Choiseul would wish it undertaken at all costs. Under prevailing conditions, however, Choiseul felt that the negotiations for such a broad commercial treaty would be really useless, since France had failed completely to establish any companies in Russia on whose behalf a treaty would operate. Choiseul decided that if such talks were one means of keeping Russia friendly to France for a little while, they should be carried on for that purpose alone. Russia might be deceived concerning French good will, and such talks cost nothing. Commercial

66. Choiseul to L'Hôpital, June 17, 1759: *ibid.* 61, 223.

67. L'Hôpital to Choiseul, Sept. 24, 1759: *ibid.* 61, 60.

negotiations served henceforth as a convenient cover for France's search for peace.[68]

The middle of the year 1760, therefore, had brought an answer to Choiseul's analysis of two years before that commercial success would be one good test of the Franco-Russian ties. Commercial relations had gotten nowhere. Projects for the Black Sea were nebulous and viewed with suspicion by France. The Russians had raised a tariff against luxury goods that was deeply felt in France. The attempt to negotiate a purchase of Ukrainian tobacco had been wrecked by the Farmers-General of France. Now even the resultant tiny tobacco trade was destroyed by exorbitant Danish charges at the Sund that French pressures could not lower. Denmark even refused to accept French complaints, insisting that duties on processed tobacco had remained unchanged since 1645. The French felt that even here their failure to effect the Holstein exchange was working against them.[69]

Proposing to deceive the Russians into thinking the French still devoted to commercial development, Choiseul permitted Saint-Sauveur to proceed with plans to appoint vice-consuls. Peter Martin, a Belgian merchant in Moscow, was appointed for that city. Christopher Berens and Jacobus Poel, both Dutchmen, were appointed in Riga and Archangel, respectively. These men were never required to engage in any business for their employer, for there was nothing to do.[70]

Choiseul sent his approval to both Saint-Sauveur and L'Hôpital to begin the motions of commercial talks with the Russians whenever the Russians felt disposed, noting always that the purpose of the talks was to indicate French good will and lead Russia toward peace. The attempts to create any real commercial ties by negotiation were now over between the French and Russians. Both countries shared the blame for the failure of these attempts.

68. Choiseul to L'Hôpital, dispatches of Oct. 16 and 28, 1759: ibid. 61, 162 and 211.
69. Memoir by Saint-Sauveur, Feb. 18, 1760: ibid. 64, 120; Bernstorff to President Ogier, June 9, 1760: AN AE B I 987, 56–72.
70. Saint-Sauveur to Ministry of the Marine, June 24, 1760: AN AE B I 987; instruction to Peter Martin, Apr. 1, 1760: ibid. B I 987.

*vi.*
### SUMMARY

The internal fabric of French resources and the external fabric of French diplomacy were disintegrating together. It was Choiseul's misfortune to have presided over this decay. France was well supplied with allies, but nowhere could Choiseul find one to bring him peace. Choiseul's first year of office had witnessed the disintegration of the Russian *rapprochement*. Choiseul could not win Russian military aid against Britain nor Russian diplomatic assistance for a Continental peace. Neither was he able or interested in generating further resistance to mounting Russian advances in Eastern Europe. From the Young Court of Russia, France received only threats and obstructions. After mutual discouragement and failure, real attempts at commercial negotiations were finally abandoned for those based on mutual deception.

Choiseul's first months in office had been used to attempt to bring Russia actively into the war against the British and thus draw some utility from the useless and costly Franco-Russian ties. Choiseul had elaborated a devious method for obtaining such help, but Russia quite reasonably considered an entry into the British war to be ridiculous. Having failed in that, Choiseul hoped that Russia would at least deliver France from the Continental war by serving as the force for peace with bellicose Vienna. By forcing Austria to a rapid compromise peace, Russia would have both ended the war and saved France from delivering unwanted advice to its Austrian ally. New Russian victories in the east and a continuing determination to have a healthy share of the fruits of war convinced the Russian Ministry to do neither. As a matter of fact, when an Anglo-Prussian proposal for a congress to discuss peace was made, it was Russia who snatched this desirable meeting from France's grasp.

In the process of negotiating for that much-needed peace, Choiseul had slowly surrendered most of former French influence in Poland and the north. Pressed by financial failure and the requirements of Swedish, Danish, and Turkish friendships, France demonstrated in numerous ways that Poland was now beyond its official defense line. The King's Secret, long devoted to the cause of Polish resistance to Russia, had been so weakened by official French diplomacy and Russian pressure as to be useless.

Choiseul could really see no future for the Franco-Russian ties. The Young Court promised only a worsening of France's position: if the Russian union was a detriment now under the sympathetic eye of Elizabeth, how much more disastrous it would be in the hands of the Grand Duke Peter or the Grand Duchess Catherine. The Young Court's stand on Holstein obstructed the war and threatened the future. Further, the Grand Duke's love of Prussia was obsessive. Choiseul's use of a French doctor to maintain the wavering life of the Empress Elizabeth was no witness to the worth of the alliance, but only a recognition of its tenuous nature and the undoubted fact that it would soon be valueless. Commercial negotiations, upon which a firmer bond for the future might have been built between the two states, had degenerated into a mask for diplomatic maneuvers.

Actually, neither France nor Russia had given its partner any reason to be confident or trustful of the relationship. France had attempted to use Russia for purposes beyond and opposed to real Russian interests: to cement France's own ties with Vienna and to wage a limited war against Prussia without major rearrangements of Eastern Europe in Russia's favor. Russia, on the other hand, had taken advantage of French misfortunes to move into the French vacuum in Eastern Europe and to keep France tied to a Continental war which served Russian purposes but destroyed France. Trust on the part of either party would have been foolhardy. Choiseul's first year in office had witnessed the disintegration of the Franco-Russian ties.

All the bitterness of Choiseul's frustrated hopes for peace, his realization that France had been maneuvered into surrender of its dominant place in Europe by enemies and allies, and his anger that not even the simplest of his plans for Russia could succeed fell on the head of the Marquis de l'Hôpital.

Choiseul's displeasure flowered more fully with each new set-back for his policy. The Minister and the Ambassador clashed first over the amount of confidence to be placed in Michael Vorontsov. Choiseul's charges, for example, that Vorontsov was responsible for "the little aid we draw from Russia, the slowness and the incompetence of the Russian army, the refusal of Petersburg to join us against the English, the public partiality of the Young Court for England and Prussia," were shown im-mediately to Vorontsov by L'Hôpital.[71] Choiseul was incensed at such stupidity, and the withering dispatches from his pen grew in number and intensity:

Permit me to tell you that you amuse yourself a little too much with the trappings of your embassy and not enough with its solid content. You think that the Russian Empire can be our ally inde-pendently of Vienna. We do not agree in this. I myself think that Russia is our ally only by accident. . . . Reflect that the Turk, the Swede, and the Dane are our natural allies and the natural enemies of Russia. France has nothing personally to gain of the Russian Empire. On the contrary, we must fear that it will extend its des-potism in the north, that it will take too much influence in Ger-many, and that England, possessing Russian commerce, will once more make an ally of that state. The English will not have the same care that we have had to guard against Russian expansion in Eu-rope. . . . Therefore it is necessary to sustain our alliance with Russia as well as we can for as long as we can, without counting too much upon it. We must profit from the Russian union at least as far as securing an honorable and solid peace on the Continent.[72]

L'Hôpital, old and weary, convinced that court honors and court pleasures passed him by while he rotted on the King's service in frigid St. Petersburg, answered irascibly that ambas-sadors dealt in the possible and foreign ministers in the im-possible. L'Hôpital found it contradictory to be ordered to

71. Choiseul to L'Hôpital, dispatches of May 8, 1759 and July 8, 1759: *AMAE CP R* 60, 275.
72. Choiseul to L'Hôpital, Oct. 2, 1759: *ibid.* 61, 103. Albert Vandal, attempting to place all blame for the failure of Franco-Russian ties on Louis XV and the French, ignores continued Russian resistance to French needs. He blames L'Hôpital's failure to win Russian cooperation for peace on the influence of D'Éon. There is no evidence that anything but Russian good sense was responsi-ble for their passivity. See Vandal, *op. cit.*, p. 359.

make peace through the Russians on one hand and to avoid speaking honestly with the Russian Minister on the other.[73] L'Hôpital had a point, but Choiseul did not appreciate it.

Choiseul would no doubt have recalled the Ambassador in late 1759 had not L'Hôpital been a particularly good friend of Louis XV, and had not Choiseul feared to disturb the Russians by a precipitate removal of a likable representative. Choiseul could only make life miserable for the Marquis, cutting his salary and expenses to the bone and increasing the general nastiness of his communications.[74]

Choiseul finally decided on a course of action. He had four tasks which he felt his Ambassador in Russia had handled badly. French policy in Russia was finally reduced to four points:

1.   The achievement of peace through Russian instrumentation.
2.   The winning of the Grand Duchess to French interests.
3.   The temporary management of the Grand Duke in order to effect the exchange of Holstein.
4.   The continuation of commercial talks as a cover for peace diplomacy.

Choiseul determined to send a Minister to the Young Court who would be charged with these tasks and who would undercut Ambassador L'Hôpital. The Marquis de l'Hôpital, unimaginative, unenterprising, and deceived though he may have been, was certainly not to blame for the failure of the Franco-Russian ties. He was merely the scapegoat for Choiseul's resentment and disappointments.

73. L'Hôpital to Choiseul, Nov. 20, 1759: *AMAE CP R* 61, 103.

74. Choiseul to L'Hôpital, May 31, 1760: *AMAE CP R* 64, 353.

CHAPTER **6**

# The End of an Alliance

THE DUKE DE CHOISEUL determined on one last attempt to draw
some aid and comfort from French ties with Russia. The man
he chose to pursue his long-frustrated policies in Russia was
the Baron de Breteuil. Louis Charles Auguste le Tonnelier,
Baron de Breteuil, began his diplomatic career as Minister to
Cologne, and was only twenty-nine years old when he received
his Russian mission. Because of the peculiar nature of the
Russian embassy, Breteuil found himself a threefold agent: an
official minister of France under the jurisdiction of the Ambassador to Russia; an agent of Choiseul with instructions to
operate unbeknownst to the Ambassador; and an agent of the
Secret of Louis XV working in favor of the Polish party unknown to either L'Hôpital or Choiseul.

Breteuil's double role for Choiseul emanated naturally
from Choiseul's distrust of the Marquis de l'Hôpital. Choiseul
was unable or unwilling to remove the Ambassador from his
post. Yet the Foreign Minister had a program that he felt was
not being pursued actively, intelligently, or successfully by the
Ambassador. Therefore, Choiseul attempted to solve his problem by sending an auxiliary minister into Russia with two sets
of instructions: the first set, the official one, providing him with

a reason to be in St. Petersburg; the second set outlining Choiseul's need and desire for Russian help toward peace. Finally, Breteuil became a member of the Secret because that dying organization saw one final opportunity to reassert its interests in Eastern Europe by recapturing the long-alienated Russian post.

Choiseul had proposed the addition of Breteuil to the Russian embassy as early as October, 1759. Bernis had left behind the recommendation that "because of the coldness that exists between the King's Ministers and the Young Court, it would be desirable that a French gentleman insinuate himself into the good graces of the couple, especially the Grand Duchess, with whom England has had so much success in this manner." [1] Choiseul found the idea intriguing. A new lover for the Grand Duchess might change the dispositions of the imperial heirs and might, more practically, effect the exchange of Holstein. Now, most important of all, Choiseul needed a clever man to bypass his Ambassador and maneuver the Russians into procuring peace for France.

Choiseul informed L'Hôpital that Breteuil was sent into Russia "to be absolutely at your disposal there," and Breteuil's official instructions mentioned simply the need of L'Hôpital for some help in managing the Young Court.[2] Actually, Choiseul provided Breteuil with secret instructions. The Marquis de l'Hôpital, wrote Choiseul, was almost completely unreliable and inactive; the Ambassador had never succeeded in anything with the Young Court and was either afraid or unable to propose Choiseul's peace plans. Breteuil was commissioned to take on both tasks without the knowledge of his Ambassador — or if necessary in opposition to him.[3] Breteuil understood his task and assured his Minister that he undertook it with enthusiasm. "As to your general system on the present and future state of Europe, I am with you. I desire strongly to be able to give you

1. Bernis to L'Hôpital, Nov. 29, 1757: *AMAE CP R* 54, 313–314; Choiseul to L'Hôpital, Oct. 2, 1759: *ibid.* 61, 99.
2. Breteuil's instructions, Mar. 16, 1760, reprinted in Rambaud, *Recueil,* IX, 193. See also Choiseul to L'Hôpital, Mar. 1, 1760: *AMAE CP R* 64, 160.
3. Breteuil's secret instructions from Choiseul, March, 1760, reprinted in Boutaric, *op. cit.,* I, 250–51.

a first proof by inspiring the Russian Ministry with a taste for peace." [4]

Meanwhile, unknown to both the Marquis de l'Hôpital and the Duke de Choiseul, the Secret had awakened to its opportunity. Since the removal of Broglie and Tercier from their official posts, the Secret in its weakened condition had come to depend more and more upon properly placed agents in diplomatic posts. The retirement of the Chevalier Douglas from Russia had left only the subaltern D'Éon representing the Secret there. At the same time Poland had been slipping from French hands. Now the opportunity had arisen to reestablish some strength in the Secret in Russia and perhaps to stem the decline of French influence in Poland. Louis, learning of Choiseul's plans for Breteuil, wrote to Broglie:

The Count de Broglie will pass the enclosed orders to the Baron de Breteuil and will receive from the Baron the communication of his instructions, either verbally or in writing, which have been given to him by the Duke de Choiseul. Do this in order that, after having examined them with Tercier, these instructions from Choiseul may be rephrased to include the secrets relative to the intentions I have for Russia and Poland. Then send them to me so that I may approve them. [5]

Breteuil received his orders from the hand of the King on February 25, 1760, "admitting him into a secret correspondence with me which I have never wished to pass by my ministers. Broglie and Tercier alone have its direction." [6] Breteuil accepted and sent his instructions from Choiseul to the King. [7] The Chevalier d'Éon in St. Petersburg was notified of Breteuil's new position in the Secret and ordered to assist the Baron in his work. This work was relatively simple in the telling: to be aware of all matters relative to Poland and to attempt to influ-

---

4. Breteuil to Choiseul, May 13, 1760: *AMAE CP R* 63, 25–26.
5. Louis XV to Broglie, Feb. 24, 1760, reprinted in Boutaric, *op. cit.*, I, p. 246.

6. Louis to Breteuil, Feb. 25, 1760: *AMAE CP R* 62, 74.
7. Breteuil to Louis XV, Mar. 1, 1760, reprinted in Flassan, *op. cit.*, VI, 190.

ence the future election of Prince Xaxier of Saxony to the Polish throne.[8]

This was the Secret's last chance to stay alive in Eastern Europe. Despite Louis XV's interest in maintaining French influence in Poland, the King was frustrated by Choiseul's lack of interest. The new French Ambassador to Poland since June, 1760, Antoine de Voyer d'Argenson, Marquis de Paulmy, was closely attached to Choiseul and therefore thought too dangerous to initiate into the Secret. Durand, French Resident in Warsaw and long an accomplice of Broglie, was also removed by Choiseul. The King was powerless to resist Choiseul's abandonment of Poland.

Choiseul read Paulmy's instructions to the last Council; they promised free choice of a King but little money to the Poles. I cannot disapprove this, since the times absolutely do not permit it. . . . If I had vetoed the removal of Durand [from Warsaw] it would certainly have aroused Choiseul's suspicions and given him the means for discovering all of this, of which he is certainly now unaware.[9]

Broglie was even more distressed for the future of Poland. "I regard the recall of Durand as the last blow, capable of overturning the edifice that we have built with so much difficulty." [10] The King and Broglie were both depending upon Breteuil to fend off that final blow.

The young Baron, bearing the burden of three separate diplomatic missions that were mutually antagonistic, arrived in St. Petersburg on June 30, 1760. The first problem to face him was a clash of the official and the Secret diplomacies. Choiseul had planned the return of Poniatowsky from Warsaw to St. Petersburg in order to demonstrate France's friendly feelings toward the young Duchess. Choiseul was convinced that Catherine no longer cared for the handsome Pole and that

8. Broglie to Louis XV, Mar. 29, 1760, reprinted in Ozanam and Antoine, *op. cit.*, I, 113; Louis XV to D'Éon, Mar. 10, 1760, reprinted in Flassan, *op. cit.*, VI, 190.
9. Louis XV to Broglie, Apr. 5, 1760,
reprinted in Boutaric, *op. cit.*, I, 252–53. For Choiseul's directives to Paulmy, see Vandal, *op. cit.*, p. 353.
10. Broglie to Louis XV, Apr. 4, 1760, reprinted in Ozanam and Antoine, *op. cit.*, I, 117.

Breteuil would already have replaced him in Catherine's affections. The Empress of Russia detested Poniatowsky and, employing her secret correspondence with Louis XV, vigorously protested the return of the former lover of the Grand Duchess. The Secret agreed with the Empress. Tercier and Broglie resented the French Ministry's attempt to restore the dangerous Pole to St. Petersburg: it was foolish to tamper with the situation and give Breteuil a rival who was formidable and experienced. The King ordered Breteuil to oppose the return. "Choiseul is operating on another principle, being ignorant of my secret intentions. He thinks Poniatowsky's return will help us with the Grand Duchess. I do not think so." [11]

Breteuil responded by doing what any normal young courtier would do in the face of contradictory orders — nothing. A letter from Louis to the Empress Elizabeth acknowledged that the return of Poniatowsky to Russia naturally required her approval.[12] Since the attitude of Elizabeth toward Poniatowsky was clear, no such approbation was forthcoming. Poniatowsky did not return to Russia, and Choiseul never knew why. It was the Secret's last victory.

Once freed of this clash of official and Secret diplomacy, Breteuil put himself to his main mission with haste but with circumspection. "Although I much desire to act on your plans for peace, I do not wish to be too hasty for fear my speed will worry and displease the Ambassador." [13] Choiseul was far less concerned than Breteuil for L'Hôpital's tender feelings. The Foreign Minister complained bitterly that he had no idea of the state of the King's affairs in Russia. The matter of Austrian guarantees of Prussian territories to Russia, already made secretly and without French knowledge, also concerned Choiseul. It seemed to him that L'Hôpital was giving the Russians the impression that France would accept without opposition any of the arrangements made by Kaunitz. Choiseul informed

11. Louis XV to Breteuil, Aug. 16, 1760: *AMAE CP R* 62, 76–77; see also Elizabeth to Louis XV, May 26, 1760, reprinted in Boutaric, *op. cit.*, I, 255–256; Tercier to D'Éon, Aug. 16, 1760: *AMAE CP R* 62, 75.

12. Louis XV to Breteuil, Aug. 16, 1760, reprinted in Boutaric, *op. cit.*, I, 257.

13. Breteuil to Choiseul, July 11, 1760: *AMAE CP R* 63, 34.

Breteuil that if L'Hôpital continued to ignore the King's interest, "you will have the kindness to tell Vorontsov that you alone have instructions from your court to deal on such matters." [14]

Breteuil finally approached Vorontsov with a veiled program designed to implement Choiseul's peace policy. France proposed that Russia mediate at Vienna to end the continental war without overwhelming rewards for the allies. Vorontsov told Breteuil that he agreed with the French plan in principle, but that the next campaign would have to determine Russian actions. The truth of the matter was that Vorontsov was not the only Russian minister who had to be won over by France. It was now no secret that the man primarily responsible for the desire of the Empress to annex Prussian territory was her favorite, Ivan Shuvalov. Shuvalov's power in the War Conference was rising, even though he was not officially a member, since he carried the wishes of the Empress to its deliberations. Further, rumors were rife that Austria and Russia had taken Choiseul at his word and were negotiating on territorial cessions without France. [15] Meanwhile, in the interests of a realistic policy, Choiseul was being forced to give more careful thought to Russian territorial demands.

The expansion of Russia by allowing it to keep East Prussia is doubtless very dangerous in its consequences, as much for Germany and the north as for France. Unhappily, it is equally dangerous for France to oppose that expansion, not for the future but for the present. We cannot strongly resist Russian claims without driving them from the number of our allies, and that we cannot yet afford to do. Our only chance is to propose some less offensive solution. We might agree to cede the sovereignty of Courland to Russia. . . . It might be possible, if the Russians are stubborn, to give them Memel also. If the Russians were ever given East Prussia, France would have to be very sure that part of Pomerania was given to Sweden, that Danzig was guaranteed in its liberties, that the exchange of Holstein took place, and that Prussia was given Mecklen-

14. Choiseul to Breteuil, July 22, 1760: *ibid.* 63, 53–54.
15. Breteuil to Choiseul, July 22, 1760: *ibid.* 63, 65; Breteuil to L'Hôpital, Aug. 2, 1760: *ibid.* 63, 75; Choiseul to Breteuil, Aug. 10, 1760: *ibid* 63, 97.

burg. Thus, Sweden, Denmark, and Prussia might counterbalance the new Russian strength.[16]

France was being slowly dragged to recognition of the accomplished facts of Russian expansion. A year earlier France had stated categorically that no expansion would be permitted. Then, seeing the difficulty of continued resistance but desiring to avoid offending France's other allies, Choiseul had relegated the decisions to Austria and Russia. Now Choiseul was being led to consider French acquiescence in those decisions. Choiseul found this situation to be a sad reflection on the whole system: he could neither grant nor refuse Russian demands without doing serious damage to French interests. An alliance, he felt, should procure mutual advantages, but "the re-establishment of relations with that court in Petersburg is worth up to now only the doubtful satisfaction of ending the coldness and anger which reigned between France and Russia for some years, and nothing else." [17]

To bend Vorontsov more surely to the idea of peace and to give the Chancellor a weapon in the Conference against Ivan Shuvalov, Choiseul empowered Breteuil to promise subsidies to Russia when the war would be concluded. Choiseul offered money, hoping to avoid the distasteful question of cessions. Choiseul felt that Russia might well bind itself to Great Britain by subsidy treaties again when the war was done, in which case immediate service was more important than future fears and France's subsidies would not be paid anyway. France wished above all to appear, in Austrian eyes, as still sincerely committed to the war, and "France is willing to pay Russia to get this business done for us. . . . All things considered, if Russia could procure peace in Germany this winter without the King of France being even slightly suspected at Vienna, we think that France cannot pay dearly enough for the service." [18]

16. Choiseul, Memoir on peace and Russian claims, July, 1760: *AMAE MD R* 31, 4.
17. Choiseul to L'Hôpital, Aug. 10, 1760: *AMAE CP R* 64, 461.
18. Choiseul to Breteuil, Aug. 24, 1760: *ibid.* 63, 122. Choiseul was determined to avoid giving Vienna cause for alarm about French determina-

tion, especially since the arrival of the strongly worded statement from Kaunitz of Jan. 30, 1760. See Waddington, *La guerre*, III, 506–7. Breteuil forwarded all of Choiseul's plans to the Secret; see Breteuil to Louis, Sept. 5, 1760: *AMAE CP R* 62, 127–129.

Choiseul could not clear from his thinking the belief that money ruled Russia. "Money is the true grease which makes that court run." [19] He deceived himself. Russia was aware of its true interests. If foreign subsidies and bribes appeared successful in determining Russian actions, it was usually when the desires of briber and bribed coincided. It was easy, in other words, to bribe the Russians to do as they wished. Breteuil saw this more clearly than his Minister: "If things go badly in this campaign, Russia will do as France wishes; if not, they will ignore us." [20] Vorontsov was more circumspect but no less clear: "I personally agree that peace would be the wisest course . . . but the Empress will not consider it, and none of those around her share my opinion." [21]

Once more external events intervened to pour salt into France's open wounds. In early October, 1760, Russian troops entered Berlin. Although their stay was brief and they departed hastily on news that Frederick was flying to the aid of his city, the Russians were entrenched in Brandenburg. The French were stunned and frightened, and Breteuil judged from the joy at the Russian court that "it is all too probable that Russian demands and intransigence will be solidified." [22]

Russia did indeed feel strengthened. The Russians began to interfere in the affairs of the coming Swedish Diet with a public declaration of support for the royal party against the French party. Even more dangerous, Vorontsov made an offhand comment to Breteuil that Poland "was a poor country which, within the next fifty years, ought to be divided among its neighbors." [23] Just three years before, no Russian would have dared make such a comment to a representative of the

19. Choiseul to Breteuil, Aug. 24, 1760: *ibid.* 63, 123. See also comments of Choiseul quoted in Anderson, *op. cit.*, p. 275.
20. Breteuil to Choiseul, Sept. 5, 1760: *AMAE CP R* 63, 128.
21. Breteuil to Choiseul, Oct. 15, 1760: *ibid.* 63, 225.
22. Breteuil to Choiseul, Oct. 28, 1760: *ibid.* 63, 253. For the general effects of this event on Russian determination, see Jesse D. Clarkson, *A History of Russia* (New York: Ran-

dom House, 1961), p. 239; Hans Rogger, *National Consciousness in Eighteenth Century Russia* (Cambridge: Harvard University Press, 1960), p. 259.
23. Breteuil to Choiseul, Nov. 16, 1760: *AMAE CP R* 63, 298. This was indeed Vorontsov's opinion; see N. D. Chechulin, *Vneshniaia politika Rossii v nachale tsarstvovaniia Ekateriny II, 1762–1774* (St. Petersburg: 1896), p. 208.

King of France: to a representative of the Secret it was the final shame.

The subsequent retreat of Russian troops from Brandenburg and the disastrous campaigns of the Austrians in the south moderated Russian activity somewhat. France, however, had seen all the lowering possibilities of Russian force. Persuaded by this demonstration of Russian ability to carry on the war, Choiseul wavered even more in his Russian policy. He still maintained that to achieve the rewards that Austria and Russia expected from the war would require an annihilation of Prussia, which the allies could not accomplish without many more campaigns. Choiseul wanted to escape either the Continental or the British war, or both, as soon as possible. Therefore, he proposed to Breteuil that France consider acquiescing in the cession of East Prussia to Russia at the peace if Austria took only Glatz and Russia helped to satisfy Denmark, Saxony, and Sweden. Choiseul felt that peace would be nearer if Russia were allowed to take East Prussia, which it held, and Austria gave up Silesia, which it could not hold. The newest element in Choiseul's plan, actually the center of his thought, was that "Russia enter into the making of peace between England and France, so that Russian power being brought to bear in our favor, France will obtain the best possible conditions." [24] French policy had been reduced by the horrors of war to its simplest terms. Choiseul would give French support to all Russian demands if Russia would intervene diplomatically in the Anglo-French war and force Britain to make a reasonable peace. It was the last service Choiseul could ask of the relationship.

Breteuil proposed Choiseul's new package to Vorontsov: Russia to receive East Prussia, Russia to provide cash payments to indemnify the Saxons, Russia to exchange Holstein with Denmark, Austria to receive Glatz but not Silesia, France and Russia to pay subsidies to the Swedes, and Russia to bring its weight to bear on Britain to procure the best possible peace terms for France. [25] Choiseul was willing to acknowledge a

---

24. Choiseul to Breteuil, Oct. 24, 1760: *AMAE CP R* 63, 248; Waddington, *op. cit.*, III, 463–65.

25. Breteuil to Choiseul, Nov. 26, 1760: *AMAE CP R* 63, 324.

major loss in European power for that last item. He had little choice. What prompted Choiseul to make the final surrender before Russian demands was clearly put by Breteuil:

The project for a general peace that we have evolved seems necessary enough. . . . I tell you plainly that I was not too interested in cementing a direct union with the Russian Empire, since I thought we could handle the war with England without its aid. But since I see the reluctance of the Spanish, the success of the English in Canada, the dangers in Pondicherry, and the impossibility of capturing the Electorate of Hanover, I sincerely believe that no one in our position ought to neglect the ties that we have so painfully and expensively created with Russia. We must above all engage Russia to share the weight of our burden against the English. . . . The problems that we will create by our cessions to Russia cannot be helped now.[26]

In addition, Choiseul persisted in holding vague ideas about negating cessions to Russia in the future. He believed that the Russian Empire would be helpless without French or British gold, that only "if financiers give it the means, could this Empire be formidable. . . . You must carry all obstacles to such events. Thus, if French financiers have a project in Russia . . . we must seek to destroy their work and decry their persons." [27]

These new programs for peace agreed upon between Choiseul and Breteuil completely removed L'Hôpital from the current of affairs. The Ambassador continued to work and to correspond with Choiseul, unaware that new projects were being negotiated under his nose. From the arrival of Breteuil until L'Hôpital's departure in June, 1761, the Ambassador was engaged with Choiseul in a correspondence of no consequence. Choiseul wrote secretly to Vorontsov in December, 1760, that "as the health of the Marquis de l'Hôpital does not permit him to pursue the details of negotiations with the necessary agility, the King will address all instructions for treating these objects to the Baron de Breteuil." [28]

26. Breteuil to Choiseul, Nov. 27, 1760: *ibid.* 63, 353.
27. Choiseul to Breteuil, Nov. 28. 1760: *ibid.* 63, 367.
28. Choiseul to Vorontsov, Dec. 18, 1760: *ibid.* 65, 241.

The next step in activating Choiseul's latest plan for Russia was a French declaration on peace to be delivered to the Empress. Choiseul was impatient for Russian support of a cessation of hostilities and the opening of two conferences to discuss peace, one at Paris for the Continental war and one at London for the naval war. Things were beginning to look more hopeful. Austria's miserable performance in the field had begun to convince Vienna that the relinquishing of some of its interests in Silesia might be required. Negotiations between Austria and France on a peace were coming increasingly to the open.[29]

Vorontsov was tempted by the French proposals to Russia, no doubt because these proposals promised Russia tangible benefits in return for intangible promises. In the Russian Conference, however, Ivan Shuvalov was still resisting proposals to make Russian territorial gains dependent on any Russian help to France against the British. Shuvalov held that any such services to France went beyond the terms of the original Franco-Russian ties and were, in any case, unnecessary. Russia, according to the favorite, had won its right to compensation by force of arms and could only be denied it by the same means.[30] Breteuil offered 800,000 livres to Vorontsov if the Chancellor could bring the conference over, but the French diplomat was not hopeful. "All the Russians now follow Shuvalov in this matter."[31] The impasse was broken by the Empress, who made one of her rare personal appearances before the Conference. The result was a counterproposal to the French.

The Russians proposed that Austria keep what its armies had already won, a small section of Silesia. Sweden would receive a tiny section of Prussian Pomerania. Russia would be guaranteed East Prussia until an indemnity was paid by the Prussians, after which Russia would cede that territory to Poland in return for a border rectification in the Ukraine. The Empress of Russia would then offer her good offices to mediate

29. Breteuil to Choiseul, Jan. 30, 1761: *AMAE CP R* 66, 60. See also R. N. Bain, *Daughter of Peter the Great*, p. 297.
30. Notes on Russian Conference of Feb. 1 and 4, 1761: *AMAE CP R* 66, 117–126.
31. Breteuil to Choiseul, Feb. 6, 1761: *ibid.* 66, 127.

between Britain and France. Meanwhile, Russia would agree to
no cessation of hostilities. The Empress then sent a letter to
Louis XV by the secret way which advocated direct ties between the two states, excluding Austria, as guarantees for the
future.[32]

Russian plans for East Prussia were now published to the
world. If Russia could hold this area, Poland would be forced
by fear of encirclement to deed away contested lands in the
east. There was, of course, no real guarantee that Russia would
live up even to the promise of ceding back East Prussia. In
return for these concessions, Russia offered, not pressure on
Britain nor a threat of war to drive Britain to a peace with
France, but merely "good offices" toward peace in London.
The Russians also vetoed the French idea of two European conferences to deal with the two wars. Ivan Shuvalov supported
the Empress Elizabeth in this preference for a general European congress, because "the Empress flatters herself to be the
first Russian sovereign admitted to a general congress on the
affairs of Europe and does not want to diminish that glory." [33]

Choiseul had again been outplayed by the Russians. Forced
finally to accept Russian claims on Prussia that would ultimately
be at the expense of Poland, Choiseul found that Russia immediately revised the price it was willing to pay. The French
Minister had exposed his weakness by his gradual acceptance
of Russian demands in return for aid against Britain. Russia
knew, as a good bargainer, that Choiseul could be forced to
accept less. In return for Russian acceptance of a European
congress and Russian "good offices" in London, Choiseul acknowledged French withdrawal from Eastern Europe. He
accepted the Russian insistence on one congress, gave over his
desire for a one-year cessation of hostilities during such a
Congress, and agreed to a Russian hold on East Prussia at

32. Response to King of France, Feb.
24, 1761: *ibid.* 66, 132–160; Bain,
*Daughter*, p. 298–99. There is no evidence that supports Rambaud's statement that "Choiseul would have accepted this alliance with joy; but
Louis XV rejected it obstinately."
Rambaud, *Russes et Prussiens*, p. 336.

Rambaud ignores the difficulty of the
Young Court. There is every evidence
that Choiseul and his King were united
at least in distrust of the Russian ties,
present and future.
33. Breteuil to Choiseul, Feb. 15,
1761: *AMAE CP R* 66, 187.

war's end.[34] In return, Vorontsov wrote to the Russian Ambassador at London, ordering him "to give to Mister Pitt a letter which will be sent to you by Choiseul, which will contain the first peace offerings of France to England." [35] With that delivery Russia considered that it had done its part.

Choiseul could not be happy with the results of his policy. He suspected that Russian assistance with the British would be only a token to satisfy the terms of the agreement. There was nothing more to give Russia and nothing more to expect of it. Choiseul determined "to follow, together with Sweden, the route we think best toward peace, and to force the Empresses to acquiesce in the accomplished fact." Frustration made him angry. "If the Empresses will not help us to make an immediate peace, we are determined to negotiate with our enemies without further submitting ourselves to the fantasies and whims of Vienna and Petersburg." [36] Breteuil continued to hope that agreements on Russian territorial gains would ultimately be worth something to France. "The Poles will not be happy with it, and the Turks will be angry enough; but these considerations must give way to the advantage of assuring or at least facilitating the return of our possessions in America." [37] But disaster had finally reached the point of diminishing returns: there was little more for France to fear because there was little more for France to lose.

The discussions concerning a European congress dragged on in London, mediated through the Russian embassy. Choiseul hoped, of course, that Russian efforts would bring peace or, in the frustration of their failure, would convince the Russians to threaten or even attack the British. Choiseul hoped for such an event, but did not believe it would ever happen. He was disappointed in his hope and correct in his belief. Russian mediation with Britain accomplished nothing.[38]

As months dragged by without results, France abandoned

34. Choiseul to Choiseul-Praslin, Feb. 22, 1761: *ibid.* 66, 252.
35. Vorontsov to Galitsin, Feb. 25, 1761: *ibid.* 66, 242.
36. Choiseul to Choiseul-Praslin, Mar. 18, 1761: *ibid.* 66, 320.

37. Breteuil to Choiseul, Apr. 10. 1761: *ibid.* 67, 45.
38. Choiseul to Breteuil, Apr. 12, 1761: *ibid.* 67, 54. See V. N. Aleksandrenko, *Russkie diplomaticheskie agenty v Londone v XVIII v.* (Warsaw, 1827), II, Section IV.

all hopes of Russian aid. Choiseul, in mid-April, 1761, made almost servile offers to Britain in the realization that the war was lost. This French willingness to surrender its empire was viewed by the Russians with "astonishment." Breteuil himself confessed to his Minister that he did not understand these extreme concessions and could only suppose that "we wish to frighten Spain and all Europe by the extent of our sacrifices." [39] Despite France's willingness to humble itself before Britain, the preparations for a peace congress at Augsburg were still incomplete. No doubt sensing the perfunctory nature of Russian interest in the French case, Pitt proposed even more degrading conditions to the French. Britain would conserve all its conquests in America and in India, and France would demolish Dunkirk and evacuate all conquests in Germany and the Low Countries. No sane and self-respecting representative of France could subscribe to those conditions, even in the prevailing state of bankruptcy and defeat.[40]

The war at home and abroad was renewed by France with sadness but resurrected determination. Choiseul notified the expectant French diplomats that "it is no longer a question of suspending hostilities. . . . I am writing by order of the King to the armies to tell them that His Majesty's intention is that they pursue their military operations with the greatest vigor once again." [41] Choiseul returned to the war with a new plan that British intransigence had finally made possible: a family compact with the King of Spain to bring Spanish forces into the war against Britain. Spain had grown more frightened each year by British gains, and the harsh terms proposed by London in 1761 only confirmed Spanish fears.[42]

39. Breteuil to Choiseul, Apr. 23, 1761: *AMAE CP R 67*, 68.

40. Memoir of Oct. 21, 1761:*AMAE MD F 571*, 36–59; printed as "Mémoire historique sur la negociation de la France et de l'Angleterre, despuis le 26 mars 1761 jusqu'au 20 septembre de la même année" (Paris: *Imprimerie Nationale*, 1761). See also Anderson, *op. cit.*, p. 249; and Vandal, *op. cit.*, p. 402.

41. Choiseul to Breteuil, May 30, 1761: *AMAE CP R 67*, 133.

42. Choiseul to Breteuil, Aug. 5, 1761: *ibid.* 67, 206. It is interesting to note that L'Hôpital had proposed what he called "a castle in Spain" in Oct., 1760. The Ambassador recommended a family compact with Spain. Choiseul at that time replied that L'Hôpital's notions were "far fetched and ridiculous." L'Hôpital to Choiseul, Oct. 14, 1760: *ibid.* 65, 91; and Choiseul to L'Hôpital, Jan. 7, 1761: *ibid.* 65, 255.

In effect, the Franco-Russian *rapprochement* was over. It is legitimate to see the family compact with Spain as the concluding act of that union. Choiseul saw plainly that Russia did not intend to threaten Britain and force a reasonable peace for France, for St. Petersburg had been unimpressed by the failure of peace negotiations. Russia's good offices to end the British war had been offered with no sincerity and no effect. France had resigned the remains of its protectorate over Eastern Europe for those good offices and had found them useless. Choiseul's approach to Spain naturally and effectively turned France's back to Russia.

Choiseul hoped for nothing more from his Russian allies. He sent orders to the embassy in St. Petersburg warning his agents "that the King's intention is that you contract no further engagements, pecuniary or otherwise, with the Russian ministers." [43] Breteuil was further instructed to inform the Russian Ministry that France had little reason to be pleased with Russia's role in the complete breakdown of Anglo-French negotiations. Choiseul was almost certain that Russia now intended neither to make peace nor to fight. Russia could await the defeat of enemy or ally with equal expectation of reward. [44]

It had been evident to the directors of the Secret that Breteuil had been on the horns of a dilemma through the whole period of disintegration. Broglie and Tercier did not like Breteuil's choice. Early in 1761, Tercier had informed Breteuil that the Secret did not approve France's part in either the cession of East Prussia to Russia or the rectification of Polish borders in Russia's favor. [45] Choiseul's program for securing Russian assistance to force Britain to peace was too dangerous for French influence in Poland. Broglie considered that Breteuil, in pursuing Choiseul's plans, had betrayed the trust of the Secret. "The Baron de Breteuil, in executing the orders of Choiseul, has lost sight of the views which were contained in

43. Choiseul to Breteuil, Aug. 27, 1761: *ibid.* 67, 233.
44. Choiseul to Breteuil, Sept. 27, 1761: *ibid.* 67, 294.

45. Tercier to Breteuil, Mar. 23, 1761: *ibid.* 62, 84.

the instructions provided him by the Secret. I think it essential that he be recalled." [46]

Breteuil had felt the contradictions in his double orders. In April the Baron replied to the Secret that he knew well enough that Broglie wished to accept no Russian claims that would work to the detriment of Poland, but it seemed to Breteuil that these cessions to Russia might lead "to the restoration of Canada and other good things." [47] The King himself saw the problem, but, as usual, could provide no sensible solution.

I have good reason to believe that any authorization to Russia to seize parts of Poland would only anger the Turks against me. . . . I would pay too dearly, in that case, for an alliance contracted with a state whose intrigues render useless the very orders of the sovereign. We can have no confidence in the most solemn Russian obligation. I see the difficulties of conciliating the instructions which I send you through the Secret and those which you receive from the Duke de Choiseul, but I exhort you to make every effort to lead Choiseul to more favorable principles on Poland.[48]

It seems impossible that Louis did not know his chief Minister well enough to see how ridiculous it was to order Breteuil to change Choiseul's principles. As a matter of fact, Louis and Choiseul had strikingly similar views on the costliness and dangers of the Russian union; they differed primarily in their analysis of the possibilities of doing anything about it. Breteuil replied sadly to the King that he really saw no way of undoing Choiseul's plans or Russian intentions. The only way for Breteuil to impede Choiseul's program for peace was for the Baron to contradict absolutely all Choiseul's orders. That Breteuil had neither the courage, the power, nor the desire to do. Breteuil further maintained that Choiseul's program was simply a recognition of the reality of Russian power. The

46. Broglie to Louis XV, June 8, 1761: reprinted in Ozanam and Antoine, op. cit., I, 128. See also Tercier to Breteuil, June 10, 1761: AMAE CP R 62, 86.

47. Breteuil to Louis XV, Apr. 22, 1761: ibid. 62, 263.
48. Louis XV to Breteuil, June 8, 1761: ibid. 62, 86. See also Vandal, op. cit., p. 400.

Baron could not manage the future of Poland, he declared, because Poland was not in his hands.[49]

Truly, the future of Poland was not in Breteuil's hands in particular or in France's hands in general. The King was operating on memories rather than realities. Breteuil was not recalled through the influence of the Secret because Choiseul was too strong. On the other hand, Paulmy, Choiseul's chosen Ambassador in Poland, had seen the need for political reform in the republic, and Choiseul had to calm "this eagerness by opposing to each of his initiatives the eternal maxims of anarchy." The remnants of the Secret's correspondence from Russia were a sad list of Russian encroachments on Poland and Russian plans for the future of the republic.[50] The official policy of France had at first unwittingly and then unwillingly abandoned Poland and destroyed the work of the Secret. The King's Secret had now to turn its attention to affairs with Britain. The organization in Eastern Europe was dead, and France would make no more Polish kings.

As to the Young Court, France was no more successful. Breteuil seemed to have been not in the least attractive to the Grand Duchess Catherine. "I can't get near the Grand Duchess; she is isolated from me." The only service which France could perform for the Grand Duchess was a minor one. The Princess of Zerbst, Catherine's mother, died in Paris during 1760. Catherine was much afraid that her correspondence with her mother would become public or at least come to the eyes of the Empress. At her request the French government found and burned the letters of the Princess of Zerbst. Catherine showed no gratitude whatever. The amorous capacities of Breteuil were transferred to less official business.[51]

Further, Breteuil's appearance had no effect on the exchange of Holstein. Denmark had continued to urge the Grand Duke Peter to exchange his Duchy of Holstein for less provoc-

---

49. Breteuil to Louis XV, Aug. 24, 1761: *AMAE CP R* 62, 351–352. The events of 1761 make it extremely difficult to accept Vandal's judgment that "France had committed a grave error in neglecting the means offered by Russia to hasten our peace with England." Vandal, *op. cit.*, p. 402.

50. Breteuil to Louis XV, dispatches of Sept. 25 and 29, 1761: *AMAE CP R* 62, 377–379 and 380–382.

51. Breteuil to Choiseul, Nov. 16, 1760: *ibid.* 63, 290.

ative lands in Germany. Denmark, sensing failure, was threatening to enter the war on the side of the King of Prussia. In July, 1760, a Danish threat to France almost precipitated that event. Only the strongest French assurances of help in the exchange averted a rupture. France was frightened. Choiseul and Breteuil knew, however, as Denmark was coming to know, that "there was not a chance in the world of succeeding with the Grand Duke in the exchange." [52]

Choiseul determined upon a double game. While actually in the process of giving in to the Russians on their territorial demands, Choiseul attempted to placate Denmark by guaranteeing that Russia would never receive territory in Poland or in Prussia. Choiseul hoped to pacify the Danes by indicating that Russia would emerge unrewarded from the war. The whole point was "to drag out these negotiations between Russia and Denmark while France makes peace. I do not think we should further embarrass or endanger ourselves by struggling for the interests of both these powers which menace us." [53] French efforts at St. Petersburg to carry out this time-consuming conciliation were at least partially successful, and thus prevented a Russian provocation of a Danish war that would have burdened France terribly. Choiseul instructed Breteuil:

Keep at this Holstein affair although it be useless. We are really convinced that this negotiation will never succeed. . . . Nevertheless, as it is essential to French interests in the present circumstances to amuse Denmark by continuing these talks, we ought to neglect no means to do so.[54]

France had come no nearer an understanding with the Young Court than in preceding years. Holstein was simply an external sign of the Grand Duke's intractability. France never had the slightest chance of winning the obstinate spirit of the Grand Duke nor the calculating mind of the Grand Duchess. The Grand Duke was too prejudiced and the Grand Duchess

52. Breteuil to Choiseul, Dec. 7, 1760: *ibid.* 63, 373; Count Bernstorff, *Correspondance du Comte Bernstorff avec le Duc de Choiseul* (Copenhagen: Ministry of Foreign Affairs of Denmark, 1871), letters for October to Dec., 1760, *passim.*

53. Choiseul to Breteuil, Jan. 18, 1761: *AMAE CP R 66, 32.*

54. Choiseul to Breteuil, Nov. 13, 1761: *ibid.* 61, 341.

too intelligent to bind themselves to French interests that could never be to Russia's benefit or to their own.

France and Russia carried on their commercial negotiations in the same spirit of mutual deception. There was little hope of arriving at a commercial treaty before the peace and little chance in finding any interest in it afterward. Choiseul now held that "the English continue to play the absolutely dominant role in Russian commerce, so it does not seem necessary or pressing to conclude a treaty. Of course, we need not tell the Russians that." [55] Broglie, avowed enemy of Franco-Russian ties, delivered an adequate summary of commercial relations:

In the alliance between France and Russia, one of the baits used to prolong the error and illusion of it was a treaty of commerce between the two powers. Negotiations for such a treaty had begun more than once. They were taken up again and again, or, to tell the truth, they seemed to be taken up; because at bottom these negotiations had never been serious nor ever would be.[56]

The year 1761 was taken up in part with discussions between the French and Russians on the draft of a commercial treaty. Breteuil bore out the contention of Broglie that the Russians were not serious. According to him, Pëtr Shuvalov and the other merchants "have consulted a crowd of ignorant and badly intentioned visionaries who produce long memoirs which prove the uselessness of commerce with France." France could not even secure a downward revision of the Russian tariffs while the talks were in progress.[57]

The commercial talks themselves were mere wrangles that extended for months over miniscule points of procedure. The Russians, for example, insisted for many weeks on a point totally unacceptable to the French: that Russian commercial fleets entering French ports should have no restrictions on the number of non-Russians employed in their crew. France in-

55. Choiseul to Breteuil, Sept. 4, 1760: *ibid*. 63, 126.
56. Broglie to Louis XV, Apr. 16, 1773, reprinted in Boutaric, *op. cit.*, II, 53.

57. Breteuil to Choiseul, Mar. 18, 1761: *AMAE CP R* 66, 324; Choiseul to Breteuil, May 13, 1761: *ibid*. 66, 106–107.

sisted that it could not allow itself to be inundated with foreigners in time of war. The Russians then insisted on being treated as well as the most favored nation. Since France extended abnormal privileges to the Swiss, this clause was also unacceptable. The Russians further insisted on the freedom of the Orthodox religion in France, which the French would not consider.[58] The talks continued into December of 1761 without result. No treaty was ever signed. Choiseul was determined that these talks should serve only to convince Russia to assist France in other more important matters. His analysis summarized the years of commercial discussions.

These commercial projects with Russia are as old as our relations with that Empire. They have been without effect and nothing real or substantial has ever resulted from the 20,000 francs a year we spend to pay a consul to do nothing. It has been seven years since the last French ship appeared in Saint Petersburg. In the last forty years there have been fewer than ten. . . . I cannot speak of what has gone on in the past few years, because it has been nothing at all. The Russians still wish to give the impression of something having been done commercially with France. . . . They send memoirs to our court and we send some to theirs. However, I must repeat, nothing has been done, nor is there anything to do.[59]

As 1761 drew to a close, Choiseul had turned France's back upon Russia. Choiseul's invocation of the compact with Spain and his determination to concentrate French attention on the naval war was an admission that the Continental system had been a disaster. French diplomacy, after the failure of British negotiations and Russian mediation, simply aimed at keeping Russia from joining the enemy; that was the last service which France asked of Russia. Yet, of course, even that was soon to be refused.

As the worth of the Franco-Russian union faded, so also, symbolically, did the life of the Empress of Russia. France

58. Memoir on Russian commerce from 1760 to 1766, Dec., 1766: AN AE B III 432: observations on commercial treaty, Apr. 11, 1761: AMAE CP R 62, 292–303; Russian counter project, July 22, 1761: ibid. Suppl.

10, 282; observations by Controller-General of France, Sept. 17, 1761: ibid., Suppl. 10, 290.
59. Choiseul, Memoir, Oct., 1761: AMAE MD R 7, 102.

had long known that the heirs of the Empress promised nothing for France but grief and upheaval. It was Breteuil's opinion that there would be no change in the succession, no regency for the Grand Duke Paul, no restoration of Prince Ivan. There was little point in the French prompting or assisting a *coup d'état,* since the French finally realized that there were no French servants in St. Petersburg. Choiseul knew "how useless it would be to pluck that cord at Saint Petersburg." [60]

The Empress suffered a grievous attack of fits and unconsciousness in early December. The lords and ladies of St. Petersburg were as confused as the French over the future. Ivan Shuvalov, sensing the near departure of his protectress, began to bank funds secretly in France through Breteuil. [61] No doubt similar precautions were underway in many St. Petersburg households. On December 24 the Empress was struck down with fever. Despite assurances given everywhere of her speedy recovery, the Empress Elizabeth Petrovna of Russia died on January 5, 1762. It is misleading to ascribe the end of the Franco-Russian alliance to the death of the Empress Elizabeth. The alliance was already over. The death of the Empress served to illustrate the fact of the union's disintegration and placed a neat and final seal on its agonized life.

On January 7 the Emperor Peter III of Russia ordered the removal and exile of all Frenchmen presently serving in his state in any capacity. [62] This also was symbolic. Within hours of his accession to the throne of the Tsars, Peter had sped emissaries on their way to Frederick of Prussia with offers of friendship and alliance. In one rapid movement Russia foresook its allies and joined actively with the enemy. [63] Choiseul took the blow calmly, an evidence that the reversal of the new Russian Emperor was no surprise. The Minister had known that the official end of the Russian *rapprochement* would come cleanly and quickly, although he was a bit shocked at the commitment of Russian troops to Frederick's cause. Still,

60. Breteuil, Memoir, Nov., 1761: *ibid.,* 265; Choiseul to Breteuil, Oct. 20, 1761: *AMAE CP R* 67, 309.

61. Breteuil to Choiseul-Praslin, Dec. 24, 1761: *ibid.* 67, 432.

62. *Archives du Théâtre Imperiale de Saint Petersbourg* (St. Petersburg, 1890–1909), II, 61.

63. Shchebalskii, *Politicheskaia sistema Petra III,* p. 27–30.

THE END OF AN ALLIANCE

France could take some consolation. All the vagaries of Russia on Holstein now belonged to the King of Prussia, and all the managements and contradictions of French policy could be forgotten by Choiseul. Would it be so surprising if such a diplomatic disaster as the loss of Russia to the war or even Russia's reversal of alliances should have been greeted in chambers of the French Ministry with a secret little sigh of relief?

CHAPTER **7**

# Conclusions

THE FRANCO-RUSSIAN *rapprochement* of 1756–1761 was a
hastily created by-product of the diplomatic revolution and
the Seven Years' War. The reopening of Franco-Russian relations in 1756, after a hiatus of eight years, had been carried
out by an obscure Scot serving as a French agent, the Chevalier Douglas. The limited nature of his two missions in 1755–
56 was indicative of the haphazard and spasmodic nature of
the reunion effected between the two states. Douglas first went
into Russia as an agent of the King's Secret and of the French
Ministry to spy out the results of recent Anglo-Russian military agreements, and then after the Treaty of Westminster he
had returned to convince the Russians to retire from those
British commitments. In neither case had the purpose of his
mission been the reopening of relations or the discussion of
any agreements. Only after Austria and France had signed the
defensive First Treaty of Versailles in May, 1756, was Douglas
permitted to treat for the renewal of Russian contacts, and
then only reluctantly and in the wake of Austrian leadership.
His first act as chargé d'affaires in Russia — the signing under
Austro-Russian pressures of a secret agreement for future

194

French aid against the Turks — showed the looming dangers of these new ties so cavalierly assumed.

When Frederick precipitated the Seven Years' War, long planned by Russia and Austria, his act invoked the defensive clauses of the Austro-French treaty and the offensive clauses of the Austro-Russian treaty and brought Russia and France together as auxiliaries of Austria. At the outset France, Austria, and Russia agreed simply and only on the necessity of waging the war against Prussia. Beneath this superficial agreement were serious disagreements as to the war's purposes. Austria and Russia were fighting for specific additions of territory of great significance to them: Austria obviously coveted Silesia and Glatz, while the Russians aimed at parts of Poland and East Prussia that would weaken Prussia and give Russia a foothold in Poland and a possible entry into the German states. Despite subsequent temporary agreement with Austria on some minor dynastic gains, French aspirations were primarily diplomatic rather than territorial. Isolated in Europe, the Abbé Bernis and his party wished to solidify an alliance with Austria which they believed indispensable to French interests. However, Prussia was not long ago a French ally, France had no major claims on the Prussian state nor any motives for its destruction, and the French court harbored a large and strong anti-Austrian party. France was primarily concerned with the British war. The French, therefore, desired the quickest possible victory in the Prussian war that would satisfy Austria, return Russia within her boundaries, and leave Prussia a reasonably strong factor in Europe. France and its allies, then, were in serious but as yet unclarified disagreement on war aims.

France accepted Russian ties with no serious determination to create a strong and enduring union. Such an attitude, accidental for the most part, was realistic. However, the French also brought into the Russian alliance the attitude that Russia could be bought, cajoled, and used for French interests. This was not realistic. Although Russian leaders had earned a reputation in Europe for excessive venality, it was a serious mistake prevalent in European courts to think that Russia was unaware of, or could be diverted from, its real interests. France, however, accepted Russia as an ally against Prussia in the belief that Russian aid could be used to bring the war to a quick end without permitting Russian expansion. France was mistaken. Russia had specific territorial ends in view, sharpened by the hatred of the Empress Elizabeth for Frederick of Prussia and directed by the intelligence and determination of Aleksei Bestuzhev. It required the six years of Franco-Russian ties to convince the French that Russia had a point to its war and that nothing short of internal upheaval or total defeat would swerve Russia from it. The Franco-Russian relationship thus had its ironic overtones. For it was France which, weakened by defeat, found the tables turned and was used effectively by Russia as an instrument toward the fulfillment of Russia's own war aims. It is to this basic disagreement on the purposes of the Seven Years' War that the failure of Franco-Russian ties must first be ascribed.

As a result of emerging tensions over war aims, France and Russia soon diverged on war programs. It was obvious to France early in the campaigns that Russian victories, with their threat of domination in Eastern Europe, and Russian defeats, with their threat of allied annihilation, were equally repugnant at Versailles. At the same time France and Russia could come to no agreements on Poland. France, whose influence had helped Poland survive against Russian pressures primarily through the King's Secret, felt that maintenance of French interests in Eastern Europe was a necessity of European stability. Russia had no such feeling. Thrusting into Europe untrammeled by any traditional views of the balance of power, Russia felt that France should leave Poland's future to its interested neighbors. France was thus faced with another dilemma created by its new ties: interest in the protection of Poland vied with the need for a Russian troop movement across the republic. Succumbing finally to bankruptcy and defeat, France began to pull in the perimeters of its influence. The Secret diplomacy in Poland was weakened by rising Russian pressures and by decisions in the French Ministry that Poland was expendable in the face of broader French interests.

Russia moved quickly to take advantage of the French retreat. Within three years there would be a Russian-made King of Poland, and within thirty years there would be no Poland at all. Having been compelled by the failures of its two-front war to abdicate the protection of Poland, France could exact no payments from Russia for Russian gains. France could only consider this product of Russian ties as a total loss. The result was the expansion of Russian influence into Europe over the corpse of French power.

France was not long in discovering that the double war it had entered so blithely was too horrible to bear. Under Bernis the country logically began to investigate the possibilities of peace. Here again French and Russian interests clashed. While it was clear and reasonable for France to seek an immediate peace in Europe, it was equally clear and logical for Austria and Russia to insist on waging the already costly war to a rewarding conclusion. Unfortunately for French diplomacy, France had nothing to gain from the Continental war and Russia and Austria had much. Thus, the Russians refused to deliver a Continental peace to France and continued to use French armies against Frederick for a war from which only Russia and Austria stood to gain. France counted another loss.

The Duke de Choiseul, newly come to power in 1758, dedicated himself to reversing the downward slide of French fortunes and sought ways of using Russia in the cause. His attempts to gain Russian military aid against Great Britain were fantastic and doomed to failure. France had been maneuvered into fighting a Continental war in which it had no real business, but this was no reason for Choiseul to believe that the Russians could be similarly deceived into joining the British war. Russia had no substantial cause for war with Britain nor could it exact any possible gain from such a venture. Britain was firmly entrenched in the Russian carrying trade, and since the first year of the war had given Russia no cause for alarm in the Baltic. Here again the Franco-Russian ties were unproductive because national interests were clear and contradictory.

Unable to use Russia in the war with Britain, Choiseul

then turned toward a Continental peace. Like Bernis before him, Choiseul learned that no Russian assistance for peace would be forthcoming until Russian territorial claims in East Prussia were approved and delivered. Such approval and delivery would themselves prolong the war far beyond French endurance. Choiseul's final attempt to gain Russian mediation in the British war, for which service he paid by virtual acquiescence in Russian territorial demands to be arranged with Austria, was also a failure. The Russians delivered a series of French peace proposals to the British through their London embassy and considered that they had done their part.

As to the durability of the alliance, France at least gauged that aspect correctly. The Young Court of Russia was and remained an enemy of France. The threat of the coming power of the imperial heirs made all Russia tremble for fear of displeasing them and made any real Russian commitment to France then or in the future impossible. In this sense, the intention of France to use Russia as quickly and as fruitfully as possible was realistic. France could not depend on, and did not plan to depend on, an empire where the ailing Empress might be replaced at any moment by successors who would reverse her policies. The fears and frustrations reaped by France for its attempts to approach the Young Court and to effect the exchange of Holstein were reason enough for lack of confidence in the future.

Commercial ties between France and Russia were not developed. French economic interests in Russia had been slight for many years, and Russian commerce was firmly in the hands of the Dutch and British. Although French manufactures were popular in Russia, it was not the French who profited from that popularity. Russia and France could come to no agreement on a Black Sea commerce because of French fears of offending the Turks. Negotiations for a tobacco treaty failed because of French indifference. The weak existing commercial ties were attacked by a prohibitive Russian tariff in 1757, which struck chiefly at French luxury items. Discussions of a general treaty of commerce, taken up at the same time that France and Russia were parting ways over the peace, were never serious. Through the fault of both parties, no economic ties were created between France and Russia that could have served as a foundation for future cooperation.

France had become entangled in a system in which it did not belong. To hold, as Albert Vandal and Alfred Rambaud have firmly held, that France could have benefited from the Russian alliance would have required at the start that France have some interest other than fear of European isolation to motivate its war with Prussia and that France and Russia share some common aim in the abasement of Prussia. There was no such common aim. If French participation in the European war was an error, then the Russian ties were products of error. For either Russia or France to have benefited from their relationship required that one of them sacrifice its real national interests. Although just such a sacrifice occurred, neither party entered the relationship for that purpose.

Another central thesis as to how France could have benefited greatly from its Russian ties, a thesis advocated also by Vandal and Rambaud — holds that France and Russia, allied cleanly and directly, could have saved the peace of Europe, restrained Prussian power, and freed France for a victorious British war. Criticism is here leveled at all French leaders who failed to commit France wholly to the new system by creating a direct alliance with Russia. Thus, Russia would have replaced the weak power of Sweden, Poland, and Turkey as a French counterweight in the east, and the aggressive German Empire would never have emerged subsequently to plague Europe. The whole relationship of the two states during the six years of war belies any such possibility, and the existence of the Young Court alone destroys the myth. On the matter of preserving the peace of Europe, such a possibility would have required that both France and Russia be committed to peace. Such was not the case, since Russia and Austria were determined to enter into a Prussian war. France's mistake was surely not in neglecting Russian dispositions for peace but in misjudging the Russian determination for war.

The most serious misfortune for France was that once having entrapped itself in its new ties, it could find no harmless way out. France had sprung a trap upon itself from which it could not escape without serious injury, and the six years' duration of those ties was the time it took to prove it. The keynote of the Franco-Russian relationship of the Seven Years' War, then, was its inherent conflict of national interests. Beyond the original intent to wage war on Prussia, France and Russia could not agree on war conduct, on war aims, on the necessity of peace, on the building of commerce, or on the future of Eastern Europe. The union of France and Russia was less an alliance than a contest to determine who could make the best use of whom. In contests of this nature there is usually a winner. France, at first unwittingly and then unwillingly, took the loser's part.

# BIBLIOGRAPHY

## Bibliographies and Guides

Artsimolovich, E. V. *Ukazetel' knig po istorii i obshchestvennym vopro-sam*. St. Petersburg, 1910.

*Biographie Universelle*. Paris: Calleman-Lévy, 1811–1862.

Brockhaus and Ephron. *Entsiklopedicheskii slovar'*. 6 vols. St. Petersburg, 1890–1907.

Garnier, E. A. *Repetoire met odique des ouvrages en langue français relatifs à l'Empire des Toutes les Russes qui se trouvent à la Bibliothèque Nationale de Paris*. Paris: Imprimerie Nationale, 1892.

Horn, David Bayne. *British Diplomatic Representatives: 1689–1789*. (Camden Third Series. Volume XLVI.) London: Royal Historical Society, 1932.

Kerner, Robert J. *Slavic Europe: A Selected Bibliography in Western European Languages*. Cambridge: Harvard University Press, 1918.

Marion, M. *Dictionnaire des institutions de la France aux XVIIe et XVIIIe siècles*. Paris: A. Picard, 1923

Mezhov, Vladimir. *Russkaia istoricheskaia bibliografiia*. St. Petersburg, 1881 and 1892–93.

Morley, Charles. *Guide to Research in Russian History*. Syracuse: Syracuse University Press, 1951.

*Ruskii biograficheskii slovar'*. 25 vols. St. Petersburg, 1896–1918.

Saulnier, E., and Martin, A. *Bibliographie des travaux publiées de 1866 à 1897 sur l'histoire de France de 1500 à 1789*. 5 vols. Paris: Limman, 1900.

## Archives

Archives du Ministère des Affaires Etrangères, Paris.

*Correspondance politique: Danemark, Pologne, Prusse, Russie, Suede.*
*Mémoires et documents: France, Russie.*
*Dossiers personnels.*
*Correspondance consulaire.*

Archives Nationales, Paris.

> *Affaires etrangères.*
> *Ministère de la marine.*
> *Correspondance consulaire.*

Bibliothèque de la Comedie Française, Paris.

Bibliothèque Nationale, Paris.

> *Manuscrits françaises.*
> *Nouvelles acquisitions françaises.*

Bibliothèque du Ministère de la Marine, Paris.

Bibliothèque de l'Opera, Paris.

## Collections of Documents

(Included here are some historical works that have reprinted documents extensively.)

Arneth, Alfred von. *Geschichte Maria Theresia.* 10 vols. Vienna, 1863–79.

*Archives du Théâtre Imperiale de Saint Petersburg.* 90 vols. St. Petersburg, 1890–1909.

Bartenev, P. I. (ed.) *Arkhiv Kniazia Vorontsova.* 40 vols. Moscow: Imperial Academy of Sciences, 1890–95.

———. *Vosemnadtsatyi vek.* 4 vols. Moscow, 1869.

Chulkov, Mikhail. *Istoricheskoe opisanie rossiiskoi kommertsii pri vsekh portakh i granitsakh ot drevnikh vremën do nyne nastoiashchego.* 7 vols. St. Petersburg, 1781–88.

Favier, Georges. *Politique de tous les cabinets de l'Europe pendant les regnes de Louis XV et de Louis XVI.* 2 vols. Paris: Chez Buisson, 1793.

Flammermont, Jules. *Les correspondances des agents diplomatiques etrangères en France avant la Révolution, conservées dans les archives de Berlin, Dresde, Genève, Florence, Naple, Lisbonne, Londres, La Haye, et Vienne.* Paris: Imprimerie Nationale, 1896.

Flassan, Gaëtan de Raxis de. *Histoire général et raisonné de la diplomatie française depuis la fondation de la Monarchie jusqu'à la fin du regne de Louis XVI, avec des tables chronologiques de tous les traités conclus par la France.* 2nd ed., 7 vols. Paris: Treuttel et Würtz, 1811.

Geffroy, Michel. *Recueil des instructions donnés aux ambassadeurs de France depuis les Traités de Westphalie.* Paris: Imprimerie Nationale, 1884.

Kurakin, J. A. *Le dix-huitième siècle: des documents historiques en français et en russe.* Moscow, 1904.

Martens, F. F. *Recueil des traités et conventions conclus par la Russie avec les puissances étrangères.* 15 vols. St. Petersburg: Ministry of Communications, 1874–1909.

*Mémoire historique sur la negociation de la France et de l'Angleterre; depuis le 26 mars 1761 jusqu'au 20 septembre de la même année.* Paris: Imprimerie Royale, 1761.

Pipin, A. N. (ed.) *Socheneniia Imperatritsy Ekateriny II.* 30 vols. St. Petersburg: Imperial Academy of Sciences, 1907.

Rambaud, Alfred. *Recueil des instructions données aux ambassadeurs et ministres de la France.* 12 vols. Paris: Felix Alcam, 1890.

*Russkaia Starina.* St. Petersburg, 1874–89.

*Sbornik Imperatorskago Istoricheskago Obshchestva.* St. Petersburg, 1867–1916.

Solov'ëv, Sergei M. *Istoriia Rossii s'drevneishikh vremën.* 26 vols. Moscow, 1871.

*Starye Gody.* St. Petersburg, 1909–11.

Turgenev, Alexander I. *La cour de Russie il y a cent ans: extraits des dépêches des ambassadeurs anglais.* Paris: E. Dentu, 1858.

Vitzthum Von Eckstadt, K. F. *Geheimnisse des Sachsischen Cabinets.* 2 vols. Stuttgart: J. G. Cotta, 1866.

## Memoirs and Letters

Barbier. *Journal historique et anecdotique du regne de Louis XV.* 8 vols. Paris: Didot frères, 1857.

Bektiev, F. D. *K istorii nashikh snoshenii s frantsuzskii; iz donesenii F. D. Bektieva Imperatritse Elizavete Petrovne 1756–1757. Russkii Arkhiv.* ( Volume XLI, Book 3.) Moscow, 1931.

Bernis, Cardinal de. *Correspondance du Cardinal Bernis avec Paris du Vernay: 1752–1769.* Paris, 1790.

————. *Mémoires et lettres du Cardinal Bernis,* ed. Frederic Masson. Paris: Plon, 1882.

Bernstorff, Count. *Correspondance de Comte Bernstorff avec le Duc de Choiseul.* Copenhagen: Ministry of Foreign Affairs of Denmark, 1871.

Boutaric, Émile. *Correspondance secrète de Louis XV sur la politique étrangère, avec le Comte de Broglie, Tercier, etc.* 2 vols. Paris: Plon, 1866.

Boutry, Maurice. *Choiseul à Rome, 1754–1757: lettres et mémoires inedits.* Paris: Emile Paul, 1895.

Choiseul, Duc de. *Mémoires du duc de Choiseul, 1719–1785.* Paris: Plon-Nourrit, 1904.

*Correspondance secrète de l'Imperatrice Elisabeth avec Louis XV, 1758.* Moscow, 1875.

D'Argenson, Marquis. *Journal et mémoires.* 2 vols. Paris: Badouin, 1825.

Duclos, C. P. *Mémoires secrètes sur les regnes de Louis XIV et de Louis XV.* 2 vols. Lausanne: Mourer, 1791.

Frederick II. *Correspondance de Frederick II, Roi de Prusse, avec le Comte Algarotti.* Berlin: Gropius, 1837.

————. *Histoire de mon temps.* 1747 edition. Leipzig: Prussian State Archives, 1879.

————. *Oeuvres de Frederic le Grand.* 30 vols. Berlin: Prussian State Archives, 1846–56.

————. *Politische Correspondenz 1741–1762.* 20 vols. Berlin: 1879–1939.

Gaillardet, M. *Mémoires de la Chevalière d'Éon.* Paris: Treuttel, 1866.

Ilchester, Earl of. *Correspondence of Catherine the Great While Grand Duchess.* London: Thornton Butterworth, 1928.

Lefevre, Georges. *Discours sur le progrés des beaux-arts en Russie.* St. Petersburg, 1760.

Luynes, Duc de. *Mémoires du Duc de Luynes sur la cour de Louis XV: 1735–1758.* Paris, 1865.

Marmontel, Jean François. *Mémoires.* 6 vols. Paris: Firmen, 1804–5.

Maroger, Dominique (ed.) *Memoirs of Catherine the Great.* New York: Collier Books, 1961.

Montalambert, Marquis de. *Correspondance du Marquis de Montalambert employé par le Roi de France à l'armée Suedoise: 1757–1761.* London, 1777.

Ozanam, Didier, and Antoine, Michel. *Correspondance secrète du Comte de Broglie avec Louis XV: 1756–1774.* 2 vols. Paris: Societé de l'Histoire de France, 1956.

Shakhovskii, J. P. *Zapiski.* St. Petersburg: Balasheva, 1887.

Thévenot, A. (ed.) *Correspondance du Prince François-Xavier de Saxe.* Paris: Plon, 1874.

## Secondary Works

Aleksandrenko, V. N. *Russkie diplomaticheskie agenty v Londone, v XVIII v.* 2 vols. Warsaw, 1897.

Amburger, Erik. *Russland und Schweden, 1762–1772.* Berlin: Emil Ebering, 1934.

Anderson, M. S. *Europe in the Eighteenth Century.* New York: Holt, Rinehart and Winston, 1961.

Bain, R. N. *The Daughter of Peter the Great: A History of the Russian Diplomacy and of the Russian Court Under the Empress Elizabeth, 1741–1762.* New York: E. P. Dutton, 1900.

————. *Gustavus III and His Contemporaries: 1746–1792.* 2 vols. Westminster: Constable, 1894.

————. *The Pupils of Peter the Great: A History of the Russian Court and Empire from 1697 to 1740.* London: Constable, 1897.

————. *Peter III, Emperor of Russia.* New York: E. P. Dutton, 1902.

Bamford, P. W. *Forests and French Sea Power 1660–1789.* Toronto, 1956.

Bang, Nina Ellinger, and Korst, Knud. *Tabeller over Skibsfart og Varentransport gennem Øresund 1661–1783.* Copenhagen: Lars Schmidt, 1930.

Benois, Albert. *Tsarskoe Selo v tsarstvovanie Elizavety Petrovny.* St. Petersburg: Imperial Academy of Sciences, 1910.

Borschak, Elie. *Hryhor Orlyk: France's Cossack General.* Toronto: Burns and MacEachern, 1956.

Bourgeois, Emile. *Manuel de politique étrangère.* 2 vols. Paris: Firmen-Didot, 1901.

Bourget, Alfred. *Etudes sur la politique étrangère du Duc de Choiseul.* Paris, 1907.

————. "Les debuts d'un ministère – le Duc de Choiseul et l'Autriche," (Paris) *Revue Historique*, LXXXVII (1905).

Broglie, Albert, Duc de. *L'alliance autrichienne, 1756.* Paris: C. Lévy, 1895.

————. *Frédéric II et Louis XV.* 2 vols. Paris: C. Lévy, 1883.

————. *Histoire de la politique exterieure de Louis XV: 1741–1756.* Paris: C. Lévy, 1899.

————. *La paix d'Aix-la-Chapelle: 1748.* Paris: C. Lévy, 1895.

————. *Le secret du roi, 1752–1774: Louis XV et ses agents diplomatiques.* 2 vols. Paris: Cassell, 1878.

Broglie, Jacques de. *Le vainqueur de Bergen et "le secret du roi."* Paris: Louvois, 1957.

Brousson, Jean Jacques. *Le chevalier d'Éon: ou le dragon en dentelles.* Paris: Flammarion, 1934.

Brückner, Alexander. *Istoriia Ekateriny Vtoroi.* 5 vols. St. Petersburg: A. S. Suvorina, 1885.

Carré, Henri. *La regne de Louis XV.* (*Histoire de France depuis les origines jusqu'à la Révolution,* ed. Ernest Lavisse, Vol. IV.) Paris: Hachette, 1911.

Chambrun, Charles. *A l'école d'un diplomate, Vergennes.* Paris: Plon, 1944.

Chechulin, N. D. *Vneshniaia politika Rosii v nachale tsarstvovaniia Ekateriny II, 1762–1774.* St. Petersburg, 1896.

Chevalier, Émile. *Histoire de la marine française jusqu'au traité de paix de 1763.* Paris: Bibliothèque d' Histoire Illustré, 1902.

Clarkson, Jesse D. *A History of Russia.* New York: Random House, 1961.

Doria, Comte Arnauld. *Louis Tocqué.* Paris: Edition Beaux Arts, 1929.

Dorn, Walter L. *Competition for Empire*. New York: Harper & Brothers, 1940.

Fabre, Jules. *Stanislas Auguste Poniatowski et l'Europe des lumières*. Paris: C. Lévy, 1952.

Fagniez, Gustave. "Les antecedents de l'alliance Franco-Russe, 1741–1762," *Revue Hebdomadaire* (Paris, August, 1916), 316–38.

Fain, Baron. *Politique de tous les cabinets de l'Europe pendant les guerres de Louis XV et de Louis XVI*. 3 vols. Paris, 1801.

Feoktistov, E. M. "Otnosheniia rossii k Prussii v tsarstvovanie Elizavety Petrovny," *Russkii Vestnik* (Moscow), CLIX and CLX (1882).

Foust, Clifford. "Sino-Russia Trade Relations from 1727 to the End of the Eighteenth Century." Unpublished Ph.D dissertation, University of Chicago, 1957.

Furcy-Renaud, Marc. *L'engagement de Tocqué à la cour d'Elisabeth*. Paris: A. Colin, 1903.

Gaxotte, Pierre. *Louis XV and His Times*. Philadelphia: Lippincott, 1934.

Gideonese, Max. "Dutch Baltic Trade in the Eighteenth Century." Unpublished Ph.D. dissertation, Harvard University, 1932.

Gooch, G. P. *Louis XV: The Monarchy in Decline*. London: Longmans Green, 1956.

Grunwald, Constantin de. *Trois siècles de diplomatie russe*. Paris: Callman-Lévy, 1945.

Hautecoeur, Louis. *L'architecture classique à Saint-Petersbourg à la fin du XVIIIe siècle*. Paris: Bibliothèque de l'Institut Français de Saint Petersbourg, 1912.

Haumant, Émile. *La culture français en Russie (1700–1900)*. Paris: Plon, 1910.

——. *La Russia du XVIIIe siècle*. Paris: Bibliothèque d'Histoire Illustré, 1904.

Homberg, Octave, and Jousselin, Fernand. *Un aventurier au XVIIIe siècle, le Chevalier d'Éon*. Paris: Plon-Nourrit, 1904.

Horn, David Bayne. *Sir Charles Hanbury-Williams and European Diplomacy: 1747–1758*. London: George Harrap, 1930.

Horowitz, Sidney. "Franco-Russian Relations 1740–1746." Unpublished Ph.D. dissertation, New York University, 1953.

Immich, Max. *Geschichte des Europäischen Staatensystems von 1660 bis 1789*. Berlin-Münich: R. Oldenbourg, 1905.

Johnsen, Albert. "Le commerce entre la France meridionale et les pays du nord sous l'ancien regime." *Revue d'histoire moderne*, II (1927), pp. 81–98.

Kaplan, Herbert H. *The First Partition of Poland*. New York: Columbia University Press, 1962.

Kirchner, Walter. "Relations économiques entre la France et la Russie au XVIIIe siècle," *Revue d'histoire économique et sociale*. (Paris), XXXIX, No. 2, (1961), 158–97.

Klochkov, M. V. "Rossiia, Avstriia i Prussiia v seredine XVIII v" *Istori-cheskii Vestnik* (Petrograd), No. 3 (1915), 839–55.

Koehl, Robert L. "Heinrich Brühl: A Saxon Politician of the Eighteenth Century," *Journal of Central European Affairs*, XIV (Jan. 1954).

Konopczynski, Wladyslaw. *Polska w dobnie wojny siedmioletniej.* 2 vols. Krakow and Warsaw: W. L. Anczyca, 1911.

Lambert, Francis X. "The Foreign Policy of the Duke de Choiseul, 1763–1770." Unpublished Ph.D. dissertation, Harvard University, 1952.

Masslowski, E. I. *Der Siebenjahrige Kreig nach Russischer Darstellung.* 3 vols. Berlin: R. Eisenschmidt, 1889–93.

Masson, Frédéric. *Le Cardinal Bernis.* Paris: Plon, 1884.

Masson, Paul. *Histoire du commerce français dans le Levant au XVIIIe siècle.* Paris: Hachette, 1911.

Maugras, Gaston. *Le Duc et la Duchesse de Choiseul.* Paris: Plon-Nourrit, 1902.

May, Louis Phillipe. "La France, puissance des Anteilles," *Revue d'histoire économique et sociale.* (Paris), XVIII (1930).

Mediger, Walther. *Moskaus Weg nach Europa.* Braunschweig: G. Westermann, 1952.

Mooser, R. Aloys. *L'opera comique française en Russie au XVIIIe siècle.* Geneva: René Kister, 1954.

Osipov, K. *Alexander Suvarov.* Translated by Edith Bone. London: Hutchinson, 1941.

Ozanam, Didier. "La disgrace d'un Premier Commis: Tercier et l'affaire de l'Esprit, 1758–1759," *Bibliothèque de l'Ecole des Chartes* (Paris), CXIII, (1955).

Ozanam, Didier, and Antoine, Michel. "Le secret du Roi," *Annuaire bulletin de la societé de l'histoire de France* (Paris, 1954–55), 328–47.

Portal, Roger. *L'Oural au XVIIIe siècle.* Paris: Institut d'Etudes Slaves, 1950.

Potemkin, V. V., *et al. Istoriia diplomatii SSSR.* 3 vols. Moscow, 1941.

Price, Jacob M. *The Tobacco Adventure to Russia.* American Philosophical Society Transactions, LI (March, 1961).

Rambaud, Alfred. *Russes et Prussiens: Guerre de Sept. Ans.* Paris: Firmen-Didot, 1895.

Ramsey, John Fraser, *Anglo-French Relations 1763–1770: A Study of Choiseul's Foreign Policy.* ("University of California Publications in History," Vol. XVII, No. 3.) Berkeley: University of California Press, 1935.

Reading, Douglas K. *The Anglo-Russian Commercial Treaty of 1734.* New Haven: Yale University Press, 1938.

Reddaway, W. F., *et al. Cambridge History of Poland.* 2 vols. Cambridge: Cambridge University Press, 1941–50.

Réau, Louis. *Histoire de l'expansion de l'art français*. Paris: Firmen-Didot, 1924.

————. *L'art russe de Pierre le Grand à nos jours*. Paris: H. Lavrens, 1922.

————. *L'Europe française au siècle des lumières*. Paris: H. Lavrens, 1938.

Rogger, Hans. *National Conciousness in Eighteenth Century Russia*. Cambridge: Harvard University Press, 1960.

Rojdestvensky, S., and Lubimenko, I. "Contributions à l'histoire des relations commerciales franco-russes au XVIIIe siècle," *Revue d'histoire économique et sociale* (Paris), XVIII, 389–401.

Rulhière, Claude Carloman de. *Histoire de l'anarchie de Pologne et du démembrement de cette republique*. 4 vols. Paris: Desenne, 1807.

Sée, Henri. "Les relations commerciales et maritimes entre la France et les pays du nord au XVIIIe siècle," *Revue maritime* (Paris), New series, No. 71 (November, 1925), 599 ff.

Shchebalskii, Pëtr Karlovich. *Politicheskaia sistema Petra III*. Moscow: Moscow University Press, 1870.

Shchepkin, Yevgenii N. "Padenie Kantslera Grafa A. P. Bestuzheva-Riumina," *Zapiski, Imperatorskoe Odesskoe obshchestvo istorii i drevnostei* (Odessa), XXIII (1901), 207–60.

————. *Russko-Avstriiskii soyuz vo vremia semiletnei voiny 1746–1758*. St. Petersburg: V. S. Balashevi, 1902.

Soltau, Roger H. *The Duke de Choiseul; the Lothian Essay, 1908*. Oxford: B. H. Blackwell, 1909.

Sorel, Albert. *La question d'Orient au XVIIIe siècle*. Paris: Plon, 1889.

Svanstrom, Ragnar and Palmstierna, Carl F. *A Short History of Sweden*. Oxford: Clarenden Press, 1934.

"Tainaia Kantseleria," *Russkaia Starina*, XII (1875), pp. 523–39.

Tinirzaev, Vladimir. "Doch Petra Velikago," *Istoricheskii Vestnik* (July, 1900), 485–523; (September, 1900), 825–59.

Vandal, Albert. *Louis XV et Elisabeth de Russie*. Paris: Plon, 1882.

Waddington, R. *Louis XV et le renversement des alliances: préliminaires de la guerre de sept ans (1754–1756)*. Paris: Firmen-Didot, 1896.

————. *La guerre de sept ans: histoire diplomatique et militaire*. 5 vols. Paris: Firmen-Didot, 1899–1914.

Waliszewski, Kasimir. *La dernière des Romanov*. Paris: Plon, 1902.

————. "L'evolution de la politique française en orient au XVIIIe siècle," *Revue d'histoire diplomatique*, (Paris), II (1888), 410–661.

————. *Potoccy i Czartoryski: Walka stronnictw i programow politycznych przed upadkiem Rzptej 1734–1763*. 2 vols. Krakow, 1887.

————. *The Romance of an Empress*. New York: Appleton, 1905.

Wassiltchikov, Vladimir I. *Les Rasumovski*. 6 vols. Halle, 1893–95.

Wilson, Arthur M. *French Foreign Policy During the Administration of Cardinal Fleury, 1726–1743.* Cambridge: Harvard University Press, 1936.

Zeller, Gaston. *De Louis XIV à 1789. (Histoire des relations internationales,* ed. P. Renouvin.) Paris, 1955.

# INDEX

Adolphus Frederick, King of Sweden, 74 f.

Aix-la-Chapelle, Treaty of, 1748, 1, 2, 3, 4, 5

Alsuviev, Adam V., 118, 159

Anglo-Russian Subsidy Treaty, 1755, 11, 12, 13, 15, 19, 21, 23, 29, 30, 31, 43, 47, 54, 194

Anna Ivanovna, Empress of Russia, 4, 8, 106

Anna Leopoldovna of Brunswick, Russian Regent, 3

Apraksin, Stepan Fëdorovich, Field Marshal, 31, 72, 78, 79, 80 ff., 83, 85–87

Augustus III, King of Poland, Elector of Saxony, 9, 52, 64, 66, 103, 106, 156

Austria, 48, 49, 83, 94, 95, 115, 122, 134; in Bestuzhev's programs, 4, 17, 19, 33, 86; and Choiseul's appointment as Secretary of State for Foreign Affairs, 136; in Choiseul's programs, 137, 143, 146–47, 168, 177, 180–82; and defense of Russia against Prussian invasion, 79 n; and First Treaty of Versailles, 54–58; and Grand Duke Peter, 110; and the King's Secret, 9, 26, 52–53, 96–97; in L'Hôpital's instructions, 72; negotiations for an offensive alliance with Russia, 32, 33 n; negotiations with Britain, 11; negotiations with France, 29 n; and opposition to a peace congress, 154 n; at outbreak of the Seven Years' War, 44–45, 46; party at the French court, 11–12; and peace policy of Bernis, 91–93; policy after 1725, 1; policy after 1748, 2; policy in 1748, 2; and Polish succession, 64; reaction to Anglo-Prussian talks, 28;

and Second Treaty of Versailles, 83; summary of role in Franco-Russian relationship, 194, 195, 197, 199; and Swedish Treaty of March, 1757, 75; and territorial cessions to Russia, 149–52; and Third Treaty of Versailles, 143–44; and Treaty of St. Petersburg, 58, 91; war aims, 77–78. *See also* Esterhazy, Kaunitz, Maria Theresa

Austrian Succession, War of, 8

Baltic Sea, 76, 77, 106, 114, 123–24, 125, 138–40, 150, 161, 167, 197

Baudouin, Nicholas, of Rouen, 126

Beaujon and Goosens of Paris, 125, 126

Bektiev, Fëdor Dmitrievich, Russian chargé in France, 35, 36–37, 37 n, 38

Berens, Christopher, 167

Berlin, 87, 93, 179

Bernis, François Joachim Pierre, Abbé and Cardinal de, 137, 139, 142, 155, 159, 198; appointment as Secretary of State for Foreign Affairs, 70–71, 173; and appointment of Consul in Russia, 129–30; and Apraksin's retreat, 78, 81; and Bestuzhev, 86; determination to seek a continental peace, 92–93, 93 n; and the exchange of Holstein, 115–17; intervenes between Broglie and L'Hôpital, 99–100; and the Poissonnier mission, 119; and Poland, 95–96, 97, 100, 107–108; policy on Courland, 106–107; policy on Danzig, 104 f., 105; policy on the Young Court, 110–17; prepares to retire, 95; recalls Broglie from Warsaw, 101–102, 103; refuses to accede to Austro-